MODERN
GRANTMAKING

MODERN GRANTMAKING

A Guide for Funders Who Believe Better Is Possible

GEMMA BULL &

TOM STEINBERG

Copyright © 2021 by Gemma Bull and Tom Steinberg

Modern Grantmaking:
A Guide for Funders Who Believe Better Is Possible

moderngrantmaking.com

All Rights Reserved. No part of this publication may be reproduced, stored or transmitted in any form without the permission of the authors. If you would like permission to use material from the book (other than for review purposes), please contact hello@moderngrantmaking.com.

First edition: June 2021

Paperback print edition ISBN 978-1-8384879-0-4
Hardback ISBN 978-1-8384879-1-1
eBook 978-1-8384879-2-8

Text designer: Andrew Chapman.
Cover designer: Jamie Keenan.
Copyeditor: Jacqueline Harvey.
Proofreader: Catherine Dunn.
Indexer: Rosie Wood.

Set in Sabon and Trade Gothic.

How to cite this book: Gemma Bull and Tom Steinberg, *Modern Grantmaking: A Guide for Funders Who Believe Better Is Possible* (London: Modern Grantmaking, 2021).

To the reformers

CONTENTS

Introduction		9
1	What is Modern Grantmaking?	25
2	What are the no-brainers of Modern Grantmaking?	45
3	What should I do about privilege?	75
4	How do I help my funder develop a good strategy?	107
5	What big questions should all funders debate from time to time?	139
6	How can I improve the experience of grantseekers and grantees?	173
7	How should I make use of research?	205
8	How do I manage well both upwards and downwards?	243
9	How do I keep developing my skills?	267
10	How do I become a grantmaking reformer?	287
Acknowledgements		299
Notes		301
Index		320

INTRODUCTION

> I went looking for a book on grantmaking that challenged my thinking and posed difficult questions, to help me to become a better grantmaker.
>
> I couldn't find one.[1]
>
> — LISA WEAKS, assistant director and head of Third Sector, The King's Fund

This book is for anyone who is employed in the curious world of grantmaking, whether you work for a private foundation, a government funder or a corporate donor.

Grantmaking is such an unusual occupation – *giving away freaking money* – that we have encountered people who don't believe that anyone actually gets paid to do it. But grantmaking is a real job, and if you're reading this book then the odds are that it's your real job.

We've written it because *giving away freaking money* turns out to be a great deal more difficult than it sounds. Not only is it a hard job to do well, but the challenges involved are not widely understood – or widely empathised with – by people who haven't done grantmaking themselves.

We know how hard it can be to do funding well because we've both been grantmakers and have experienced those moments of deep self-doubt that come with the terrain.

To work out what good grantmaking means these days, we met with a wide range of grantmakers working for funding organisations that were large and small, old and new, private and public. We also learned a lot from people who work for organisations that benefit from grant funding – the crucial partners without whom all our work would be totally pointless. We're incredibly grateful that so many people were willing to talk to us.

One thing we heard from our many conversations with grantmakers stands out: there is deep and widespread unease about the lack of training and skills development that most grantmakers receive. Underpinning this discomfort is the strong feeling that 'doing grant funding the way it's always been done' is not good enough for professional grantmakers working in the 2020s.

If grantmaking is a profession, it's a funny one – a profession without the sort of standardised training, qualifications or rules that make sure, for example, certified engineers can design planes that fly, and that qualified architects don't design buildings that fall down.

Given this gap, we wanted to help. Our aim in writing this book was to produce a practical guide that grantmakers can open and refer to whenever they are looking for some support. To make it quick and easy to use, we've filled the book with answers to real-world grantmaking questions such as:

- How do I know if I'm getting the basics right?
- How can I make sure that our funding is accessible to all prospective grantseekers?
- How do I manage well both upwards and downwards?
- How should I deal with power and privilege?

This guide focuses on questions like these because we observed that the grantmaking sector doesn't currently contain much in the way of concrete, easily accessible day-to-day advice on how to be good at our curious occupation.

This gap in helpful guidance would be bad enough at the best of times, but these haven't been the best of times. We're writing in the midst of the COVID-19 pandemic and in a time of terrorism and natural disaster that is the early 2020s.

Against this backdrop, nonprofits around the world are struggling to balance the books and still support the communities they serve, while many funders have been innovating and trying to make grants more quickly and with fewer of the usual bureaucratic strings attached than ever before.[2] These challenges are taking a huge toll on both nonprofits and grantmakers: in the words of one grantmaker we spoke to, 'All I do is read applications and sleep.'[3]

A lot of people have been doing a lot of grantmaking very fast, in very stressful and emotionally draining situations, and the need for advice and support that is quick and easy to digest has never been greater. We hope this book can be an asset for a cohort of people who have been working very hard, often without much recognition.

Introduction

Does this book have an agenda?

Absolutely! Thanks for asking.

We believe that a lot of what we call traditional grantmaking is problematic and needs reform. That's why this book is expressly about Modern Grantmaking, a term that we explain and define in Chapter 1.

We think that a lot of the criticism that grantmaking gets is justified, despite the fact that funding organisations as a whole employ large numbers of talented, hard-working and highly motivated people, including some of our dearest friends. This is because grantmaking is mostly a field of dedicated employees trapped within creaking systems and outdated conventions. (If you want to skip straight to the bit where we set out our critique of what happens as a result of these problems, you can turn to Chapter 1.)

Despite being critical about some current practices, we don't believe that the solution is to tear down grantmaking and salt the earth. Unlike some more radical voices, we're not calling for governments to end megaphilanthropy. Even if they did the world would still contain a lot of public service grantmakers who would also need training, advice and support. We do not want people to give up on grantmaking entirely but we do want to encourage more people to be Modern Grantmakers.

We think that a revolution of norms and practices in grantmaking *should* be within our shared grasp, especially since our institutions have a lot of money, power and influence. However, such a reformation can happen only if we, as grantmakers, are willing and courageous enough to push for change. It can also happen only if we get down from our pedestals and start to treat grantseekers, grantees and communities as indispensable partners and not simply as recipients of money.

We believe that grantmaking will benefit enormously from the rising community of grantmakers who are self-identifying as reformers – people who recognise the problems with the status quo, and who have chosen to prioritise improving grantmaking. These include members of the Grant Givers' Movement,[4] supporters of #ShiftThePower[5] and people who have decided to set up entirely new funds, such as the Resourcing Racial Justice fund.[6] At the end of this book (in Chapter 10) we discuss these grantmaking reform movements and explain how you can get involved.

This book recognises all the hard transformation work that's currently going on in funders and communities, and attempts to celebrate it by telling stories of innovation and success.

So is this book some sort of rallying cry?

At its heart, this book is a deliberate, unashamed attempt to be a unifying point for aspirational grantmaking reformers, in the way that 20th-century environmentalists bonded over Rachel Carson's *Silent Spring* (1962) and 21st-century tech entrepreneurs circle around Eric Ries's *The Lean Startup* (2011).[7] We've written this book to be a focal point for people who believe that grantmaking can and must be done better.

We understand that it's an ambitious goal, and that we may not succeed. We also acknowledge that in this aspiration we're showing ourselves to have a degree of ego and hubris. But we believe unashamedly that the many different grantmaking reformers around the world who are doing this hard work would benefit from a shared identity, a home or community to call their own. If it doesn't come from this work, we hope it emerges somewhere else.

If being part of an international grantmakers' reform community sounds like something you want to be part of, please take a look at Chapter 10 for practical advice on how to connect with us and others. To understand what reforms we're actually talking about and why we're not content with the status quo, please read Chapter 1.

Who is this book for?

The primary audience of this book is employees of grantmaking organisations. These are the often underappreciated people who talk to grantees, assess proposals, move money, write strategies, commission research and run board meetings, as well as anyone who is considered part of the staff of a funding organisation. These individuals have job titles like 'grants officer', 'director of funding', 'programme officer' and others that are synonymous with 'grantmaker'.

The book may also be of value to the chief executives or executive directors of funding organisations. It includes lots of strategic advice and management advice, as well as more day-to-day stuff.

The book is also for people who are on a career track to become those CEOs or executive directors. We know that lots of people in the rising generation of reforming grantmakers want these top positions not so much for the money and prestige they bring but so that they can shake things up and do better than what has come before. If this sounds like you, we think you'll find a lot here to inspire you as you work out what kind of leader you want to be.

Employed grantmakers, then, are the central focus of the book. However, grantmaking organisations also employ lots of other critical team members, who also deserve to know about good grantmaking practices. So this book could be suitable for funder employees who are lawyers, accountants, human resources (HR) people, comms people, administrative staff, digital specialists and so on. Essentially, if you get a pay cheque to work for a grantmaking organisation, this book is to help you with workplace dilemmas.

Finally, while the book is written in English and has a UK and US focus (because we know more about grantmaking in these contexts), we hope that it includes insights and stories that will be of help to virtually any grantmaker anywhere in the world.

Aren't funders too different for a single book to be useful to all grantmakers?

There are over 10,000 funding organisations in the UK, 11,000 in Canada and 120,000 in the US, and they vary in a lot of different ways.[8] For example, the world of grantmaking includes:

- large funders;
- small funders;
- civil society funders;
- arts funders;
- science funders;
- private funders run by highly engaged donors;
- private foundations whose founders are deceased;
- government funders;
- corporate funders;
- funders that accept unsolicited proposals;
- funders that are invite only;
- funders that focus on one city or area.

A helpful way to visualise and understand the differences between funders is the following diagram. We think it's useful because the types of skills that a grantmaker will have to major in will be different in different parts of the diagram overleaf.

Modern Grantmaking

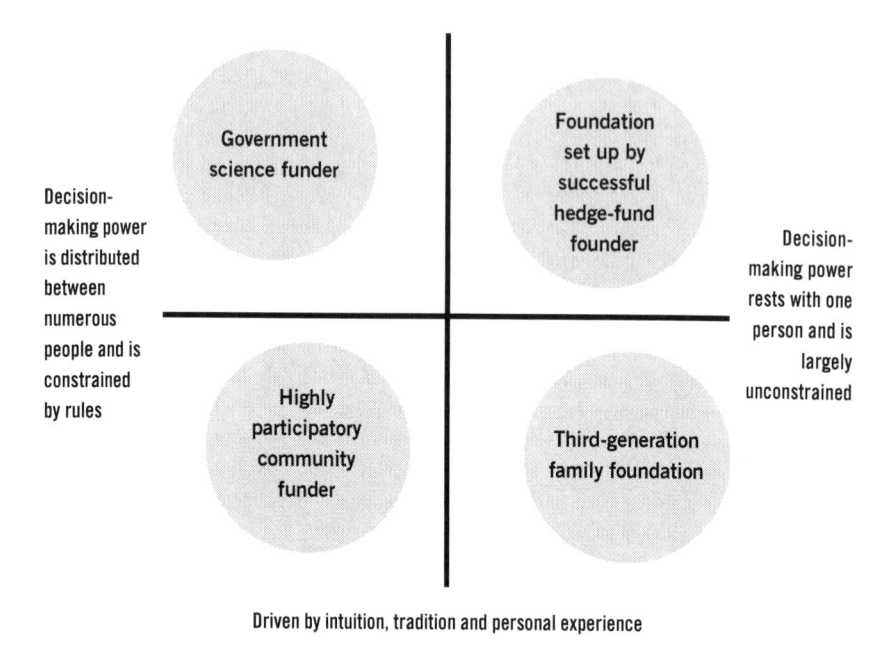

Driven by data and research

Decision-making power is distributed between numerous people and is constrained by rules

- Government science funder
- Foundation set up by successful hedge-fund founder
- Highly participatory community funder
- Third-generation family foundation

Decision-making power rests with one person and is largely unconstrained

Driven by intuition, tradition and personal experience

A simple way of differentiating kinds of funding organisations. Note that the positions are indicative and that individual funders may vary greatly.

Funding organisations that lean towards the top left (on the diagram) are more bound by rules and checks and balances, while those that lean to the right are able to make quicker decisions but are less accountable. Working for a funder on the left side of the diagram requires you to be better at bureaucratic navigation, whereas the skills required in funders on the right are more likely to be managing upwards and catching ideas coming downwards.

At the top of the diagram are the ultra-data-driven funding organisations, filled with scientists and statisticians, while at the bottom are the more community-rooted grantmakers. Again, the skills that will help a grantmaker succeed are different at the different ends of the vertical axis.

Pause for a moment. Where does your funder sit in this diagram? What about other funders you admire? Wherever your organisation sits, there will be some shared basics that are as important to you as to a funder in another quadrant. For instance, you'll both need to pay grantees quickly, to communicate with them clearly and respectfully, and to have good managers supporting and challenging teams to do their best. In short, despite the immense differences between funders, there are some key values, skills and behaviours that really do matter for everyone – these are at the heart of the book.

Who is this book not for?

This book is not aimed at helping a private individual to work out how to make charitable donations that have an impact using their own money. There are some terrific books on this subject, but it involves a different skill from being a grantmaker. If you want a book to help you with your own giving, we suggest:

- *Giving Done Right: Effective Philanthropy and Making Every Dollar Count*, by Phil Buchanan.

- *Doing Good Better: How Effective Altruism Can Help You Help Others, Do Work that Matters, and Make Smarter Choices about Giving Back*, by William MacAskill.

- *It Ain't What You Give, It's the Way that You Give It*, by Caroline Fiennes.[9]

Second, this book is not aimed primarily at the donors or board members who sit at the top of most funding organisations, usually in non-executive roles. Instead, we have chosen to write directly for grantmakers working in full- or part-time roles, who seem especially underserved when it comes to advice and guidance. While we hope this book will also be useful to board members of grantmaking organisations, we acknowledge that it has not been written specifically for them. Who knows – maybe that could be the topic of our next work?

Third, we are not experts in social investment and other ways of deploying capital to create social and environmental impact through loans and equity investments. We do, however, understand that some funders both make grants and engage in these kinds of investments. If you want to develop your skills in these areas, we recommend the following reading:

- *Real Impact: The New Economics of Social Change*, by Morgan Simon (for US readers).

- *After the Gold Rush: The Report of the Alternative Commission on Social Investment* (for UK readers).
- *Futurebuilders Learning Project Data Deep Dive*, a slide deck by the Social Investment Business (for UK readers).[10]

Lastly, this book has not been written for people who are absolute beginner grantmakers learning how to assess a proposal or scrutinise a budget for the first time. We assume that if you're reading this book you already know a bit (or perhaps too much) about the 'game' and that you've ushered at least a few grants through the grantmaking process. In short, this book isn't for total novices: it is for people who have been doing the job for at least a year, and who have worked out that not everything in grantmaking always smells of roses.

Is it even moral to work for Big Philanthropy?

To begin with, we need to separate grantmaking from philanthropy. A huge amount of grantmaking that happens in different countries is actually done by people working on behalf of democratically elected governments, not private foundations. You may not always like those governments or what they do but they're still, in a sense, controlled by 'the people'. This book has been written for government grantmakers as much as for their private foundation equivalents.

Private foundations are quite a different kettle of fish. They are usually controlled by a wealthy individual or by a board of people who have in some way been entrusted with money by someone else (very often someone who is very well off themselves).

These organisations have few legal obligations about what they must do and how they must behave: the legal obligations of trusts and foundations are different in the United States and the United Kingdom, but what they have in common is that they're very minimal. As long as the money doesn't go to impermissible places (e.g. back into their founder's pockets) there's really nothing much to stop a funder deciding to spend money on whatever they choose, even if it's bad for humanity or the planet.

This largely unaccountable status has not gone unnoticed. Searing critiques of the role and behaviour of big US foundations have been published and widely read in recent years. The most well known of these are probably Rob Reich's *Just Giving: Why Philanthropy Is Failing Democracy and How It Can Do Better* and Anand Giridharadas's *Winners Take All: The Elite Charade of Changing the World*.[11] In his book

Decolonizing Wealth: Indigenous Wisdom to Heal Divides and Restore Balance, Edgar Villanueva also writes extensively on the connection between major funders, people of colour and indigenous peoples whose stolen labour and land underpin some endowments.[12]

High-profile journalists have also been flagging concerns.[13] *The Washington Post*'s Roxanne Roberts and *The New Yorker*'s Elizabeth Kolbert have been raising critiques that have been read by much larger audiences than most books can reach.

These writers haven't been limiting themselves to criticism but have been actively pushing for tougher legal restrictions on the wealth and power of private foundations. For example, several voices have been arguing that the tax benefits of mega-philanthropy should be lowered or capped, and that private foundations should be forced to spend their endowments more quickly.

We think that anyone who works for a private funder, especially a large funder with a highly engaged founder, should read a range of writers such as those we cite, and regularly ask themselves and their colleagues challenging questions about where they work and how they work. In particular, employees of private foundations should be aware that a sizeable proportion of the money they give away would – all other things being equal – be paid as taxes to the government. This means that every grantmaking decision in a private funder needs to be underpinned by the question 'Would a range of people agree that it's acceptable to spend the money in this way rather than pay it as taxes?'

Lastly, the employees of private foundations need to continually ask themselves whether their positively intended grantmaking props up or provides cover for activities with negative social consequences. It may not be immediately obvious what we mean by 'cover', so consider a scenario where a philanthropist funds a lot of schools and hospitals in their hometown. Imagine that this same philanthropist owns a business that, because of lax environmental regulations, pollutes the local drinking water. If local lawmakers feel that they cannot legislate to protect the water for fear of losing the funding to schools and hospitals, this act of philanthropy is clearly deeply problematic, and the people who deliver it are partly culpable too.

So it is your responsibility, as a grantmaker working for a private funder, to be aware and to take action if you ever suspect that your organisation is providing shielding for social ills from your founder(s). This might mean complaining, whistleblowing or even quitting, if that's what it takes, although we understand that these choices are easier to make for some than others. For more on what underpins positive, values-driven grantmaking, check out Chapter 1.

Why should I pay any attention to your advice on grantmaking?

We're a British woman and an Anglo-American man who cut our teeth working for a range of nonprofits for over a decade each before switching lanes to work for funding organisations. Our own experiences as often exhausted, disappointed and sometimes angry grantseekers shaped our belief that grantmaking can be better, and our experience when we became grantmakers confirmed what we had often suspected from the outside.

We met while working together as executives at the biggest community funder in the UK, what is now called the National Lottery Community Fund, an arm's-length government funding organisation that distributed about £650 million (about $900m) in 2020. Since then we've both moved on, working for other funders and settling down to write this book together.

We are different people, of course, with different lived, learned and practical experiences. But what we have in common is a passion for supporting and challenging grantmaking organisations to be more equitable, inclusive and quite simply better run.

Grantmaking is exhausting enough – do I really have to continually develop my own skills too?

Yes, it *really is* very important that you as a grantmaker take the time and effort to develop your own skills. We're sorry. We know it feels like yet another burden. But as grantmakers we all have a duty to strive to continually improve our own skills because lazily or ineptly misdirected grant money can hurt people. Rogue cash can fund projects that destroy jobs, undermine children's education or expose people to real harms.

We also have to work hard to do our best because opportunity costs really exist and really matter: money given to organisation X cannot be given to organisation Y. As the Indigo Trust's chief executive Paul Lenz puts it, 'As a grantmaker, it's so tempting to coast, to not be self-critical. But to do so would be to squander the opportunity of making the greatest positive impact possible upon thousands or even millions of lives.'[14]

Our goal in writing this book is to make the process of steadily building up your grantmaking skills a bit more fun – and a bit less lonely.

How do I use this book to improve my grantmaking?

We've written this book so that it can be used as a practical tool. It absolutely doesn't have to be read through from start to finish. Here are a couple of approaches we recommend.

First, you can use the book as a reference guide to dip in and out of when you have a specific problem, a bit like a DIY manual. We have structured the book as a set of questions and answers. You should be able to find your way to most questions pretty quickly using the contents and index.

Second, you can use each chapter as a discussion tool with your colleagues or board members to stimulate debate and reflection on key issues. We've attached exercises to the end of most chapters to help you use it in this way, and there will be more available on our website at ModernGrantmaking.com.

Finally, you can just read or listen to this book. Preferably with a cat on your knee, a dog by your feet or whatever works for you.

Will this book tell me what causes and organisations to give money to?

While this book is all about helping you to develop your skills as a grantmaker, we won't be telling you whether to spend money on kittens or cancer research. We have two reasons for dodging this big question.

First, most people reading this book won't actually have the power to set the overall strategic priorities of their funding organisation. That's because this book is mainly for employed grantmakers and not for board members or donors. One important way that this book differs from many other books on grantmaking is that we don't assume that anyone reading it calls all the shots at their funder.

Second, if we were to set out all the priority areas we think should receive money, this book would be a political manifesto and not a professional guide. That would just be an entirely different kettle of fish.

None of this means we believe that it's not important to think very carefully about where a funding organisation spends its money. It is so important to do this right that we've dedicated an entire chapter – Chapter 4 – to explaining how to run a strategy development process for a funder. It just means that we're not going to tell you what we think the conclusions of your strategy process should be.

Do you really have no opinions on where the money should go?

OK, you've got us. We will make one exception to our 'no spending priorities' rule for the biggest issue in the world: climate change. We think this deserves an exception because, if it is not meaningfully managed in the next decade, the climate crisis could ultimately undermine funders' attempts to achieve everything else they care about.

We think that every single funder should review its strategy, rules and processes and the way it manages its savings in light of the climate crisis. Then, having reviewed these diverse issues, it should consider whether it needs to take further action.

Given the importance of the issue, it seems very likely that funders could generally be doing more. For example, the best available data suggest that only a small fraction of philanthropic funding in the UK is currently focused on climate change.[15]

We recommend that all funders consider revising their organisational strategy to factor in the climate crisis, especially since climatic changes are already impacting marginalised groups, as well as our planet's biodiversity. You could, for example, consider holding an emergency board meeting to discuss how the organisation's current strategy and practices should change.

At such a meeting the discussions you have should be much broader than just 'Are we funding the right green organisations?' There are many ways in which funders can have a positive impact on climate change. Consider the following:

- If you have an endowment or other investments, should they be moved around to ensure that you are not financially propping up the types of business that contribute significantly to climate change?

- How much of your giving should be focused on the kind of direct climate activism that will ultimately persuade governments to change policies? What coalitions can you join or support to scale up the overall impact?

- Have you actively offered to help your grantees adapt to more climate-friendly practices, or to bring them into campaign networks?

- Can you help your grantees with suggestions for reducing their carbon emissions? A funder is in a strong position to persuade grantees, for example, to migrate from high-carbon energy suppliers to low-carbon suppliers.
- Can you fund projects that will enable those whose voices are not being heard in the climate change debate to be heard and, even better, included at tables of power?

There is also much to learn from networks such as the Global Alliance for Green and Gender Action, or the Global Greengrants Fund which has been supporting grassroots-led efforts to protect the planet and the rights of people for decades.[16]

What is the structure of this book?

This isn't a single 'big idea' book, which takes a single glitzy concept that just about fills a magazine article and stretches it thinly across a couple of hundred pages. I'm afraid we're not here to tell you that there's one simple trick to grantmaking. Instead, it's an intensely practical guide that covers a mass of good and bad practices, using real-life stories wherever possible.

Each of our 10 chapters tackles a different question. Each chapter is practical except for the first, which is about the values that underpin good grantmaking. In other words, the book starts with the *why* of Modern Grantmaking, and then examines the *what* over the next nine chapters.

In Chapter 1 we ask the question 'What is Modern Grantmaking?' In answering this we look at the most common critiques of traditional grantmaking and identify some core values that underpin the rest of this book.

In Chapter 2 we keep things simple, asking 'What are the no-brainers of Modern Grantmaking?' In this chapter we focus on the importance of doing straightforward things well, like paying quickly and listening carefully.

In Chapter 3 we explore a question currently making many grantmakers rightly uncomfortable, 'What should I do about privilege?' We consider how avoiding difficult conversations about race, ethnicity, class, disability and gender may ultimately undermine your overall mission as a funder, and we provide practical examples of funders that have been brave enough not only to talk about these issues but also to act on them meaningfully.

In Chapter 4, 'How do I help my funder develop a good strategy?', we demystify one of the most important tasks a grantmaker can carry out for a funder. We show that a good strategy is simple, concrete and essential, and we set out a path to getting hold of one yourself.

In Chapter 5 we explore perennial big questions in funding that don't have easy right answers, such as 'Should we accept unsolicited proposals?' This is a chapter full of old chestnuts, which will hopefully look different when exposed to a new light.

In Chapter 6 we ask, 'How can I improve the experience of grantseekers and grantees?' We look at how well-meaning funders can make nonprofit staff and volunteers deeply unhappy, and we give lots of advice on how to make sure that your applicants and grantees don't find dealing with you to be 'worse than dying' (to quote an actual grantseeker).

In Chapter 7 we dig into research and evaluation. 'How should I make use of research?' is the question, and we take readers on a quick canter through both the *why* and the *how* of using research to make a real difference.

In Chapter 8 the focus turns inwards: 'How do I manage well both upwards and downwards?' Few managers in funding organisations are given formal management training, and there's often more managing up than down! How do you lead and how do you ensure your grantmaking has more and more of an impact when you're sandwiched in the middle?

In Chapter 9 we explore, 'How do I keep developing my skills?', that is, how to keep developing the skills and experience that are essential in Modern Grantmaking.

Finally, in Chapter 10 we talk about becoming (or continuing to be) a grantmaking reformer, including prioritising changes in your own workplace, and how to join the wider Modern Grantmaking movement.

A quick note on anonymity

In aiming to write a book that is enjoyable to read, inclusive and honest, it was important for us to gather the views and stories of a diverse array of people from both sides of the grantmaking table, primarily in the US and the UK. So we asked a lot of people to talk to us in interviews, and a great many gave their precious time to share with us both their thoughts and their often personal and painful experiences (see our Acknowledgements section at the end of the book).

Unfortunately, the inescapable power dynamics within the funding sector are such that many people have good reason to be afraid of going on the record, and are justifiably uneasy about having their names attached to certain quotes and stories. Why the fear? Well, a nonprofit that truthfully reports bad treatment by a funder has every reason to fear that this will stop them getting future funding. An individual grantmaker who speaks painful truths about the bad behaviour of a leader or philanthropist may find that it's hard to get a new job with another funder. This isn't a theoretical danger either. We've spoken to people whose frank speech has cost them dearly.

Because of these worries we have quoted a large number of interviewees anonymously, and in some cases we've altered stories in small ways so that it is not possible to guess where they came from or who they refer to. It is sad that we have had to do this, but as this book will show, power and money can have a distorting impact on human relationships. Our having to anonymise our sources is, in some ways, just another reflection of how power makes it difficult to be a good grantmaker.

A few notes on tone and language

The tone of this book may seem a bit less formal than is often the norm in writing about grantmaking and philanthropy. This is partly because that's our authentic voice, but mainly because we wanted to write something that is, hopefully, fun and engaging to read or flip through. Most grantmakers spend a lot of their lives reading very serious documents, and the last thing we want to give them for their leisure time is even more earnest verbiage to slog through. If the lighter tone works for you, great. If it doesn't, we're sorry. Either way, we thought it best to give you fair warning up front.

Now to a few key points about words and phrases.

- Throughout this book we use 'funder' to denote an institution, not a person, and we use 'grantmaker' to mean a person, not an institution.

- Although we're an Anglo-American author team, we're both UK educated and so we've written the book in British English.

- Further, we use 'nonprofit' to denote any organisation that is organised and operated for a collective, public or social benefit, such as a voluntary group or a charity. We're not referring to a specific legal status, such as 501(c)(3) in the US or registered charity in the UK.

- The language that people use to describe themselves is also extremely important. Throughout the book we have referred to people using the words they have chosen to use to describe themselves and their organisations. This includes people who have self-identified as being a 'disabled person' or a 'person with disability', and also people who talked about 'disabled-led' organisations or organisations run by 'people with disabilities'.

- Whenever we have included stories or scenarios relating to disability we have used the language in the UK's Equality Act 2010, which legally protects people from discrimination in the workplace and in wider society.[17]

And, with that, it's time to get down to business. First on the agenda: what the heck is Modern Grantmaking?

1
WHAT IS MODERN GRANTMAKING?

This is not a book about how to be a grantmaker: it is a book about how to be a *Modern Grantmaker*.

Now, there's only really one good reason to take a portentous word like 'modern' and stick it in front of a profession, and that's because you think it may be possible to do things better than they've been done before.

We are guilty as charged. We think better grantmaking by private, government and corporate funders is most definitely possible. Happily, it turns out we're not alone in this. As we developed the book we spoke to dozens of grantmakers from funding organisations of all types and sizes in the US and the UK, and we think it's safe to say that a series of energetic reform movements were already well under way before we picked up our pens.

You may be someone who already identifies as a grantmaking reformer. Or you may have just picked up this book because you want to solve a problem that has come up in your work as a grantmaker. Whatever your story, we've done our best to write a book that will help you.

What's been brewing?

In the last decade a host of new ideas about how grantmaking should be done differently have been growing up like green shoots through cracks in a pavement. These shoots are now so numerous and so vigorous that the paving slabs of traditional grantmaking practice are threatening to buckle. This book is partly about giving those slabs a gentle tap of the toe to help them break apart more quickly.

New ideas about what 'better' looks like come from diverse peoples and places. Perhaps the strongest and most vibrant new wave of ideas about grantmaking comes from social movements demanding more power for marginalised communities. Other innovations come from researchers with a passion for using evidence to create social impact. The sectors of design, participatory democracy and management have also offered up ideas and practices that could make grantmaking better.

In this book you'll find stories and recommendations relating to all the above ideas. What's most striking about the ideas that have emerged is that they are *not* sitting in heavy books on dusty shelves or in journal articles that nobody will ever read. They're out there being implemented right now.

Many bold ideas and practices have already been adopted by grantmakers who aren't content to just do it the way it has always been done. For example, the Ford Foundation's BUILD programme is a 'five-year, $1 billion investment in the long-term capacity and sustainability of up to 300 social justice organizations around the world'.[18] This is a fundamentally high-trust approach that contrasts with how things have often been done in the past.

We're not alone in feeling that a wave of change in grantmaking is already well under way. You can see this in the perspective of experienced grantmaker Jayne Engle from Canada's McConnell Foundation who told us:

> Philanthropy and grantmaking is coming to the end of another cycle. The key question is, what are the next generation of funders doing to create the next one, and who is making those kinds of strategic decisions of utmost importance?[19]

One answer to Jayne's question comes from a private foundation CEO in the UK who told us anonymously that 'There are now a number of new leaders who talk much more clearly about what they're doing, using the same language that is used by the people they're trying to support'.[20]

We heard similar things about the US. One grantmaker was illuminating about the change, telling us:

> In the US democracy funding space, at the programme officer level, we've seen a shift in the people involved, especially in terms of women and people of colour. Just a few years ago, there were more white men named John leading programmes than people of colour.[21]

So change is absolutely afoot. But how does that connect with this book and with the idea of Modern Grantmaking?

What we call 'Modern Grantmaking' is fundamentally a collection of ideas and practices that are already out there in the wild. We don't claim to have invented any of these ideas: indeed we owe our own grantmaking education to many people quoted in this book.

Our contribution to this growing reform movement is simply to tie a bow around the ideas and give the whole package a name: Modern Grantmaking. And, because a slogan won't make any meaningful difference, we've also written a whole book – this book – about what Modern Grantmaking means in practice.

However, before we get started on the tips and hints, we must first address the elephant in the room. Why are grantmaking reform movements needed at all? What's wrong with how things work at the moment?

What do you mean by traditional grantmaking?

There are plenty of critiques out there about the evils of grantmaking, and especially about the alleged sins of certain types of mega-philanthropy. This book isn't another one of those. However, we cannot explain what Modern Grantmaking is and why anyone should care about it if we don't start by explaining what it is a response to.

Traditional grantmaking is the business of taking money that someone powerful has secured, and giving it away to what are believed to be 'good causes'. In most funding organisations the people who decide on who gets the money are normally the board members of the legal entity that controls all the money. This basic model tends to be similar for government grantmaking and private foundation grantmaking, which means that they are not always as different as they seem.

The board members who make the key decisions in traditional grantmaking organisations typically work on funding decisions for a handful of days a year, most often alongside another job or activity that takes up most of their time. Generally, these individuals come from privileged backgrounds and tend to be highly educated and solidly middle class. As board members they are often supported by paid staff members – from one person to over a thousand – who source and vet funding proposals to put before the board for approval.

The staff who support boards are what we call grantmakers. Hugely powerful in relation to grantseekers and grantees, they can often appear invisible in relation to board members or to their own CEOs. They also rarely have formal training in grantmaking – most live by their wits and learn on the job. We have been these people, we know the work they do is very important, and we've written this book for them.

Traditional grantmaking as described here is most often associated with private philanthropic foundations, and sometimes the words 'grantmaking' and 'philanthropy' are treated as meaning the same thing. But they don't. Philanthropy primarily refers to individual donors choosing to give away their own money, whereas grantmaking refers to the process of an organisation awarding a grant. A substantial amount of the kind of traditional grantmaking described above is done by government funding agencies and by businesses, not just private foundations.

What are the weaknesses of traditional grantmaking?

Before we start to pick holes in it, we should say that traditional grantmaking as described above has achieved a range of great things. From Carnegie libraries to the contraceptive pill, traditional grantmaking has made a huge, positive mark on the world. We enjoyed *Philanthropy: From Aristotle to Zuckerberg* by Paul Vallely – if you want a fun romp through this history.[22]

But, talking of history, we're not here to praise Caesar: we're here to bury him. Or, more accurately, we're here to point out that traditional grantmaking suffers from a range of problems that need to be recognised and addressed.

But where to start? Traditional grantmaking has been subject to a range of criticisms from a lot of different directions. In his book *Decolonizing Wealth*, Edgar Villanueva doesn't hold back:

> It is (we are) a period play, a costume drama, a fantasy of entitlement, altruism and superiority. Far too often, it creates (we create) division and suffering rather than progress and healing.[23]

During our interviews and research we collected mountains of grumbles and rivers full of woes. We could have written a book filled just with these gripes and critiques but that would have distracted us from our goal of helping grantmakers to do better.

So we boiled down most of the criticism we heard and read to just five common themes that came up time and again in our research.

- *Money follows social ties at the expense of need.* Often the people who most need the money do not have social relationships that would connect them with funders. This can result in too little money going to communities where it would make the biggest difference.

- *Trying to get money out of funders is too often a miserable experience.* Funders have a bad reputation for making the experience of applying for money much more stressful, exhausting and confusing than it needs to be.

- *Funders too often steer grantees to do unhelpful things.* Grantmakers often influence what grantees do with the money, either by making suggestions or by imposing restrictions. This sounds reasonable until you consider that it means that a person who is an expert in their job (e.g. a youth worker or care specialist) is being told what to do by someone who has likely never done that job. This form of back-seat driving leads to services that waste time and produce lower-value outcomes than would otherwise be possible.

- *Too many grants are made without using evidence to inform decisions.* Traditional grantmakers are often criticised for failing to commission or exploit the sort of high quality evidence that makes a real difference.

- *Bad grantmakers never get fired.* If you're a bad chef or a bad train driver, you will get found out sooner or later, and you might very well get fired. But if you're a bad grantmaker the chances are that you won't even get criticised, let alone moved on.

To cap this list of complaints, we also acknowledge the widely voiced criticism that grants made by the world's most privileged people are unlikely to be spent on supporting work that undermines their social position and power. If you want to know where we stand on this huge issue, and how we think grantmakers who work for private foundations should think about it, please see our Introduction.

What about the worst kinds of money?

There is one very important criticism levelled against some funders which is a failing of a completely different kind from the day-to-day problems listed above.

As has been highlighted by recent news stories and protests, the money given out by some notable philanthropists was raised historically through exploitative, racist or anti-competitive behaviours. In 2020 a statue of a 17th-century British philanthropist named Edward Colston was torn down by protesters in the city of Bristol because he had made his money primarily through slave trading.

The ties between slavery and philanthropy in the UK run deep. The Cass Business School, which today teaches a respected course on philanthropy, is in the midst of renaming itself because Sir John Cass, after whom it had been named, profited from the slave trade.

There are numerous private foundations operating today whose money was made through activities that are now illegal or considered profoundly immoral. Some of these activities occurred long ago, but others are much more recent. For example, at the time of writing many institutions are debating removing the philanthropic name 'Sackler' from buildings over that funder's connections with the US opioid crisis.[24]

Even if you don't work for a funder whose money comes from troublesome sources, you shouldn't rest too easy. As Sufina Ahmad, director of the UK-based John Ellerman Foundation, observes:

> Even newer funders that are only decades rather than hundreds of years old still perpetuate traditional grantmaking methods. It can be a closed, carbon copy sector with a lot of rotation of approaches and people.[25]

Where does Modern Grantmaking come into this?

The main motivation behind naming and promoting Modern Grantmaking is to discourage and ultimately eliminate some of the worst aspects of traditional grantmaking.

One way of understanding what we are arguing for is simply to take the criticisms of traditional grantmaking listed above and flip them on their heads. Using this method, we can say that Modern Grantmakers should:

- ensure that all organisations, including those led by and supporting marginalised communities, are empowered to get money, not just those with strong social connections to funders;
- practise trust-based ways of working with grantees as partners;
- make grant decisions based on evidence, and take active steps to overcome their own biases and prejudices;
- allow grantees to decide how the money should be spent rather than micromanaging them from afar, including spending on core costs such as organisational development.

So what is the definition of Modern Grantmaking? After much head-scratching, we decided that this is the definition we like best:

Modern Grantmaking is grantmaking that embodies the values of humility, equity, evidence, service and diligence.

You'll note that our definition doesn't name day-to-day practices or rule specific activities in or out. Instead we have rooted Modern Grantmaking in a set of values that we think all good grantmaking practices are already in touch with. In the rest of this chapter we'll explain what each of these values means.

What are the values that underpin Modern Grantmaking?

This book is full of practical advice and stories about how to be a better, more Modern Grantmaker. But the advice needs to be founded on a solid base for it to be worth listening to.

The foundations that we offer are *values* – concepts that people find intrinsically motivating. Modern Grantmaking is informed by five core values:

- humility
- equity
- evidence
- service
- diligence.

These values are not just philosophical abstractions – they can help you solve problems. For example, almost every grantmaker is permanently overstretched, trying to decide between competing priorities for their time. Values can help you to prioritise, when there's simply too much to be done and not enough time.

Each value is a big idea, so we'll spend the rest of this chapter looking at each one in turn.

Why is humility the first value of Modern Grantmaking?

> Humility is one of the key values for grantmaking. I remember thinking before I joined a funder that I never wanted to lose the stuff I felt when I was in the charity sector because that's what gives you some of the humility and not thinking you know all the answers as a grantmaker. As time's gone on, I've lost a bit of that and it does make me worry a little bit.[26]
>
> — ANONYMOUS GRANTMAKER

Humility is the quality of being aware of your own failings – of not thinking you know it all. People with humility behave without arrogance and without self-importance in their relations with other people.

Humility in grantmaking means entering every conversation with an assumption that you are no better or wiser than the person on the other side of the table (or screen). It means engaging in every conversation with a willingness to listen and to adjust your views in response to what you hear.

It is a value that can be hard to maintain – we all have a certain amount of ego. But we cannot overstate how important an attitude of humility is to the job of being a grantmaker. If you close this book now and take nothing else away from it, the critical importance of humility is what we would like you to remember.

At this point you might be wondering, 'Yes, yes, but what does it actually look like for a funder to display humility?' Well, the Ford Foundation's president, Darren Walker, wrote about it thus:

> Humility is characterized by an accurate sense of self-assessing not just our weaknesses but also our privileges and strengths, being honest with ourselves about both. The root of the word is related to the soil, like the word 'humus'. Humility literally means being close to the ground.[27]

Another way to illustrate what we mean by humility is to paint a picture of the opposite, that is, what we are trying so hard to avoid: arrogant grantmaking.

Arrogant grantmakers feel that they have nothing left to learn. They 'just know' when a grantseeker is a great organisation or when a funding proposal sucks. They read a funding application and judge its quality with their gut – they 'feel' if it's good or bad in their bones, and then make decisions on the basis of those feelings. They sit in decision meetings and declare 'If I ran this organisation, I'd do X', even though, as one of our anonymous interviewees put it, 'They are in no way qualified to make that assessment.'[28] Unfortunately, the sheer power that grantmakers have can fan the flames of the ego and arrogance that lurk within our souls. As the CEO of a private foundation told us: 'If the primary virtue of grantmaking is humility, the primary vice is hubris.'[29]

In contrast to arrogant grantmakers who are comfortable in their self-assurance, funders who value humility worry all the time. They worry that their judgement may be flawed or wrong, or prone to biases. They worry that none of their grants are making any impact – not even the ones given to 'star' organisations that are being showered with awards and plaudits. And they read post-grant evaluation reports with a cautious, doubtful eye, looking for weaknesses in the evidence rather than for vindication of their own brilliant decision making.

Humility doesn't just drive the best grant decisions. It also helps grantmakers to be nice, decent human beings in their interactions with grantseekers and colleagues. It also encourages grantmakers to listen more than they speak, which is good for everyone. We recognise that humility takes hard work, and that it doesn't come naturally to most people (we're still working on it!). It's even harder to stay humble when, because you are a funder, people tend to flatter you, laugh at your jokes and tell you how clever you are.

Humility isn't just about being a lovely, warm, virtuous person. It's about cold, hard results too. Humility reminds us as grantmakers that we can't create any impact at all without nonprofits and other grantees. They do all the actual work out there in the world. They make the difference while we mainly provide the cash. In a world without partner organisations that deliver services, run campaigns and innovate, we grantmakers would be as useful as a chocolate teapot.

Humility is also critical to improvements in performance. Humility is the value that puts funders on track to making this year's grants routinely more effective than last year's. An overabundance of grantmaker self-confidence, however, leads to stasis: this year's grants will always have about as much impact as last year's grants because arrogant grantmakers never really learn. As Stephen Bediako, founder and chair of the Social Innovation Partnership, told us: 'Grantmaking is done well when the grantmaker can see, learn and grow themselves from giving that grant.'[30] No learning means no improvement.

Finally, and somewhat unfortunately, some arrogant grantmakers have worked out that talking about humility – but not practising it – is good for their careers. One experienced foundation grantmaker told us a sorry tale:

> We had this director of a foundation who spoke continuously about the need to be humble and to be aware of 'our privilege' but was notorious for not allowing people to state another point of view and for railroading them into decisions.[31]

So watch out – just dropping the H word is not enough. If you want some practical advice on how to make sure you're practising humility in your work as a grantmaker, we suggest checking out our section on listening well (in Chapter 2) and on collecting and responding to feedback (in Chapter 6).

Why do Modern Grantmakers value equity?

> In an ideal world, funders shouldn't be allowed to practise unless they are taking positive and explicit steps to check their power and privilege and promote equity.[32]
>
> — MAGGIE JONES, CEO of Consortium of Voluntary Adoption Agencies and experienced funder board member

One of the biggest problems Modern Grantmakers have with traditional grantmaking is that it is frequently inequitable. This can manifest itself in quite a few ways, including:

- grant money being awarded disproportionately to organisations run by relatively privileged people;
- decisions being made on the basis of a simplistic understanding of the generations of disadvantage, discrimination and underfunding that have kept non-traditional

nonprofits from reaching a 'standard' that many funders deem to be what 'good looks like';

- endowment investment decisions being made by people who are protected from the ugly sides of the ways in which some companies make money;

- grantmaking power can become just another kind of power that is hoarded by a very tiny slice of society;

- grant money being awarded to people who have social connections with funders – connections that are not available to people outside certain social groups.

Valuing equity in grantmaking means looking at all aspects of what a grantmaker does and constantly asking the question 'Does this seem fair and just, in a broad social sense?'

Here are a few more specific examples of what can happen when a grantmaker takes equity seriously:

- Mechanisms are consciously put in place to ensure that grants are made not only to organisations that have pre-existing relationships with board members and grantmakers.

- Less than perfect spelling and grammar in a funding proposal will not lead to its being automatically seen in an unfavourable light.

- Even within invite-only funders, the funding process will be designed and tested to make it accessible to all potential grantseekers and grantees regardless of their education or any disability, and whether English is their first language.

- Data on the demographics of staff, board, grantseekers and grantees will be collected, analysed and made public to keep the question 'Are we working with the right people?' at the forefront.

We believe that grantmakers are most able to meaningfully put equity at the heart of their thinking and practice when they have a clear sense of their own privilege and the relative privilege of others. If you're not sure what equity means in a grantmaking context, check out Chapter 3 where we explore it, and explain how you, as a grantmaker, should respond.

Why does Modern Grantmaking value the use of evidence?

> I think that the most important thing for anybody, whether it's a foundation or a grantee, is to have the ability to be curious and to update your thinking based on experience and new evidence.[33]
>
> — RUTH LEVINE, former programme director of global development and population at the William and Flora Hewlett Foundation

Nobody in the grantmaking universe is ever going to admit that they don't really care much about using evidence when making grants. Even people who love to make gut decisions feel the social pressure to deny that this is their preferred way of working. As one anonymous US grantmaker told us, 'There's a lot of theatre built up around evaluation and learning.'[34]

Despite many protestations that 'evidence matters', an awful lot of traditional grantmaking decisions still get made without much real evidence being involved at all. In the heat of a board meeting it is often anecdotes, hunches, prejudices and sheer force of character that sway decisions.

Modern Grantmakers value evidence and research because they know that there's simply no other way to find out whether money being spent is making the world a little better or a little worse. Valuing evidence doesn't mean that Modern Grantmakers have to be highly trained research experts with lots of expensively acquired university degrees. This would exclude all sorts of people and we'd never endorse it. Valuing evidence *does* mean that grantmakers need to understand that scientists, social researchers and statisticians have developed an array of methods that can help us to understand when some grants are having an impact and when others aren't. Grantmakers need to value these skills and to understand when they need to deploy them even if they don't fully understand the ins and outs of research methods themselves.

Modern Grantmakers also know that, while most site visits to grantees are fun and interesting, they are a poor way of discovering the impact of a grant and are subject to all sorts of biases and distortions that conceal the truth. As we were told by the grantmaking research expert Dr Genevieve Maitland Hudson:

Site visits tend to play into funders' sense of specialness. This is often why volunteer trustees have become involved with a trust or foundation, but it feeds a dynamic of poor decision making. They tend to think that a single visit confers a deep knowledge that it doesn't and cannot without good comparative knowledge of similar delivery across multiple settings.[35]

So what does it look like, in practice, to be a grantmaker who values evidence? Here are some specific examples:

- When you first assess a funding proposal, you should take the time to ask yourself the question 'Is there any evidence of the impact of similar initiatives?'

- Where it is important to evaluate the work done by a grantee, you should arrange for it to be evaluated independently rather than asking the grantee to mark their own homework.

- You could partner with other funders to commission high-quality research that will ultimately enable you to make better grants.

Thoughtful grantmakers will also acknowledge that the research establishment, like the rest of society, is the product of a world that contains much discrimination and structural inequality. As a consequence, they will always try to work with researchers in ways that are consistent with the other values in this chapter, especially equity.

A Modern Grantmaker will bear in mind that some funding proposals come from organisations that cannot possibly supply evidence of prior impact from day one. They will understand that new organisations and organisations that lack resources will need long-term support and assistance before they can provide the same kinds of evidence that more established and wealthier grantees can easily provide.

Using research and evidence successfully and equitably is such an important issue that we've written a whole chapter – Chapter 7 – on how to get hold of research, how to use it and what to watch out for as you do so.

What does it mean for Modern Grantmakers to value service?

> One day one of the veteran grantmaking directors said to me, 'What we do is really all about the ideas – we want to be known for our ideas, not our money.' I didn't say anything but I thought that was crazy: giving out money responsibly, respectfully and quickly is essential for the health of the sector. It's how philanthropies add value. But some of our people clearly thought of it as secondary.[36]
>
> — ANONYMOUS FORMER CEO of large US foundation

'Service' may mean different things to different people. For Americans, 'service' frequently includes a moral component, as when a person stops a passing soldier on the streets to say, 'Thank you for your service.' To those in the UK, it tends to relate more to the way you're treated in a shop or restaurant.

When we say that Modern Grantmakers value service, we mean that they think of themselves as professionals who will willingly be inconvenienced to make life better and easier for applicants and grantees. This is in contrast to grantmakers who think grantseekers are lucky to even have a shot at 'their' funding.

Consistently treating grantseekers like valued customers and partners can be challenging because grantmakers are often more powerful than the people seeking money. In extremis a funder can have all the power in a relationship very much like a medieval monarch had absolute power over their subjects. As one anonymous grantmaker said wryly, 'Hello grantees! My name is Catherine the Great and you must put on a show. Show me the village!'[37]

This is where the value of service comes in, and why it's so important to think and talk about it in your workplace. If we see ourselves as *serving* grantseekers, rather than as their bosses, we will feel a moral duty to do things we wouldn't otherwise do. Grantmakers who really value service will be polite to grantseekers and show tolerance and patience when they can't express themselves quickly and clearly. An ethos of service encourages us to bend over backwards to make our criteria or processes easy for grantseekers to understand and to make application forms easy

What is Modern Grantmaking?

to fill in. It also encourages us to make sure that our funding organisations are easy to find and easy to understand by the people we hope to serve, even when it costs us more.

A service mindset is especially important to keep us doing the job that grantseekers desperately want us to do: give organisations money. Some grantmakers have aspirations to become known as intellectuals or activists, and start to see the business of handing over cash as slightly demeaning, whereas what nonprofits want from funders is to be given money quickly and simply. Valuing service means that we see the business of handing out the money as the priority and an essential part of what we do, rather than as a distraction from something grander that we'd rather be doing.

So that's what valuing service means. At this point you may well be wondering why we should behave like this when our control over the money means we *could* behave like medieval monarchs. As one of our interviewees put it, 'Our survival doesn't depend on our customers – we don't have any competition.'[38]

Nevertheless there are three reasons why funders should act as if grantseekers were paying customers who can afford to walk away.

The first is simply respect. We should show respect for the hard work that nonprofits and other grantees do to make the world a better place because that's simply the right thing to do.

The second reason is that a service mindset forces us to remember that we *need* grantees – they are our essential partners. As Phil Buchanan, president of the Center for Effective Philanthropy, says in his book *Giving Done Right*:

> Funders and nonprofits need to work collaboratively in a relationship that, by virtue of the challenges they face, is unique. Each party brings distinct strengths to the effort: the nonprofits as the doers and the funders as the ones who have the resources.[39]

The third reason is that a service mentality leads to greater impact. If we don't adopt a service mentality – if we are high-handed, superior and hard to approach – we will only end up hearing from and granting to applicants who can scale our fortress walls. A service mentality means that we will be more receptive and ready to hear when a grantee says, 'Your processes are in danger of ruining our impact.'

Why is diligence the final value underpinning Modern Grantmaking?

> Grantmaking is easy – I don't know why you need to pay people to do it.[40]
>
> — ANONYMOUS BOARD MEMBER of a private UK foundation

> You have a duty to be informed about what you're doing.[41]
>
> — ANNA DE PULFORD, director of the Dulverton Trust

One of the worst, most deeply embedded problems with traditional grantmaking is that too many crucial grant and strategy decisions are made by people who simply haven't put much time or effort into learning how to be good grantmakers. This is a big problem because grantmakers make choices that affect lives. Where grantmaking is carried out well it can dramatically improve lives, but where it is done badly it can really hurt people. Give a grant to charity A and you may be dooming charity B. The decisions are serious.

Within traditional grantmaking it has long been the norm that most of the people who make most of the decisions do so having gone through no more focused grantmaking training than the 'school of life'. Decisions are often also made by board members who dedicate perhaps 5% or 10% of their working lives to evaluating proposals and making grants. Why is so much power traditionally wielded by people who invest so little time in it? Perhaps it's because, as one of our anonymous interviewees told us, 'Many people treat grantmaking as a very easy job.'[42]

This is why Modern Grantmakers place a real premium on the value of diligence. They feel that anyone who either works for a grantmaker or serves as a board member for a grantmaker should put time and effort into developing the skills required to do the job well. This doesn't mean that everyone needs to be working full time as a grantmaker for their views to count, but it does mean that everyone – including board members – needs to treat grantmaking as something that cannot be done well without specific training, focused effort and frank feedback. For complete clarity, we should now say that when we use the word 'diligence' we're talking about the virtue of hard, focused work, not the legal practice of 'due diligence'.

You may be wondering what it looks like for someone to be a diligent grantmaker. Here are a few examples that you can learn more about elsewhere in the book:

- A diligent grantmaker does a research trawl to find out if there are any relevant studies or evaluations that might shed light on the likely impact of a proposal under consideration (Chapter 7).
- A diligent grantmaker regularly undergoes training and skills development to ensure that they keep getting better (Chapter 9).
- A diligent grantmaker regularly solicits honest feedback from colleagues and people outside their organisation to help them to improve (Chapter 8).

Lastly, diligence isn't just about how hard you personally work on grantmaking. It's also about how you work as a team. Diligence is *not* another name for lousy management behaviours like micromanagement and obsessing over relatively trivial details. For more on being a grantmaking manager who lives up to the values set out above, we suggest you skip ahead to Chapter 8.

How do I know if I'm living up to these values in my grantmaking?

> A colleague of mine once joked about the importance of humility to our funding organisation. 'We're so humble,' they said, 'if there was a league table of how humble funders were, we'd crush all the others.'[43]
>
> — ANONYMOUS GRANTMAKER

So we've just set out five values that we think all grantmakers should hold dear – especially those who aspire to be Modern Grantmakers.

- humility
- equity
- evidence
- service
- diligence.

These values underpin everything in the rest of this book, as well as our own attempts to be good grantmakers. You may be wondering how you are supposed to know whether you're living up to these ideals.

One of the simplest mechanisms is to conduct anonymous surveys of your grantees and others in the sector. It may be something you already do. If you conduct such a survey you can ask all sorts of things about your performance, including the extent to which your organisation's actions are seen as aligning with the values in this chapter.

Grantee surveys of this type have to be anonymous because grantees are at an enormous power disadvantage in relation to funders, and may not be wholly truthful about the failings of their 'paymasters' if their future funding is at stake. So you should make it very clear that nobody is going to lose funding for being honest.

One well-known method for studying the way in which grantees see you is to commission the US-based Center for Effective Philanthropy (CEP) to produce a Grantee Perception Report (GPR) for you. This involves surveying grantees in a safe and anonymous way, and producing results that compare you with other funders. These reports have been produced for over 300 funders around the world, and grantmakers often speak positively of them. For example, the CEP website quotes Meghan Barp, president and CEO at United Way of Greenville County: 'The GPR provides an opportunity for our grantees to give us candid, anonymous feedback, [and] launched us into refreshing our strategy and process.'[44]

The Center for Effective Philanthropy is not the only specialist that can be commissioned to produce this kind of perceptions research, although it does have an advantage in that it holds a lot of existing data on other funders. But almost any high-quality social research company will be able to get you useful results on how you are perceived by the people you are trying to serve.

However, before forging ahead, consider any ways in which this kind of research can potentially be distorted. For example, if grantseekers are not given anonymity they are likely to express much more positive sentiments about your organisation than they actually feel.

So remind me again – what is Modern Grantmaking?

Modern Grantmaking is grantmaking that embodies the values of humility, equity, evidence, service and diligence.

This may sound as though you have to be a saint to be a Modern Grantmaker. But we talked to numerous people during the writing of this book whose work clearly demonstrates all the values that underpin the idea. One of these was Sufina Ahmad, director of John Ellerman Foundation. Sufina's drive to address her organisation's past and present is exemplary, and she put into words the challenge that the rest of the book tries to address: 'Modern Grantmaking requires a transformation of values and processes. It requires breaking the standard model and rebuilding and remaking it *with* those we are set up to support.'[45]

We believe that anyone working for a funding organisation who doesn't already identify as a Modern Grantmaker should consider it. Even if your organisation is a bit behind the times, and even if you don't have the most powerful or senior role, there is nothing to stop you.

In the next chapter we'll start you on your journey to being a Modern Grantmaker via a series of basics or no-brainers that every grantmaker should practise.

An exercise on Modern Grantmaking values

Gather your colleagues together, either in person or online, for between 90 minutes and two hours. Ask them to come with an open mind, and potentially ready to tackle some uncomfortable issues about being a grantmaker.

Start by asking people to spend a couple of minutes privately writing down the bad or sub-optimal things they have experienced in grantmaking that they'd really like to see stopped or reduced. You should stress that these don't have to be problems witnessed in your organisation. If possible, these ideas should be written on sticky notes, whether the paper kind or the virtual variety.

Once everyone has written down at least a couple of these each, spend 20 minutes getting people to share their examples, and stick them on a wall. Don't worry about clustering notes at this stage, but do get people to expand on their examples.

After this, spend 10 minutes introducing people to the key ideas of Modern Grantmaking, as described in this chapter. You should run through our criticisms of traditional grantmaking and the five values that underpin Modern Grantmaking – humility, equity, evidence, service and diligence.

When you've set out what Modern Grantmaking is, write on the wall the five values that underpin modern grantmaking. Make them nice big headings under which you can cluster notes.

Then spend about 30 minutes asking people to pick an issue that has already been stuck on the wall, and to put it under one of the value headings, explaining their thinking as they do so. For example, if someone says, 'Funders giving money to their friends', consider putting it under 'equity' (because it's unfair) or 'diligence' (because it's lazy). Try to match as many of the issues on the wall to the five values as you can in the available time. If possible, cluster all of them.

When you have clustered the notes, ask everyone to stand back and consider. What patterns emerge? Do some of the values have lots of issues under them, while others have only a few? Why might that be so?

Finally, ask people which value they think they themselves would like to work on in their own working lives. Ask them to explain why they chose that value. Finally, wind up by challenging your colleagues to name specific things that they could do after the meeting to ensure that some real change happens as a result of this session.

2

WHAT ARE THE NO-BRAINERS OF MODERN GRANTMAKING?

Try not to be an asshole.[46]

— ANONYMOUS GRANTMAKER

Grantmaking is full of genuine dilemmas and often imponderable questions. We recognise this complexity throughout the book, and Chapter 5 is essentially a blow-by-blow guide to some of the biggest puzzlers out there.

But not everything about grantmaking is so conceptually tricky that it needs to be debated in a seminar. There are all sorts of no-brainers that Modern Grantmakers should just get on with.

In this chapter we'll take you through our top 15 no-brainers for Modern Grantmakers. We call them no-brainers not because they're easy to implement (some are and some aren't), but because, if your organisation fails to do enough of them, it has little chance of realising its grander ambitions.

To get the most value out of this chapter we suggest that you read it first, then find some colleagues with whom to run through the list. You may find that there's some illuminating disagreement over what you think is a no-brainer, what we think is a no-brainer and what your colleagues think is a no-brainer.

No-brainer no. 1: Make most of your grants unrestricted

> Every time we've been able to make an enormous step change it is because we've had unrestricted funding.[47]
>
> — ANONYMOUS FOUNDER of an international development nonprofit

Like most other grantmaking reformers, we argue strongly that the majority of grants made by most funding organisations should be unrestricted. You probably already know what we mean by unrestricted grants but, for complete clarity, we're talking about giving money to organisations without asking the grantees to spell out in advance exactly how all the money will be spent. Unrestricted grants are also sometimes called 'core grants' or 'general support grants'.

Unrestricted grantmaking is the opposite of restricted grantmaking. This is where money is handed over only after a grantseeker signs an agreement in which they promise to use that money only for certain clearly defined purposes.

We have two key criticisms of restricted grantmaking:

1. *Restricted grantmaking can lessen the positive impacts that can be made with funders' money.* It was an open secret, even before the COVID-19 pandemic, that grantmaking restrictions stopped grantseekers from responding quickly and smartly to surprising events and new opportunities. Once the pandemic struck it was obvious that many grant restrictions were now worse than useless, and funders around the world rushed to remove them.

2. *Restricted grantmaking uncomfortably echoes structural inequalities.* All forms of restricted grantmaking are a way of a funder saying to a grantseeker, 'We are capable of making certain better choices than you are.' Sometimes grantees do benefit from a funder's knowledge. But in relationships where a grantmaker comes from a position of immense power and a grantseeker comes from a position of having very little, the implicit message of restricted funding can simply be: 'People like us are cleverer than people like you.' This embeds and sustains an 'us' and 'them' culture that is the opposite of equity, one of our five Modern Grantmaking values (see Chapter 1).

Placing restrictions on grantseekers is, nevertheless, very common in the funding world – there are even some government funders whose rules limit them to making exclusively restricted grants. This norm hides just how strange a behaviour restricted grantmaking is, since most real investors – the ones who want to make money – almost never hand over money with such restrictions.

Most of the money in business and finance is unrestricted by default. For example, as an investor you can't buy shares exclusively in the part of Apple that makes iPhones – you can only buy shares in Apple Inc. This is because corporations know that they have to be ready to redeploy their assets at any time, for instance, to defend themselves from unexpected competition or to cope with an unexpected pandemic. If their resources were restricted in the same way as many grants are, those businesses wouldn't last long at all.

Happily, things are changing, and 2020 in particular saw a significant widespread move to making unrestricted funding more common across funding organisations. In that year over 800 funding organisations signed the Council on Foundations' pledge to 'loosen or eliminate restrictions on current grants' and to 'make new grants as unrestricted as possible'.[48] It was primarily driven by the COVID-19 crisis, but this change was already under way before the dam was breached.

The pledge appears to have worked: 66% of funders who took part in a survey about their responses to the pandemic so far said that they had offered unrestricted funding for the first time.[49]

One of the most tireless champions of unrestricted grantmaking is John Rendel, director of grants at the Peter Cundill Foundation. Here are a selection of comments from a spicy Twitter thread in which he lists some of the reasons he champions unrestricted funding:

No. 1   If you don't trust the organisation you're funding, why trust a project they're running? ...

No. 3   Efficiency. Restricted funding substantially increases the stress, time and costs involved in: Reporting, accounting, audit, fundraising (because grantees still need unrestricted funds and the fewer funders providing it, the higher the fundraising costs of getting it). ...

No. 5   Long-termism. Restricted funding encourages the creation of finite projects that 'neatly' open and close. But in the real world this creates massive amounts of waste. Unrestricted funding helps organisations invest for the future.[50]

We should probably say that we're not fundamentalists when it comes to unrestricted grantmaking. There are a few situations where grant restrictions make sense, and it's good to be clear about these.

The most common such situation is where you are trying to help an organisation that is doing important work, but that also has a weakness it does not really understand. So, for example, a nonprofit may need to get better at doing its accounts or at listening to those it serves, but it is simply unaware that it has this problem. In such a case, if you give the organisation an unrestricted grant they may never fix the problem because they just don't know about it.

There can also be situations where you are considering a grant to a branch of a very large organisation. If you were to give unrestricted funding to the parent organisation, the branch that sent you a proposal may never receive any of your money at all. In such a situation it would make sense to impose some restrictions on which part of the organisation can use the money, while taking care not to make the restrictions so tight that you limit the grantee's ability to adapt to a changing world.

Can you give me some examples of funders who make unrestricted grants, so I can learn from them?

- Headwaters Foundation (Montana, US) offers multi-year unrestricted funding for strategic initiatives.[51] Furthermore, the foundation's automatic GO! Grants of up to $5,000 are given to any organisation that meets its initial eligibility requirements. Yes, you read that right, *automatic*. Headwaters is also a founding member of the Trust-Based Philanthropy Project, which we discuss in Chapters 5 and 10, and which we think is a great example of Modern Grantmaking.

- The Blagrave Trust (UK) provides unrestricted multi-year funding to youth charities who give young people a meaningful voice.[52]

- Luminate (US and multi-country) has made a public commitment to 'wherever possible – provide unrestricted funding to our grantees and investees'. We also like their sharing of data on the proportion of unrestricted funding they award.[53]

- The Peter Cundill Foundation (Canada, Bermuda and UK) offers funding partnerships of three-year unrestricted grants that are extended by a year each year, 'subject to partners making sufficient progress against their own organisational milestones'.[54]

- Pears Foundation (UK) believes in long-term core funding and builds relationships that develop over time.[55]

- The Trans Justice Funding Project (US and Puerto Rico) is a community-led funding initiative founded in 2012 to support grassroots trans justice groups. The project makes grants annually by bringing together a panel of six activists to review every application received. All the money raised goes to grantees with no restrictions – an approach designed to show that they believe in trans leadership.[56]

- Esmée Fairbairn Foundation (UK) has changed its approach to provide larger and longer-term grants. It has also very helpfully published analysis and commentary on the debate on restricted and unrestricted grantmaking.[57]

No-brainer no. 2: Adopt a clear mission and make grants that support it

A mission is a simple thing: it's a short, clear description of what you're trying to achieve and why you're trying to achieve it.

Every grantmaking organisation needs a good mission, one that's easy to remember and easy to communicate with grantseekers, grantees, colleagues and board members. Why is this so important? Because every funder needs something to keep it heading in a purposeful direction when temptations and distractions are all around.

Without a clear mission your funding organisation is likely to spray grants wildly all over the place, like an out-of-control fire hose. Once the excitement has passed the world will probably look much the same as if your organisation had never made any grants at all.

So, how do you get hold of a good, clear mission statement? Well, we have an entire chapter on that coming up (Chapter 4). Just go on ahead if you can't wait.

The 'Magna Carta excuse' for a weak funder mission

Some funders have a weak, outdated or missing mission statement.

One of the reasons for this, especially in older funders, is what we call the 'Magna Carta excuse', named after a bit of medieval British law on which many countries' legal systems are based.

In old funding organisations it's inevitable that the people who came up with the original mission are dead and gone, sometimes for hundreds of years. In such cases we've heard the excuse from trustees that 'Our founders are departed. Their original aims don't seem so relevant now but it seems like so much work to revise and update our mission. And sort of disrespectful of the people who set up the organisation, too.'

We don't have a lot of sympathy with this. It uses sentimentality and laziness to avoid the hard work of making sure you have a focused and relevant mission. If you hear an argument like this in your board or staff meetings, it's time for emergency action. You should either figure out how to run a robust and inclusive strategy refresh process (see Chapter 4) or consider spending down your endowment and winding up the shop (see Chapter 5, dilemma no. 9).

No-brainer no. 3: Make more long-term grants

> No one can really achieve change across the windows within which most funding is offered.[58]
>
> —DAN PASKINS, director of UK Impact, Save the Children, and former senior grantmaker

Most grants are made to last for a pre-specified period of time, often one year. We believe that most grants should last much longer than this, and that in most cases funders should offer grants that are much longer term – 3, 5 or even 10 years.

Why are we against short-term grants? Well, we're not always. We think they make perfect sense in some cases, such as a grant to celebrate a big day in a community, for example. But, ultimately, most things that almost all grantees are trying to achieve take time. For something to have a lasting impact it usually requires effort and funding to be sustained over considerable periods of time, whether it's discovering a new drug, helping young people into employment or lobbying for new laws.

We're not alone in our view. Ruth Levine, who was for eight years a director at the William and Flora Hewlett Foundation, told us unambiguously that grantmakers 'should give multi-year grants whenever possible: virtually nothing can be accomplished in a twelve-month period.'[59] Echoing this view are the Bridgespan Group, the widely respected social impact consultancy, which reported that 90% of attempts to change systems take 20 years.[60]

Consequently, we applaud the position adopted by the Boston-based Cummings Foundation. This foundation, whose money had been made through canny real-estate investments, seems to appreciate the value of long-term funding. In 2017 the foundation, which was already making regular multi-year awards, started a programme called Sustaining Grants.[61] It is explicitly stated that these grants are up to 10 years in duration, something that is almost never formally announced by funders, even those that privately plan on long-term backing.

The Cummings Foundation deputy director Joyce Vyriotes explained the choice, noting that

> Long-term financial support is rare for nonprofits, making fundraising a constant and time-consuming task. The Sustaining Grants are intended to provide some relief, allowing these organizations to focus more of their time and energy on delivering and enhancing their important services.[62]

Before considering a move to make a larger proportion of longer-term grants, a funder must ensure that this kind of change aligns with both its mission and its strategy. For those that operate a mixed portfolio of shorter- and longer-term grants, moving to a new operating model based on longer-term grants will take time and require a range of adjustments, the most difficult of which is likely to be financial planning.

Despite the possible difficulties of making this kind of change, we believe that funders who are serious about making a deep, lasting impact in the world must be willing to make long-term grants on a more regular basis.

No-brainer no. 4: Don't fund alone

There are a great many reasons why funders should try to collaborate regularly with other funders, and very few good reasons for always going it alone.

The three main reasons why we think funders should take the time and effort to collaborate with others are:

- Really big problems are too large for any single institution to have any chance of affecting, let alone resolving.

- Funders who collaborate will gain valuable new knowledge and make better choices.

- It will make life easier for applicants who can, in the case of pooled funds, write a single funding proposal and then receive grants from several organisations.

Collaboration is not always a bed of roses, though. Time-wasting collaborations do exist (trust us, we've been there). One anonymous grantmaker we spoke to lamented the number of collaborations that were 'a lot of talk and no action'.[63]

The first step to joining or starting a successful collaboration with other funders is to be very clear about the type of partnership you want. The funding experts at GrantCraft, an online repository of knowledge for grantmakers, have helpfully created three broad categories,[64] which represent the different types of collaboration you may want to consider:

- *Learning Network* is a group of funders who come together to hear what's happening in a field or issue area, share information, and explore potential strategies for making more effective investments.

- *Strategic Alignment Network* is made up of funders who share a mission, strategise together, and work in concert to obtain publicity, traction, and impact – but who still do all their grantmaking independently.

- A *pooled fund* is a 'pot' of money to which funders contribute and from which grant dollars (or programme-related investments) are disbursed. Money from the pot is used without distinguishing the original donor. The day-to-day work of the collaborative is often carried out by staff

or consultants, with donors serving on steering
committees, setting strategy, and making decisions.

One recent example of a pooled fund is the approach taken by the music star and businesswoman Rihanna's Clara Lionel Foundation (CLF) to co-fund rapid emergency grants in response to COVID-19.[65] Working with other funders, CLF organised pooled funds and swiftly made joint funding decisions, including with Jay-Z's Shawn Carter Foundation, to provide support for marginalised communities in New York City and the Los Angeles area.

Once you have chosen the type of collaboration you want to be part of and decided on its purpose, you still need to make it a success. We asked a lot of people who'd been involved in funder collaborations what they felt made the difference between good and bad partnerships. We were told that it is important to:

- clearly identify a shared cause or a 'common enemy' (preferably a disease or a social ill rather than another funder who has more Twitter followers or a more charismatic CEO);

- make time for grantmaking colleagues to work on a collaboration – don't assume that they can be a successful part of a collaboration and do all their other duties at the same time;

- involve senior decision makers – it wastes everyone's time if your funder is represented at a collaboration by someone who can't actually decide anything or doesn't really understand how the ultimate decision makers think;

- put in place mechanisms, ideally outcome measures, to gauge whether the collaboration is achieving anything (see Chapter 7);

- establish informal meetings alongside the formal ones (even in in an era of online meetings, there's a lot of value in a cup of coffee);

- join a collaboration only if you're willing to change how money is spent: funders who become part of collaboratives and whose spending is totally unchanged afterwards have missed the point, or may have joined just to add their name to something or to look good. One former CEO of a private foundation lamented the funding partnerships where nobody commits any actual money, saying, 'Too often funders behave like a collection of small children standing around the edge of a cold swimming pool too scared to jump in'[66] – don't be those people;

- beware of herding: sometimes funders copy each other's actions not because it's the right thing to do, but because it's the easy thing to do – it makes them feel included. Be vigilant that you don't fall for this – it's a very human temptation to succumb.

If you're really serious about dipping your toes in the collaboration pond, an essential piece of reading is Bridgespan's report, *Value of Collaboration Research Study: Literature Review on Funder Collaboration* by Alison Powell, Susan Wolf Ditkoff and Kate Hassey.[67] Their monumental work of analysing over 125 articles and reports on partnerships, plus a huge survey of over 400 grantmakers and nonprofits, is a benchmark in terms of what grantmaking as a sector knows about collaboration. Their conclusions, as you'd expect, are subtle: collaboratives can work but also often fail. Their analyses and conclusions are well worth reading carefully: our advice here is a pencil sketch compared to their oil painting.

Case study of a good funder collaboration: The Thomas Paine Initiative[68]

Through the 1990s and 2000s human rights actors in Europe enjoyed a striking series of legislative successes which enshrined human rights in international and domestic laws.

However, by 2009 it was clear that a general backlash against human rights was under way. More specifically, it was clear that the relatively new human rights legislation in the UK was under serious threat.

A series of meetings between human rights funders was arranged by the network Ariadne, which had been set up to facilitate collaboration between human rights funders across Europe. Invitations to the meetings were shared as broadly as possible to ensure that as many potential collaborators as possible were in the room. The main topic of discussion was the rising challenge of politicians who saw that political capital could be gained by weakening or repealing human rights laws.

During these conversations the idea emerged of a formal funder collaborative specifically to defend human rights in the UK. But it was just an idea, and without nurturing it seemed unlikely to ever make it off the drawing board. Fortunately, Jo Andrews, who had set up Ariadne, was willing to put a lot of hours into being a 'sheep dog' (in her words), gently herding the various interested funders towards a more formal collaboration. She called it the Thomas Paine Initiative.

Eventually a group of seven funders were tentatively lined up who had expressed interest in and enthusiasm for the idea. But – alas – none of them was willing to be the first to put money into a collaboration that was new and untested. The project stalled.

Deploying a piece of Machiavellian ingenuity to break the deadlock, Jo asked a friendly programme officer at a relatively large funder to say that they were simply 'considering inviting this collaborative for a proposal'. This wafer-thin non-commitment was then shared around the rest of the potential funders who, feeling somewhat comforted, were then willing to make more formal commitments. The collaborative was born, funding human rights defenders across the UK.

The Thomas Paine Initiative ran for a decade as a result of the hard work of Neil Crowther, who was its director, and James Logan, then of Oak Foundation, its chair. The real lesson for readers of this chapter, however, is the story of its birth, which was a tribute to Jo Andrews's determination and people skills.

No-brainer no. 5: Invest to make applying for your money easy and accessible

It is easy for funders to set up an application process that is dire for grantseekers. This is true for both funders that welcome unsolicited proposals and those that are invite only. Here's an illustration from the founder of a nonprofit organisation:

> When our organisation was small and new, we came across a foundation that loved our work, and which quickly gave us £10K. They liked what we did with the money and asked us to submit for a larger amount through their website.
>
> The application form was immensely long – it just kept asking more and more questions. Because we were new we really didn't have real answers to many of the questions, but I drove on through this barrier using the skills and confidence I got from my privilege and my education.
>
> What I witnessed was clearly a huge systemic barrier to less privileged applicants that the funder just wasn't aware that they'd put in place. In the end we submitted 60 pages for a £60K grant – a most unfortunate symmetry.[69]

No matter how small a funder you work for, we believe that you should put time and energy into making sure that your grant application process is as easy and accessible as it can be.

There are two reasons why this is a no-brainer rather than a 'nice to have'. First, you should provide a clear, accessible application process so that your employer does not become a *de facto discriminatory* funder. The more confusing the questions you ask and the more impenetrable your funding guidance, the less likely you are to get good applications from diverse applicants. A bad application process is like a strongly scented flower that has evolved to attract highly confident, over-educated applicants while scaring everyone else away.

Second, you need to make sure that you're not costing applicants more money than you're actually putting into the sector you are supporting. A study of grant application forms by the University of Bath found that they contained anything from 21 to an astonishing 193 questions, and that the average registered charity studied was submitting 22 applications per year.[70] Another study claimed that the average cost of applying for each grant is £6,600 (about $7,500).[71] While the robustness of all these figures may be contested, one thing is certain: the worse designed your submission process is, the more it will cost grantseekers to engage with you. If you want to do something about your application process but you don't know where to start, never fear: Chapter 6 is all about this and is full of practical advice.

No-brainer no. 6: Say 'no' clearly and quickly

Telling people that your funding organisation is not going to give them a grant is probably the worst single part of the job. We hate saying 'no' to grantseekers because we hate upsetting other people. Making people upset is generally not why any of us became grantmakers. And rejecting lovingly crafted funding proposals that contain people's deepest hopes and dreams is a surefire way of making people sad.

People get upset for good reason too. It really does hurt to have put a lot of effort into a proposal and then get a 'no' in return. It's also often more than just a professional disappointment – it's also a personal one. Having your grant proposal rejected can feel like being rejected as a human being.

We as funders tend to loathe this part of the job. So it can be tempting simply to avoid it by never quite saying 'no', and instead disengaging, while we hope the grantseeker will just give up and leave us alone.

Stringing people along whom you know you will never fund is one of the grantmaker habits that most frustrated the nonprofit leaders we interviewed for this book. It's bad practice for a lot of different reasons, not least because most grantseekers will not simply give up and go away if you don't say a clear 'no'. As social enterprise founder Wietse van der Werf told us, 'It isn't fair for a funder to keep talking to a nonprofit whom they think they are unlikely to fund. It wastes time and builds hopes unnecessarily.'[72]

So one of the golden rules of grantmaking is to say 'no' straight away, as soon as you know that a grantseeker is not likely to receive any money. Don't beat around the bush and don't obfuscate the reason for your decision. As the Luminate CEO Stephen King put it with helpful clarity, 'It's really important to have the courage to give a quick "no".'[73]

It is also much better and more useful to grantseekers if you can give a reason for your rejection at the same time as you say 'no' to them. Far too many funding organisations, we think, fall back on the excuse that they don't have the time to give feedback. We think these funders should ask themselves whether it is more important to save this time than to invest it in giving grantseekers potentially priceless feedback about their ideas.

If you really cannot make the time to give an explanation for your decision, you should still always endeavour to answer 'no' as quickly as you can. If you are struggling with what to say in a hurry, here are some

Modern Grantmaking

suggestions from our interviewees and from our own experience:

- 'I'm sorry to tell you that your proposal has not been successful. We have to weigh up many competing priorities, and there were other proposals that simply matched our goals more closely than yours.'
- 'I'm sorry that the answer is "no". We looked at your proposal, and despite some strengths we decided it was not a priority for us at this time.'
- 'Unfortunately, we do not have the financial or strategic flexibility to support the important work you propose.'[74]

> ### A 'saying no slowly' horror story (don't do this!)
>
> The following tale was shared with us by the CEO of a successful activism nonprofit.
>
> 'We first approached a really big beast funder with a carefully thought through proposal. We had an initial conversation, but then everything got very confused and slow. We were glacially punted between different bits of the funding team, never quite getting a clear interest.
>
> Eventually, after about two years, we were asked to revise our proposal to make it bigger than we originally envisaged. This was a good sign!
>
> Encouraged by this positivity, we revised the plan, and had another chat with the funder. The grantmaker we spoke to said they thought it was about 80% likely that our proposal would get approved by their decision-making board. But, several weeks later, it didn't: the board shot it down pretty brutally showing that the programme officer actually didn't really understand what the board wanted after all. The "no" arrived via an extremely awkward phone call about two and a half years after our conversations with this funder had started.
>
> We could have coped with this rejection but what was really damaging to our organization is that after we were asked to increase the size of our proposal, other funders stopped considering granting to support that project. Medium and small funders thought we were about to be given a big grant by a big funder, and so went "why bother?". New money dried up. So when we got rejected by the big funder we were really stuffed, and we had to inform our staff they might be laid off. It was awful.'[75]

No-brainer no. 7: Tell people what they want to know when they want to know it

It can be hard for a grantmaker to empathise with how complicated and stressful life is for most grantseekers. Grantseekers almost invariably work for overstretched organisations, most of the time in underpaid or unpaid roles, with little of the support and infrastructure that come from working in a company, a government or a funder. As Phil Buchanan puts it in his book *Giving Done Right*, 'Nonprofit leaders are like Ginger Rogers, who – as a cartoon famously described her – did everything Fred Astaire did, but backwards and in high heels.'[76]

One especially miserable part of the job is waiting for a 'yes' or a 'no' from a funder. It can be a form of mental torture. This may sound like a slightly tasteless exaggeration but it isn't: we've witnessed the effects on people as they obsess over pending decisions, and it's really grim. So please have some sympathy with people you've put in this position.

Waiting for decisions also tends to be worse for smaller and less experienced organisations, because they tend to make fewer funding applications and will therefore be more dependent on each one. The key thing that funders can do to alleviate this misery is to keep up regular communication so that grantseekers know where they are in the funding process.

There are many ways in which you can communicate with grantseekers during the grantmaking process. For example, you can talk to prospective grantees:

- before they have even decided to apply, giving them useful information about things such as turnaround times and success rates;
- after they have applied, to confirm that you have received their application and will process it;
- during the proposal vetting process, to give them information on the dates of decision meetings, who attends them and what criteria will be used;
- after decisions have been made, to explain those decisions – this is especially important if a grantseeker is unsuccessful.

You should never simply assume that a grantseeker won't want to know a piece of information about your organisation or the process. They almost certainly have an appetite for this knowledge. And if you want to know what information does and doesn't matter to grantseekers, do user research instead of guessing: check out Chapter 6 for lots more on how to do this.

As a general rule, you can safely assume that grantseekers are very keen to have every scrap of information you can share with them that relates to the decision-making process and their proposal. However, if you have said 'no' and explained why, you shouldn't feel obliged to keep talking to them. Time is scarce, and new grantseekers deserve your time more than rejected applicants who are simply trying to work out what to say so that you will reconsider their proposal.

Be aware too that the need to keep up friendly, regular communication doesn't stop when a grantseeker is successful and becomes a grantee. Regular check-ins will help put grantees' minds at rest and stop them making bad choices because they've mistakenly second-guessed what you want. Regular communication also helps make changes to grants easier and less painful. It's not rocket science. It's just being decent to people.

No-brainer no. 8: Practise having conversations that are mutually beneficial

> The No. 1 thing that nonprofits have said to me over the past 14 years when I asked them, 'What do you wish funders would do more?' is just listen.[77]
>
> — EDGAR VILLANUEVA, author of *Decolonizing Wealth*

On the whole, funders have a reputation among nonprofits for talking too much and listening too little. You may have witnessed this yourself if you have ever attended a meeting or been at an event where a powerful funder dominated the floor, even though there may well have been more interesting speakers who merited the time more.

It's important that, as a funder, you take steps to make sure that your conversations with grantseekers and grantees are valuable both to you and to the applicant or grantee you're talking to. A successful conversation should have the tone of two people building something together, not one person awkwardly trying to chat the other up.

What are the no-brainers of Modern Grantmaking?

There are various ways you can try to make sure your conversations are mutually beneficial:

- You can explicitly name 'listening' as a crucial behaviour in your internal rules and culture, as the William and Flora Hewlett Foundation does, which instructs staff to 'Listen more than you talk in grantee conversations'.[78]

- You can ask your colleagues to shadow you in meetings with grantseekers and grantees, so they can give you feedback on the quality of your conversations.

- When you are gathering feedback from grantseekers and grantees, you can ask them for anonymised feedback on how well you talk and listen.

- You can review your grant-making processes to see whether there are things about the rules and structures you have in place that prevent listening (see Chapter 6).

The COVID-19 crisis has made some funders think more about what it means to listen to grantseekers. As one US private foundation leader quoted in a research report observed, 'We're really just beginning to learn how to develop the culture and practices to listen more effectively to communities least heard and most affected by inequity. As we look ahead, it's going to be critical for our organization.'[79]

There are signs that this pattern of funders working on their listening skills is more than a one-off. A 2016 study by the Center for Effective Philanthropy found that, for foundation CEOs, 'listening to and learning from the experiences of intended beneficiaries' was ranked first in a list of 'practices for increasing impact', while listening to and learning from grantees was second.[80]

No-brainer no. 9: If you don't accept unsolicited proposals, explain how grantseekers can get noticed by you

There are a lot of funding organisations in the world that do not accept unsolicited proposals. The choice to be invite only is an entirely reasonable position (we discuss whether or not the choice is right for your organisation in Chapter 5).

If you work for this type of funder, which doesn't accept proposals through an application form or by email, there is one extremely important grantmaking no-brainer: you have to make it clear and transparent how people are supposed to get money from you.

What this means is that you should have a short, clear explanation somewhere on a website of how your funder finds and chooses grantees to give money to. It will give grantseekers who could potentially be brilliant grantees for your organisation a chance to understand what they have to do to get noticed by you in future.

You may be thinking, 'Isn't this a bit of a pain? Can't we just be totally private about what and how we choose who to grant to?' While we sympathise with this position – it's obviously less hassle for us as grantmakers – we just don't think it's OK in this day and age.

It isn't acceptable to be completely secretive about how you find and fund organisations because this way of working actively contributes to social exclusion and inequality. Groups led by people from less privileged backgrounds or actively marginalised communities may well not get invited to the right parties, may not have easy access to key conferences or may just not bump into your grantmaking colleagues or your board members. The result is that your money will tend to go to more privileged people, and probably more privileged causes, at the expense of those who aren't already in your network.

In short, opaque grantee identification processes come with major risks of distortion that strongly disadvantage the most marginalised groups. We therefore believe that all funders, even very small and very private ones, should publish an honest account of how successful grantees have come to their attention over the years. If nothing else, this gives newer, more marginalised groups a playbook: they can learn how to get your attention and ultimately have a better shot at getting your money.

For many funders, publishing an explanation of what a funder is for and how it chooses grantees will mean building and launching a website

What are the no-brainers of Modern Grantmaking?

for the first time, as a huge number of funders have no online presence. Given the low cost of simple websites nowadays, and the pro-equity reasons for publicly explaining your mission and way of working as a funder, we think virtually every funder should have a website.

If having a website is something you haven't discussed for a while, it's time to open up that conversation again, particularly in the context of discrimination, diversity and inclusion in your society. In the words of one anonymous foundation chief executive we spoke to:

> I was talking to someone who runs a foundation that's got nearly a billion dollars in the bank. They told me they didn't have a website. And I thought 'Why the hell don't you have a website – what's that about?'[81]

We couldn't have put it better ourselves.

No-brainer no. 10: Don't bounce grantseekers into doing things that aren't their priorities

> It's very easy for a funder to make a minor request that massively distorts the focus and mission of a grantseeker, for example: 'Ooh, this proposal would just be a bit stronger if you could add in under-represented voices from Tanzania.'
>
> And now you've potentially just ruined everything.[82]
>
> — HELEN TURVEY, executive director of the Shuttleworth Foundation

As Helen Turvey says, it's the easiest thing in the world to accidentally nudge grantseekers towards engaging in activities that aren't their priority. This happens because grantmakers have power.

Power can be defined as the ability to get other people to do things they wouldn't otherwise do. One of the most damaging manifestations of grantmaker power is where a funder persuades – or intimidates – a nonprofit that is excellent at doing thing X to do thing Y instead, which is nowhere as important or impactful as carrying out their original plan.

What's so self-defeating about making grantees do work on which their hearts are not really set is that it leads to a double failure, all at the funder's expense. First, it distracts nonprofit organisations from their core business – the activities that they've really thought about and that they believe will

Modern Grantmaking

have maximum impact and value. So good things can stop happening just because an organisation got a grant, which isn't a brilliant outcome.

Second, the productivity of nonprofits may decline when they are working on ideas that they don't fully own. Who can blame them for not working as hard on someone else's passion?

If this seems fanciful, consider for a moment the following sad – but true – story from a successful nonprofit founder:

> Pre-COVID, our nonprofit ran several face-to-face training sessions a year, heavily focused on the kind of community building that happens best in a shared physical space. An interested funder emerged and said 'We want to support this, but we really want it to scale. Could you please do this teaching via a Massive Open Online Course (MooC)?'
>
> We replied to the funder and said: 'Look, we're not technophobes but we have lots of reservations about pure online training to meet our organisation's goals, especially around the diversity and inclusion problems experienced by other MooCs.'
>
> Eventually it became clear that if the funder was going to support this work we'd have to set some ambitious numbers, which we were worried about achieving, given it was such a new project. We were clear from the start that we couldn't achieve the same sort of numbers as MooCs, and it seemed the funder accepted that.
>
> However, they clearly hoped that we would change our mind in time – so every meeting we had with them ended up with them putting more pressure on us to go back to their idea (do a MooC) and they never really accepted our plan.
>
> So in the end, after three years of very awkward funding we mutually agreed to end the funding arrangement. We arranged a debrief with them, and to our pleasant surprise they revealed that this experience had taught them that it might be best to just fund organisations for the work they know needs to happen, delivered in the way they think is best! I was delighted they'd come to that realisation, and that our feedback was heard, but ultimately sad that we had to endure three years of a very challenging relationship.[83]

The lesson here is very simple. As a grantmaker you should back grantees to deliver on their own missions. If you don't think a grantee is capable of delivering on their own mission, you should either fund the strengthening of that organisation or look for someone else to fund.

But what you shouldn't ever do is misuse your power to turn a good thing into a bad thing. That's grantmaking at its worst.

No-brainer no. 11: Pay grantees up front

We'll keep this one short, since it's really simple. Grant payments to grantees should always be made up front – not paid in arrears after the work is delivered. This doesn't mean that you should pay the entire value of a grant in one go (although you can), rather that your first tranche of grant funding should always be made quickly and early on.

A payment schedule that isn't quick and early assumes that a nonprofit organisation can just use imaginary 'spare cash' to tide it over till you make the payment. If your organisation routinely works on this assumption, you should read Chapter 3 on learning to check your privilege.

No-brainer no. 12: Don't short-change your grantees

> One time, a funder looked at my salary as the executive director, which was $1,500 a month not including any benefits or health insurance, and they thought that was a bit too much for a nonprofit. Meanwhile, their own salary was orders of magnitude more than that – and Global North grantees also had EDs [executive directors] that were compensated in six figures despite being much newer and without any track record.[84]
>
> — ESRA'A AL SHAFEI, founder of Majal and creator of *Philanthropi$$ed* podcast

Even though we started this chapter with a strong endorsement of unrestricted funding, we understand that you may find yourself managing a lot of restricted project funding for the foreseeable future.

If you do make restricted grants for specific bits of work, it's incredibly important that you allow grantees to use your money to pay for the true costs of running their organisation. This is vital because one of the most

Modern Grantmaking

common and entirely justified complaints levelled at funders is that they insist on paying only for certain parts of an organisation's work, and refuse to pay for others.

This is especially curious since nobody does this in their own personal life. You don't walk into a restaurant and say, 'I'd like to pay for the chef but not the waiter, please.' If your boss said they'd like to pay you only for every other piece of work you deliver, they'd pretty soon find that they weren't getting any work from you at all.

However, this bizarre practice is almost normal in grantmaking, and is hidden in language that conceals just how weird it is. Consider:

- 'We don't cover "indirect costs"; we only fund direct project-based activity.'
- 'We only pay 10% or 15% for overheads.'

In both cases the funder is essentially saying, 'I'd like to have a lovely thing please, but I don't want to pay for it.' In our daily lives we'd call that extortion, and we'd probably call the police if someone persistently tried it out on us.

Failing to cover the true costs of your grantee's operations actively harms their financial health and stability, and as a funder you should never do anything like that. What's more, not investing in core costs also means not investing in upcoming and current leaders of grantee organisations, networks and movements, and that is likely ultimately to undermine your own organisation's mission.[85]

We're pleased to report that this practice is slowly dying. Over the past few years, a number of US-based funders have agreed to support a 'pay-what-it-takes' approach to philanthropy – a more flexible approach grounded in real costs that would replace the rigid 15% cap on overhead reimbursement followed by many foundations.[86] As Jen Bokoff, director of development at Disability Rights Fund, says, 'Multi-year general operating support is working. I believe it's something every single funder should be doing in a big way, even if they still choose to offer some more focused funding.'[87]

So, if you want your organisation to pay the real costs of getting things done you have to:

- make the case for a change with your leadership;
- design and implement changes to your back-end processes, staff training and all the guidance you put out;

- borrow tools like budget templates from other funders that are already working in this way (there's no need to always develop lots of new stuff from scratch);
- communicate the change to your current grantees but don't expect them to change how they interact with you overnight – building up new ways of working will take time and patience.

Simple but hard – like so many things in this book.

No-brainer no. 13: Fund quickly

> Working with the Center for Effective Philanthropy we secured a lot of frank, anonymous feedback from our grantees. It turned out we were much slower to make decisions than we thought we were – something we're now working to improve.[88]
>
> — STEPHEN KING, CEO of Luminate

One of the most fundamental differences between how grantmakers and grantseekers perceive the world is how each group thinks about time. For grantseekers time is a crushing machine, a terrifyingly fast conveyor belt ceaselessly dragging them towards a zero bank balance and bankruptcy.

For grantmakers the opposite is true. As funders we worry that rushing too quickly to make decisions will result in worse grants being made. We feel that a stronger proposal or a better use of our money might appear from somewhere if we were to wait just a few more weeks: we fear the potential pangs of regret. In short, grantmakers feel numerous pressures on them to move slowly and deliberately. They don't have to worry about going under if they don't move quickly – that simply isn't a possibility for them as it is for most grantees.

We should always remember that our perspective as grantmakers is hugely distorted because we experience far less time pressure than the organisations to which we make grants. We therefore tend to act slowly – even as we feel incredibly busy – and, perhaps more importantly, we often seem slow to the organisations we serve.

'Sure,' you might say, 'but our purpose is not to look good to others. Our purpose is to create impact, so what's the harm in taking a little more time to make good choices?' Put this way, taking our time to make the right call sounds very reasonable. But, from the grantseeker's point of view, slow grant decisions are awful and can even be deadly for organisations. For example, the more slowly a nonprofit acquires sufficient grants, the more overall time, money and energy its leadership has to put into raising money. If grantmaking is sufficiently slow, organisations could simply fold and lay off their staff before funding decisions are made.

Furthermore, while we as grantmakers dither about our funding choices, the people running nonprofits are spending their time raising money and bolstering our egos rather than delivering impact. By making them wait, we are making them less productive.

We must therefore set and enforce a pace of grantmaking for funders that is quicker than we would naturally feel comfortable with, while not being absurdly quick and driven purely by hunch.

To make this kind of commitment to a faster pace, you'll need:

- to take time to understand the internal barriers that currently stand in the way of working quickly, and get senior management to remove them;
- to work with grantseekers and grantees (not just your own colleagues) to understand what a better pace and timescale might look like.

As one anonymous grantmaker put it to us, 'Maybe it doesn't have to take 9 to 16 months to do a grant.'[89]

No-brainer no. 14: Take safeguarding seriously

A lot of nonprofits work with children or elderly people who are potentially vulnerable to abuse. Funders have a unique responsibility to ensure that the organisations they support have appropriate processes and systems in place to protect these individuals from the very people who are supposed to be helping them.

What does this mean in practice? First, it means that every funder should make sure up front that grantseekers are effectively addressing the safeguarding needs of those who work for and with funding beneficiaries. This means asking probing questions about what safeguarding measures they take and, if appropriate, seeking assurance from independent reviewers.

What are the no-brainers of Modern Grantmaking?

A very common mistake that funders make is to assume that an organisation that used to be good at safeguarding still is – this isn't necessarily so. Funders with a responsible approach to safeguarding will have regular updates and checks by safeguarding organisations, not just one-offs.

The Association of Charitable Foundations (ACF) in the UK has developed a helpful safeguarding framework specifically for funders which considers three areas.[90] This is well worth a look even if you operate in another country or in a legal context with different rules. Some of the questions it encourages you to ask are critical, including:

- Is your current assessment process adequate and proportionate to the nature of safeguarding risk in the organisations you support?

- Do staff have sufficient understanding of safeguarding (what to look for or what questions to ask) to be sure that a grantseeker's approach to safeguarding is adequate?

- How would you respond if you had concerns about a grantseeker's safeguarding policy, process or implementation?

The full ACF checklist on safeguarding is considerably longer and more thorough than this. We also recommend reviewing the free International Child Safeguarding Standards produced by the independent nonprofit Keeping Children Safe.[91] These standards have been designed to ensure that all organisations working directly for and with children have comprehensive safeguarding measures in place. They have been recognised by the United Nations and may be highly relevant if your funding supports this kind of work.

Our grantmaking no-brainer here is simple: you either put in place steps to safeguard vulnerable people or you don't make grants to organisations that work with vulnerable people. There's no shortcut. Of course this may mean introducing restrictions on grants up front and potentially supporting organisations to improve their safeguarding processes too, but these kinds of restrictions are very different from those that fundamentally rob grantees of their autonomy.

It's not only about knowing and following the correct process, however. It's also about ensuring that you have the right culture in place to enable people to get this right and to feel supported. An experienced grantmaker for one of the largest community funders in the UK offers this advice:

> You don't go into grantmaking thinking you're going to manage safeguarding. You go into grantmaking thinking you're going to be happily sitting behind a desk and not getting involved in the difficult, gritty, nasty stuff.[92]

While there's a lot of good guidance about policies and how you do the process, the difficulty we found was more about giving people the confidence, the right questions to ask and knowing what their role is. It was more around support and providing pastoral care and recognition. We need to remember to say 'thank you' to the people leading on safeguarding in our organisations, because it can be relentless.

No-brainer no. 15: Be transparent about what you do and don't fund

People who work for nonprofits and other grantseeking organisations are constantly stumbling across funders who may or may not be right for them – squinting at oblique guidance or eavesdropping on rumours about the types of grants that have been made in the past.

These grantseekers then very often spend quite a lot of time and effort – and money – slowly and painfully establishing that a particular funding organisation is not even *remotely* interested in what they do. But, by the time this has happened, both sides have often spent weeks or months in a time-consuming dance.

This enormous waste of time and money happens because too many funding organisations have concluded that they like and even enjoy a bit of vagueness and mystery in their public identity.

Some of the reasons for keeping funding criteria secret are practical. Grantmakers sometimes fear being buried in funding applications or personally hassled for money. But other funder motivations are not so pure, and may be based more on the thrill that comes from holding all the cards when the other player holds none. This is a straightforward case of revelling in power, and if you catch yourself feeling this way you should take a cold shower, and then start to make amends.

You should put the information on what you do and don't support on a website – even if you don't accept unsolicited applications – so anyone who needs to read it can do so. The only exception is situations where sharing information publicly could put other people at risk. In such cases, we would still suggest that you provide a short, readable briefing containing relevant information on what you do and don't fund, which you can email to people privately.

At this point, it's worth saying that the overall state of transparency of funding organisations is rather weak. Only one in 100 funders in the US currently shares information on past grants, and only 10% of US foundations have a website.[93] Our view is that you should adopt a policy of de facto secrecy only if your goal is to waste the time of prospective grantees.

Once you have made clear your funder's purpose through a website, including what you do and don't fund, you should consider going further. For example, it is becoming increasingly common for funders to publish data about the grants they have made in the past.

The best way of being transparent about past grants is to publish the data in such a way that they can be included in grantmaking databases online, which grantseekers and funders regularly use to help plan their activities. In the UK you should sign up to 360Giving, which runs the excellent GrantNav website,[94] and in the US you should take a look at GlassPockets.[95]

Both of these organisations support funding organisations in publishing their grants data in an open, standardised way. This helps both nonprofits and other funders to make better-informed choices about how to spend their time and money. We strongly encourage you to look them up and get in touch with them.

All that said, we don't underestimate the challenge of trying to be more transparent. The road to routine transparency for most funding organisations is long and hard, but it is ultimately worth it.

What is GlassPockets?

GlassPockets is an initiative from the US-based Foundation Center. In their own words, 'GlassPockets provides the data, resources, examples, and action steps foundations need to understand the value of transparency.'

GlassPockets works specifically with private foundations to improve their openness. It ascribes different levels of openness to partner organisations including 'core transparency' and 'champion transparency', and provides tailored assistance to foundations that are trying to improve their transparency. As of autumn 2020, 102 funders, with total assets of $214 billion, have signed up to GlassPockets.

Am I really supposed to put all these no-brainers into practice?

We understand that many grantmakers on their own won't have the power to engage in the full range of practices recommended in this chapter. We have set them out so that you can ensure these issues form part of the ongoing debate about how your organisation is run, and not because we expect anyone to implement them all in a weekend.

We have called these practices no-brainers not because they're easy to implement, but because, if too many of them are missing from your organisation, even the smartest of grantmaking strategies are likely to be undermined.

Speaking of mistakes that can undermine a funder's impact, in the next chapter we shall discuss the reform challenge that has given rise to some of the greatest resistance in contemporary grantmaking: what to do about privilege and power.

Chapter 2 checklist

1. Are the majority of your grants unrestricted?
....
2. Does your organisation have a strategy based on a clear mission, and do you make grants that support that mission?
....
3. Do you make long-term grants?
....
4. Do you work in a partnership?
....
5. Do you invest in making the process of applying for your money easy and accessible?
....
6. Do you say 'no' clearly and quickly?
....
7. Do you tell people what they want to know when they want to know it?
....
8. Do you practise having conversations that are mutually beneficial?
....
9. If you don't accept unsolicited funding proposals, do you explain how grantseekers can get noticed by you?
....
10. Have you bounced nonprofits into doing things that aren't their priorities?
....
11. Do you pay up front?
....
12. Do you pay full cost recovery?
....
13. Do you fund quickly?
....
14. Do you take safeguarding seriously?
....
15. Is your organisation transparent about what it funds?
....

3
WHAT SHOULD I DO ABOUT PRIVILEGE?

> The sheer power of grantmaking! People laugh at your jokes when they're not funny. If you convene 100 people, 150 will show up. But this kind of power can be dangerous.[96]
>
> — NGOZI LYN COLE, experienced senior UK grantmaking executive and board member

Gather round the campfire, everyone – it's time for a horror story. As with any good scary tale, we leave it up to you to speculate on which bits are real …

Picture a boardroom in a large funding organisation. The deep lustre of the mahogany table and the discreet, expensive lighting hint at the volume of wealth lurking in institutional bank accounts.

A board meeting is just getting started. Eight of the great and the good are sitting around the table studying the agenda, which includes a never-before-seen session called 'Diversity, equity and inclusion awareness training', scheduled just before lunch.

The morning passes as it usually does in board meetings, with presentations, finances and decisions. Late morning, around the time appetising lunch smells start to waft into the room, there is a knock at the door. An assistant informs the chair of the board that their guests are here. With great fanfare, members of a training organisation run by disabled people are ushered in to run the scheduled awareness training session.

Over the course of the allotted 25 minutes, the training organisation takes the board members – none of whom are disabled – through an exercise focused on helping them understand how modern professional organisations should think about equity, power and privilege.

But, although they take part and nod along politely, the board members are not really engaged in the exercise. Their minds are elsewhere. There's a lot of other stuff on the agenda, and some tricky funding choices to be made – plus the allure of a three-course meal is strong when you had to get up early to travel to the meeting. This appears to be especially so of the chair, who smiles a lot but does not steer the board to discuss any actual decisions or commitments they could make. Then it's lunch-time.

The board meeting ends a few hours later. The official minutes of the meeting show that diversity training was delivered and appreciated by the board who were grateful to the trainers for coming in to run the session. There's consensus around the table that it was a good thing to do the training and that everyone is better off for it. The board meeting concludes and everyone goes home.

Then ... *nothing changes*. Or, to be more specific:

- No changes are made to the organisation's priorities or strategy.

- Nothing changes to make this funder's application process more open and welcoming to different sorts of people.

- Nobody reviews the funding strands and programmes themselves to make sure that they don't exclude certain groups.

- No changes are made to the composition of staff, board members or, ultimately, the mix of grantseekers who are awarded funding.

To the board members the diversity awareness training has been like water off a duck's back. But, despite the total lack of impact, it has been minuted as a great success and the organisation officially plans to return to it in three years' time.

And so, with a great, silent scream of missed opportunity, our horror story draws to its close.

How does this story help me be a Modern Grantmaker?

> If you're a funder who brings in Black and brown expertise to 'help trustees' and yet doesn't take that next step and look at who needs to give up some power, step down and allow new and different faces in, you're the problem.[97]
>
> — RUTH IBEGBUNA, founder of RECLAIM Project and The Roots Programme

This is fundamentally the story of an organisation making a costly mistake. It is a mistake that all Modern Grantmakers should work hard to avoid.

We call it a mistake because the board members in the story had an opportunity to make their own funding organisation better, but they passed it up. They had the opportunity to make changes that would have led to new applications from potentially impactful grantseekers, but they ignored it. They had the chance to make the funder's own team stronger and more capable, but they passed that up too. They also had the chance to make sure that their funding wasn't perpetuating problematic inequalities in the society they served, but they didn't. They thought the exercise was about ticking a box and feeling good about themselves.

Why didn't the board members in the story think any change was needed?

> In ten years working for disability charities, I have yet to meet a person with lived experience of disability, representing a strategic funder.[98]
>
> — ANONYMOUS SENIOR EXECUTIVE of a UK disability nonprofit

In the story the board chose not to make any changes to the way the organisation worked because they didn't understand or couldn't empathise with the very different life experiences of people who weren't like them. They just couldn't comprehend how the way in which their funding organisation worked could present barriers to people whose lived experience of things like money, education, discrimination and employment was profoundly different from their own.

This kind of mistake has already been given a name: *unchecked privilege*. It's called 'privilege' because it relates to the advantages some people have, and others don't, that are a result of accidents of birth. This privilege is 'unchecked' because in our story the people around the board table didn't take any steps to better understand and act on what the trainers from the disabled-led organisation had shared with them.

Grantmakers need to be aware of the role of privilege in their organisation and in society at large. They need to know how to acknowledge and manage privilege – this is often known as 'checking your privilege'. To get you started, we will look more into what privilege is and why it matters so much to good grantmaking. Then in in the second half of the chapter we'll look at what other funders are doing to stop unchecked privilege from undermining their mission and strategy, and what this could mean for you.

What are privilege and power, and why do they matter to a grantmaker?

This chapter is about the problems that privilege gives rise to and the problems that power creates.

This book mentions power quite a bit, often in passing. Therefore it's important to be clear about what we mean by 'power' and why power can be a problem.

Power is basically the ability to get people to do things they wouldn't otherwise do. When a teacher tells a rowdy classroom full of students to be quiet and they shut up, that's power. Grantmakers have power over grantseekers and grantees because they can make them do all sorts of things that they would never do otherwise, such as writing long proposal documents or developing new projects and plans that weren't on their original list.

For most people in grantmaking, the fact that they have more power than grantees and grantseekers is unremarkable – it's just part of life. Even for those who don't have megalomania, it's still quietly satisfying to be the actor and not the person who is acted upon.

But – party poopers that we are – we're here to encourage you as a grantmaker to think about the power that you have as a burden that you need to be worried about rather than as a gift to be enjoyed. For example, an individual grantmaker can deploy their power to create real harms by making 'helpful suggestions' that grantseekers find impossible to refuse, such as:

What should I do about privilege?

'Maybe to increase the bang for your buck of your proposal, why not expand your carefully designed and evaluated therapeutic support programme to also include ... army veterans / elderly cats / everyone in California?'

These idle comments can – and do – lead nonprofits to embark on whole programmes of work to which they're not really committed, which aren't central to their own mission and which do not make the best use of their capabilities. Power can indeed be dangerous.

The definition of *privilege* we use in this book is by writer, journalist and editor Sian Ferguson. She describes privilege as 'A set of unearned benefits given to people who fit into a specific social group.'[99]

To understand this definition we have to unpack its two halves – the 'unearned benefits' bit and the 'specific social group' bit. We'll start with the latter.

What are the 'specific social groups' that have privilege?

Various characteristics of a person can give them greater privilege than some other people. These are all accidents of birth and not the result of personal choices. They will be different in different places and at different times. The following list includes some of the factors within contemporary Western society that tend to give some people a greater advantage in life than others:

- being born white;
- being born non-disabled;
- being born male;
- being born into a middle-class or wealthy household;
- being born heterosexual;
- being born neurotypical;
- being born English-speaking;
- being born into a family or society that guarantees you a good education;
- being born into a body that you feel matches your gender identity;
- being born into a loving family.

While an individual may have certain kinds of privilege, such as being white, they may not be privileged in other ways. For example, they may be middle class, male and heterosexual but still have experienced early childhood trauma.

We quite like the way Erving Goffman put it in 1963:

> There is only one complete unblushing male in America: a young, married, white, urban, northern, heterosexual Protestant father of college education, fully employed, of good complexion, weight and height, and a recent record in sports.[100]

Some people, then, are born with advantages that make their lives easier. But what exactly do these advantages consist of? What exactly is in their goody bag?

What are the 'unearned benefits'?

The unearned benefits of privilege vary widely but can include:

- receiving less or no hassle from the police, compared to other people;
- having skills and confidence as a result of a good education;
- benefiting from racist bias in hiring practices, which give preference to a name that doesn't look 'different';
- being attentively listened to in meetings rather than talked over or ignored.

Is privilege a widely accepted idea?

The unearned benefits of privilege are, as a general rule, never written down or codified. The people who supply the benefits – employers, colleagues, police officers, judges and teachers – often have no idea that they're treating some people better because of characteristics over which these people have no control. Moreover, privileged people will often strenuously deny that these unearned benefits actually exist at all.

Those who deny privilege commonly argue that they have worked very hard during their lives, and therefore privilege doesn't exist and is not real. In answer to this, we would simply encourage them to have a conversation about the nature of hard work with the cleaners in their own offices.

John Amaechi, a former NBA basketball player who is now a psychologist and a best-selling author, explains why some people feel a strong urge to push back when they hear others speak of privilege:

> Privilege is a hard concept for people to understand, because normally when we talk of privilege we imagine immediate unearned riches and tangible benefits for anyone who has it. But white privilege and indeed all privilege is actually more about the absence of inconvenience, the absence of an impediment or challenge, and as such when you have it, you really don't notice it, but when it's absent, it affects everything you do.[101]

If, like us, you are a well-educated middle-class white person, you may very well be riled by being told that your life must be a walk in the park. We're sure that it isn't. Having, for example, been born with the privilege that comes with being white doesn't mean that your life isn't hard, or that you've been handed everything on a plate. It simply means that your skin colour has not been the cause of your hardship or suffering.

We could dedicate pages to setting out arguments against those who claim that privilege isn't a real thing, or that the very idea is some sort of conspiracy against white people. But we're not going to waste your time debating the existence of something that very obviously does exist. That's what the comment threads at the end of news articles are for, and we don't want to muscle in on their territory.

What is 'unchecked privilege'?

Being privileged isn't a moral failing – it's just a description of how things are for some people. People who have more privilege are not automatically bad people, and people who are less privileged are not automatically good people.

Having privilege is not a moral issue because it is mostly the result of choices made by the people who raised us, before we ourselves had any agency or even before we were born. Some of us were born with a bunch of handy power-ups that make life easier, and some of us weren't. It isn't our fault.

Privilege becomes a moral issue when people with privilege make decisions that affect other people, in particular when these decisions hurt or disfavour some people. The decisions are not necessarily due to intentional discrimination but result from not asking the question 'Is what's good for me good for everyone?' Here are some examples:

- A politician advocates for a law that will harm many people not out of malice but because they have not thought enough about the lives of others.

- A school headteacher implements a rule that will cause much greater stress and grief to some pupils than others because they don't empathise with the challenging lives of some of their students.

- A boss makes a joke in a workplace without realising that it upsets a minority of their staff.

Checking your privilege isn't about some vague notion of guilt. It simply means pausing to ask if our own experience and upbringing may not be enough to enable us to make a good decision, especially one that impacts on other people. As such, 'checking our privilege' is yet another manifestation of humility – the primary value of Modern Grantmaking (see Chapter 1).

Is the concept of privilege some new, fleeting idea?

You may already know quite a lot about privilege, or you may have learned about it in the aftermath of a recent atrocity such as the killing of George Floyd by Minneapolis police on 25 May 2020. If privilege is a relatively new concept to you, you may well believe it to be a new idea. But it isn't.

The US sociologist and historian W. E. B. Du Bois published *The Souls of Black Folk* over a century ago, in 1903, in which he introduced the key concepts that we understand today as underpinning privilege.[102] His analysis showed the very different lives of white Americans and African Americans, depending on which side of the 'color line' they were on.

He highlighted that white Americans did not think much about African Americans or about the effects of racial discrimination on their lives. African Americans, in contrast, were highly conscious of white Americans and deeply aware of racial discrimination. His insight into the gap between how much different groups think about their own advantages and disadvantages made Du Bois the intellectual precursor to modern thinkers about privilege, even though he did not use the word himself.

Du Bois later expanded on his concept of privilege by defining the 'public and psychological wage' of whiteness. This meant that being white in the US was like being paid a salary that those who were not white did not receive. That's what we called 'unearned benefits' above. This wage wasn't monetary but took the form of advantages such as admittance to public functions, more lenient treatment in court and access to the best schools, as well as being treated with courtesy and deference.

Du Bois also pointed out that white people did not simply *have* advantages but also felt *entitled* to them. While he didn't use the word 'privilege', the concepts he talked about can be clearly seen in the definition of privilege we are using in this book.

Hasn't the word 'privilege' been made up by self-righteous people on Twitter?

Again, no. The American feminist and anti-racism activist Peggy McIntosh started using the term 'privilege' to build on Du Bois's concepts in the 1980s. In her much cited 1988 article 'White Privilege and Male Privilege', McIntosh acknowledged the advantages she herself enjoyed in US society as a white person, and confronted her own 'trouble facing white privilege'.[103] She compared her own reluctance to accept the advantages that come with whiteness to 'men's reluctance to acknowledge male privilege', and talked in depth about the parallels between her own experience and the 'several types or layers of denial that I see at work protecting, and preventing awareness about, entrenched male privilege'.

McIntosh listed an eye-opening 46 privileges that she as a white person experienced in the US, including:

- being able to rent or buy a house in an area she could afford and wanted to live in;
- being reasonably sure that her new neighbours would respond warmly, or at least neutrally, to her arrival;
- being able to turn on the TV or open a newspaper and immediately see people like herself positively represented;
- never being asked to speak for all the people in her racial group;
- knowing that if she were pulled over by a traffic cop it wouldn't be because of her race;
- not having to educate her children to be aware of systemic racism for their own daily physical protection.

McIntosh said that the pressure to avoid her white privilege was so strong because 'in facing it I must give up the myth of meritocracy'. In other words, she acknowledged that she didn't like confronting her own privilege because it made her question whether the advantages she had experienced had been earned or had instead been a consequence of the 'whiteness wage' that Du Bois had talked about.

If this chapter is the first time you've encountered writing on privilege, you'll almost certainly feel this discomfort yourself. We have definitely felt it, and our own acceptance of it did not come overnight.

Why should privilege and power matter to me as a grantmaker?

> Power is not intrinsically bad, but many think there is an unhealthy balance of power between funders, grantees and communities. Power imbalances can limit funders' ability to understand the issues they wish to influence and make effective decisions, undermine relationships between funders, grantees and communities, and in doing so hinder funders' ability to influence social issues and achieve their goals.[104]
>
> — KATIE BOSWELL et al., 'A Rebalancing Act', New Philanthropy Capital

Every funding organisation is established with the aim of making a positive difference. While a few may be aimed at furthering more elite pursuits (think retired racehorses or opera), far more funders focus on the welfare of people who, for different reasons, live disadvantaged lives.

However, a focus such as supporting people living in poverty sets up a fundamental power imbalance in the grantmaking profession. As a rule of thumb, the people who decide on who gets money are quite privileged, and those who get it are much less privileged. And this gap really matters.

'So what?' you may ask: 'What's so wrong with people who have means sharing with people who haven't?' The problem, in a nutshell, is one of empathy and knowledge.

Can privilege undermine good grantmaking decisions?

> I once talked to a very wealthy board member who didn't understand the difference between living in social housing – i.e., government subsidised housing – and being homeless; they had assumed they were the same thing.[105]
>
> — ANONYMOUS SENIOR GRANTMAKER

The great majority of professional grantmakers or private philanthropists we have come across in our careers are from middle-class backgrounds. They tend to have university degrees and the various other social power-ups of privilege that we mentioned above, such as being non-disabled.

By contrast, many people who directly benefit from grantmaking tend to have very different backgrounds – different experiences of education, health care and crime. They may well be members of social groups that are widely discriminated against.

This means that the lives of grantmakers and grantseekers are really different in a lot of ways. For example, funders are less likely to have direct experience of and an understanding of what life is like when your local youth club closes and your key social connection disappears. And they're far less likely to have experienced the grim realities of grinding poverty or racial discrimination.

This lack of experience makes a huge difference when we assess funding proposals in the real world. To see how, consider the following fictional story.

> A funder receives an application from a community group in a low-income area. The funding application is for a youth project that will help 100 young people to improve their prospects.
>
> The grantmaker reviewing the application grew up in a very different kind of community. They come from a different racial and socioeconomic group from most of the young people in the project, and they have two higher-education degrees, whereas most people in the community haven't been to university.
>
> The funding officer reviews the proposal. They see that the organisation is new. It doesn't even have one year of financial accounts or a properly constituted board. They note that the

Modern Grantmaking

funding application contains numerous spelling mistakes, which doesn't come across as very professional. They note that the budget isn't broken up into much detail, so it's hard to work out exactly where the money would go.

Because of this litany of 'problems', the application goes into the 'no' pile before it even gets to the decision-making board. The grantmaker has applied their critical skills and done their job. However, their privilege has resulted in their missing the following significant context:

- that the 55-year-old applicant is a self-educated community leader who dropped out of school when they were 12;

- that the applicant is the single most trusted member of the community, a combination of arbitrator, therapist and childminder for people around the neighbourhood;

- that there are no other youth schemes of any kind running in that area and there have been spates of youth violence and high levels of youth unemployment in this area for years;

- that the applicant is the only adult in the local area whom many young people respect and listen to, and the only one who can reach many other people who could otherwise end up in the criminal justice system;

- that virtually anyone in the community who was asked 'Should this applicant get the money?' would have agreed that this was obviously a sensible and trustworthy person to give it to.

With this extra knowledge, the funding proposal suddenly looks very different and considerably more impressive. The lack of knowledge about and empathy for this community has led to the grantmaker failing to identify a proposal that was going to make a big impact in a badly underserved community that really needed the money.

Worse still, some of the skills that come with privilege (such as being good at spelling) actually militated against good decision making because spelling, punctuation and grammar are unofficial, undocumented assessment criteria on which bids at this organisation are judged. On top of this, standard finance department risk management policies, such as the requirement for three years of accounts and 'well-constituted' boards, can end up excluding bids from passionate, talented people who just don't know how to play the game.

In our story the grants officer failed to check their own privilege, and their employer had not reviewed its grantmaking policies to see if they excluded organisations that could benefit from funding. Consequently, a strong proposal goes unfunded and nobody at the funder knows that it made a serious mistake.

While the story is not reportage, data show that this sort of problem affects real grantmaking all the time. In a recent survey in the UK, 70% of respondents felt that the level of diversity in board members affects which organisations get funded, and the same percentage felt that way about staff diversity.[106] More specifically, two thirds of respondents felt that the lack of ethnic diversity in foundation trustee boards had an impact on the fundraising efforts of minority-led nonprofits; only 5% disagreed. There is, in short, a widespread consensus that organisations that don't take steps to change will make less effective grants.

Why haven't funders tackled the problem of unchecked privilege and problematic power imbalances?

> There is a massive power and privilege imbalance that we have propped up and sustained and, if we're honest, we need to explore if it is something that we have sometimes liked or preferred.[107]
>
> — SUFINA AHMAD, director of John Ellerman Foundation

Some funders are taking great steps to tackle the negative impacts of unchecked power and privilege on their work – we'll talk about and celebrate them shortly. But our view is that too many funders are still not doing enough to limit the negative impact of unchecked privilege on their grantmaking effectiveness and their impact on society as a whole. This is despite the sharp, decisive action taken by many funders in response to calls for more support from the racial justice movement in the summer of 2020, where we saw promising steps forward.

The simplest explanation for the slow overall progress is that taking action to deal with the problem of unchecked privilege in funding organisations makes many of the people who call the shots at such organisations feel deeply uncomfortable. The question 'Why aren't you doing more to check problematic privilege in your organisation?' is up there with other discomforting questions such as:

- Do you really deserve to be paid that much?
- Shouldn't you do more volunteering?
- Shouldn't you phone your mother/father/sister/grandparents more often?

We all know what it's like to face awkward questions like these by simply ignoring them and getting on with other things in our lives. Grantmakers may often be very talented people but they're also just human, and they don't like admitting that they should floss more frequently any more than you do.

The reluctance to face these issues can manifest itself in unacceptable but sadly familiar behaviours by weak funder leadership, including:

- sighing, looking pained and commenting on how it's 'terribly complex' before changing subjects;
- making self-pitying jokes about how 'as an older white man I'm surplus to requirements', i.e. turning the issue into one about themselves and deflecting from a serious conversation about change;
- challenging the whole concept of privilege and turning an urgent problem into a kind of academic seminar.

These kinds of answers to questions about privilege are clear signs that some leaders are grasping at straws because it is just too unpleasant to address the problem head-on. This behaviour is what the Seattle-based nonprofit leader Vu Le has called 'funder fragility'. He defines this as what happens when:

> A group that has privilege and power is criticized, and a member of that group becomes hurt and defensive instead of reflecting on and trying to see systemic challenges and their role in it. Often times, the conversation is derailed and enormous time and energy are spent to reaffirm the offended/defensive individual and make them feel better.[108]

'Funder fragility' is, in our view, an extremely helpful concept, and one to be aware of and to watch out for whenever you raise issues of privilege and other similar topics with colleagues or board members.

What should I do about privilege?

We encourage you to try not to be a fragile funder. When you talk about these difficult topics, don't be over-defensive and don't make it all about you. Instead, try to be willing to listen – really listen – to the views of those you fund and support. And, if you find yourself with colleagues who are struggling to come to terms with their own privilege, try to take them where they need to go with empathy.

What's the scale of the challenge?

> Inherent structures within grantmaking elevate a particular experience, mindset and world-view that still puts us, grantmakers, in a senior place ... which means boards in turn tend to elevate the same things and believe that only certain types of people can have power and therefore 'do good'.[109]
>
> — JENNY OPPENHEIMER, action inquiry manager at Lankelly Chase Foundation

Funding organisations in both the UK and the US are overwhelmingly run by white, middle-class, non-disabled people. In the UK, foundation boards are 99% white.[110] In the US nearly 90% of foundation executives are white, and 40% of American foundations have boards that are entirely white.[111]

Male board members in the UK outnumber women by 2 to 1 despite the voluntary sector having a predominantly (66%) female workforce.[112] Furthermore, the CEOs of the top 20 funders in the UK are mostly male and white.[113]

In case there is any ambiguity at all, the UK's industry body for funders, the Association of Charitable Foundations, has explicitly stated that 'it [is] abundantly clear that foundations are not sufficiently diverse or representative of society'.[114]

Is the problem of unchecked privilege just about making better grants?

> My boss allows me to be bullied, marginalised and undermined, and tolerates inappropriate interference from board members.[115]
>
> —ANONYMOUS GRANTMAKER

While most of this chapter is about the negative effect of unchecked privilege on good grantmaking, there is also an issue of dignity at work. Recent surveys have suggested that illegal workplace discrimination and bullying take place in funders far more often than you might imagine.

In 2018 the Grant Givers' Movement conducted a workforce survey in the UK funding sector.[116] Over 130 grantmaking staff gave their views on the subjects of diversity, inclusion and voice in grantmaking. More than 95 instances of prejudice or discrimination in trusts and foundations were recorded by the survey.[117] In answer to the question 'Have you ever experienced or directly seen prejudice or discrimination in trusts and foundations based on age, gender, race, disability, sexual identity or any other protected characteristics?', 41 respondents (over 40% of respondents to the question) said that they had seen or experienced prejudice or discrimination on more than one occasion. Only 28% said that they had never seen or experienced discrimination in the sector. These findings are outrageous, especially for a sector that prides itself on making the world a better place.

This kind of toxic internal environment is also ruinous for funders that want to be able to connect to more types of grantees more effectively. As Paul Waters, associate director at the Democracy Fund, told us, 'The question for many Black and indigenous grantmakers is: is the harassment and second-guessing just too much for folks, and do they end up leaving?'[118]

This isn't an exaggerated concern: we have seen data from within one funder showing people of colour leaving the organisation at higher rates than white staff. People working there told us that this had been mainly driven by a mismatch between external commitments to diversity and inclusion colliding with the internal realities of an unreformed workplace.

We believe that every time a funding sector leader answers a question about privilege defensively, or shows other signs of funder fragility, an opportunity to make positive changes is lost.

What should I do about privilege?

But aren't you, Gemma and Tom, both privileged?

Yep, we're both privileged people. We are both white, non-disabled, English-speaking, middle-class people who went to university in a wealthy country.

However, as we said earlier, our privilege isn't a personal or moral failing. It's just a statement about who we are and where we have come from, and a thing we have to manage. What counts is that we have tried to take steps to ensure that our privilege doesn't make this a bad book that is full of bad advice.

We've tried to do this in a couple of ways. First, we've tackled the issue head-on – that's what has been going on in this chapter. And, second, as we developed the book we took deliberate, conscious steps to listen carefully and frequently to stories, ideas and feedback from people who have different life experiences and sometimes less privilege than we have. It will be for you to decide whether we've succeeded, and we'd welcome any feedback where we haven't.

What does it look like when funders actually check their privilege and power?

We can divide the funding universe up into two sorts of organisations: a small group explicitly set up to tackle privilege, power and inequality in grantmaking, and all the rest, which are on a journey towards modernisation.

The first sort of funder doesn't have to go through a transition from old to new ways of working because the issues were on the table from day one. The second sort has to make structural changes and put in place measures both of which may be challenging. We'll explain these challenges in a minute, but first we want to give you a picture of what the first kind of funder looks like by relating the story of the Disability Rights Fund (overleaf).

The story of the Disability Rights Fund

The Disability Rights Fund (DRF) was launched in 2008 and its sister organisation, the Disability Rights Advocacy Fund (DRAF), in 2012. Founded by Diana Samarasan, an experienced advocate for the rights of people with disabilities, they started as a pooled fund with money for multiple funders.[119]

The creation of these funds was driven by the opportunity created by the then new UN Convention on the Rights of Persons with Disabilities (CRPD). The DRF is so intertwined with this convention that it describes its own work as funding 'disabled persons organizations (DPOs) across the developing world – primarily in Africa, Asia, the Pacific Islands, and the Caribbean – to participate in ratification, implementation, and monitoring of the Convention on the Rights of Persons with Disabilities'.

A striking story told by Diana Samasaran in an interview with *HuffPost* clearly explains what this means in practice:

> In Peru, we've funded groups of people with psychosocial disabilities and people with intellectual disabilities. Both have worked very hard to see that their rights are recognized in national laws and in national disability movements. Before the 2011 elections in Peru, the electoral commission removed over 23,000 people with psychosocial disabilities and intellectual disabilities from the voter registry.
>
> There was an amazing campaign, led in part by a young woman with intellectual disabilities who went to vote and found that she couldn't. She challenged this at the legal level. She also came to New York and spoke at the United Nations, very poignantly, stating: 'I am a person too, I have political views, I have the right to vote.' She, and many Peruvians behind her, including in the larger disability movement, were able eventually to reverse the removal.[120]

The CRPD was the first significant human rights treaty of the 21st century. The Convention, which was developed in an extremely collaborative process between civil society and governments – shifted the paradigm about disability from a predominantly medicalized view to an approach based on human rights. The active role of the global disability movement, whose slogan is 'Nothing about us without us', was viewed as essential.

To support this change, the DRF and DRAF were purposefully structured as highly participatory grantmakers, with people with disabilities in decision-making roles at governance and staffing levels. For example, both funds' governance rules commit them to at least 50% representation of people with disabilities and co-chairing by a person with disability. Furthermore, the all-important Grantmaking Committee has a majority of people with disabilities representing diverse genders, ages, regions, indigeneity and impairment groups.

Most program officers at country level also come from disability movements, and the DRF and DRAF are clear that representation internally 'is not only the right thing to do; it is the smart thing to do'. People with disabilities know best which strategies work and how to ensure that funding is accessible, and both funds believe that their commitment to the inclusion of people with lived experience is a major reason why independent evaluations have shown that the organisations have been successful in their aims to grow the local and global impact of the disability rights movement.

But hierarchies of power and privilege exist even in the disability movement. Recognising this, both DRF and DRAF commit more than 50% of all their funding to persons with disabilities who are marginalised even within the disability movement, such as women with disabilities, youth with disabilities, people with intellectual disabilities and people with psychosocial disabilities. They also support grantees to connect with other human rights movements, and advocate for these movements and their funders to be disability inclusive.

What specific steps can I take if I work for a traditional funder?

Most funding organisations are, of course, not new, and their founding probably predates the relatively recent shift of privilege from a venerable but niche concept to a widespread social concern. Many of these older funders have struggled to move with the times, or in the worst cases have even been fighting it.

Encouragingly, during our research we came across numerous organisations that appeared to be serious about tackling privilege in their own grantmaking. Here are some positive examples.

- *Adopting a trust-based approach*: The Trust-Based Philanthropy Project is a five-year, peer-to-peer funder initiative that addresses the inherent power imbalances between foundations and nonprofits.[121] The initiative supports and challenges funders to 'lead with trust, centre relationships, collaborate with humility and curiosity, redistribute power, and work for systemic equity'. Some funders have begun by using the Trust-Based Philanthropy Self-Reflection Tool to understand how power dynamics play out across their own organisation before deciding to make further changes.[122]

- *Setting up new funding streams that are co-designed by people from marginalised communities and where decisions are ultimately made by people from those communities*: Multiple funders are now working closely with community representatives to determine the sort of funding that is required. We also observed some funders really let go by delegating significant decisions to panels drawn entirely from those communities.

- *Committing to making more long-term unrestricted funding available to marginalised communities*: To balance out historic underinvestment, some of the funders we studied have decided to award 20% or more of their annual grantmaking budget on an ongoing basis to activities led by Black and indigenous people and people of colour. For example, the McConnell Foundation now devotes a large portion of its funding portfolio to reconciliation and change led by indigenous communities.

What should I do about privilege?

- *Changing recruitment practices and targets to increase staff and board diversity*: Reforming funders have been removing barriers from their recruitment processes, working with communities to discuss new job opportunities and taking active decisions to make their workplaces more inclusive.

- *Updating organisational strategies to put diversity and equity at their heart*: We spoke to funders who had proactively placed diversity and equity at the heart of their missions and strategies. If this is done well, it can lead to transparent commitments to change that these organisations can be held accountable to.

- *Collecting and analysing diversity data*: Organisations that don't consider or study the demographics of their own grantseekers, grantees, staff or board members cannot start on a journey to 'moving the needle'. We witnessed organisations starting to do this for the first time or taking steps to improve their current data collection. The best of them explained why they were gathering the data and talked about how they were using them to improve inclusion.

- *Reviewing policies to ensure equity*: Some funders conducted reviews of all their policies – from recruitment to homeworking to whistleblowing – to ensure that they were inclusive. In the UK, for instance, a number of funders are working with Stonewall, a charity that campaigns for equality for lesbian, gay, bi and trans people across Britain, as part of their Workplace Equality Index scheme to make sure that all their organisational policies are LGBTQIA+ inclusive.[123] Others developed or changed their policies to ensure greater diversity at all levels, as almost 'three-quarters of [US] foundations have no written policy on board diversity'.[124]

- *Putting staff through dedicated training programmes*: Some funders had worked with organisations led by people with lived experience of discrimination and marginalisation to deliver training programmes that helped grantmakers to understand and to learn how to act on problems that stem from badly managed power and privilege. Grantmakers should be very careful to steer clear of tokenistic training schemes. In particular, any training where senior leaders seek to impose strict control and declare certain topics 'out of bounds' can be counterproductive.[125]

- *Rebuilding application processes and the whole grantmaking journey to make them more accessible and inclusive*: Many grantmakers we spoke to who were serious about addressing power and privilege saw lowering barriers for applications as important. Only a few had taken significant steps at this stage, but most knew that it was a priority if they were going to 'walk the talk'. For more on this topic, see Chapter 6.

- *Moving endowments*: Not all funders have endowments (most government funders don't), but among those that do we learned that several have already changed their investment strategy on the basis of decisions about justice and equity. A shout-out here to the UK's Lankelly Chase Foundation which has not just been making changes in this area but also publicly challenging other funders to do the same.[126]

- *Establishing or joining funding collaboratives that are specifically about recognising and addressing power and privilege issues*: We came across several funding organisations that are now part of collaboratives set up to compensate for a previous lack of funding or trust given to certain communities. If you want to know more about successful partnerships, read no-brainer no. 4 in Chapter 2.

- *Closing programmes that don't help*: We were told of one funder that had decided to close a funding programme when a review showed that the programme was not fulfilling the funder's commitment to equity, and that the money would be better spent on other programmes.

Changing who gets into grantmaking in the first place: 2027

One of the most interesting initiatives we have come across during the writing of this book is 2027 (**2027.org.uk**). 'A new, paid training programme that prepares brilliant professionals from working class backgrounds for decision making roles in the grant-giving sector', it operates in the UK and plans to continue until at least 2027, its tenth year in operation.

What's so fascinating about 2027 is that it is a conscious attempt to nurture the sort of graduate talent that would normally be hired straight from elite universities. And why would such hiring be a problem? In their own words:

> We believe that a broader spectrum of class experience at the top of foundations and trusts will lead to better decision making, happier workforces and more meaningful relationships with the communities that foundations and trusts serve.

The programme's goal is clear and ambitious: it wants talented members of working-class communities to hold 40% of grant-giving roles by 2027. By providing not only training but also a salary, 2027 helps to overcome the problem that often only the offspring of relatively wealthy families can afford to work for nothing so as to get into desirable sectors.

Various notable UK funders have funded 2027, including the Esmée Fairbairn Foundation, Barrow Cadbury Trust and the National Lottery Community Fund. This funding is critical because 2027 will succeed only if funding organisations end up employing the people it trains. By making grants to 2027, these funders both provide a living wage for participants while they train and signal a willingness to open their recruiting doors to them in the future. It's an amazing initiative, and one that every grantmaking exec team and board should know about and consider supporting.

Can you give an example of how a funder tackles privilege and power inequalities in its grantmaking?

Let's consider the Ford Foundation. Set up in 1936 with gifts and bequests from Henry Ford, the Ford Foundation is the second largest philanthropic foundation in the US. It spent over $460 million in 2019.[127]

The president of the Ford Foundation, Darren Walker, is perhaps the most widely heard voice in US grantmaking on the topics of power, privilege and inequality. A self-described Black, gay man, he has led the charge on pushing other funders to address and discuss these issues.

On taking charge of the organisation in 2013 Walker worked with colleagues and partners to update its mission to make it more explicitly about social justice. To deliver on this, Ford has made a wide range of changes including starting a programme called BUILD, 'a new six-year, $1 billion initiative to help organizations that are moving the needle on inequality become stronger, more sustainable, and more durable'.[128] What is notable about this move was the shift away from the norm of restricted funding towards a less restricted model, which showed greater trust in the organisations it was supporting.

Ford was also willing to take tough decisions to match its bold words, and during this transition it dropped from eight to six programme areas. As Walker said himself at this time, 'Almost certainly, providing deeper, more intensive support will result in fewer grants, and, most likely, fewer grant recipients.'[129] One Ford staffer we spoke to told us, 'Turning the oil tanker at Ford wasn't without some consternation on behalf of the staff. Changes were made, some portfolios and programmes were eliminated. But management was focused. They really walked the talk.'[130]

The changes relating to power and privilege have not just been external. In recruitment the Ford Foundation abides by the Rooney Rule, where 'The top three candidates in every recruitment process must reflect diversity'.[131]

But what is perhaps most symbolic about the Ford Foundation as an exemplar of good practice in a funder's approach to these issues is how it behaves when it gets things wrong. Back in 2016 Walker found himself criticised after opening up a public conversation about how the foundation intended to tackle inequality and privilege.[132] Why? Because Ford's initiative, FordForward, omitted any mention of disability. When disabled people criticised Ford for this lack of representation Walker spoke openly about having to confront his 'own ignorance and power'. He felt that the criticism was deserved because the omission reflected a lack of care or concern for disability generally within the Ford Foundation at the time.

The foundation admitted that it didn't have a person with visible disabilities on the leadership team, had taken no affirmative effort to hire people with disabilities and had not considered disabled people in its strategy. Nor were its website, social media or physical building accessible to all.

In publicly accepting his own individual privilege, Walker led by example: 'I have not been forced to consider whether or not there were ramps before entering a building, or whether a website could be used by people who were visually impaired.' By doing this, he began to 'more clearly perceive the Ford Foundation's institutional privilege' and 'narrow-mindedness [which] undercuts all of us in philanthropy'. He continued to say that if, 'despite our best intentions ... we fail to address ignorance within our organisations, we are complicit in allowing inequality to persist'. The transformation from ignorance to 'enlightenment', he acknowledged, involved 'becoming more comfortable with uncomfortable feedback ... rather than adopting a defensive posture by default'.

The Ford Foundation website now has a page on diversity, equity and inclusion.[133] It covers its ambitions and the terminology of key concepts, and provides data on diversity in its workforce as well as its annual priorities in a space-and-trend analysis of progress over time. The foundation also has a separate policy on disability inclusion, and provides public updates about its work in this area.[134]

The willingness to accept failure, to learn and to change has left Ford in a good place. As one grantmaker within the foundation told us:

> Ford's orientation, being a social justice funder and tackling inequality, gives us a lens that we use when we're making decisions. In some ways, it makes supporting PoC-led organisations easier to do, and it's a priority in the organisation.[135]

Are there any examples of funders trying to make a change in the UK?

Comic Relief is one UK funder that has started to make changes to the way it works in terms of rebalancing power in grantmaking support. Its story is worth sharing as an example of what trying to do better looks like.

This grantmaking charity was founded in 1985 on the basis of a regular comedy-driven telethon broadcast by the BBC, which became something of a national institution. In 2019 its spending was about £75 million.

In recent years Comic Relief has been criticised for perpetuating the 'white saviour' archetype.[136] This was because some of its most iconic fundraising imagery involved British celebrities (who were overwhelmingly white) visiting some of the poorest people in the world (who generally were not white).

After receiving a lot of feedback, Comic Relief decided to take steps to address this.[137] It approached Charity So White – a people-of-colour-led campaign group that tackles institutional racism within the charity sector in the UK – to discuss the latter's recommendations for more equitable funding distribution. Following this discussion Comic Relief acknowledged that they were not best placed to recognise the challenges faced by people of colour in the UK, and did not have the infrastructure to build relationships and trust quickly enough with the small grassroots organisations that were most vulnerable and most needed.

In June 2020 Comic Relief issued a funding call for people-of-colour-led intermediaries, which was boosted by their partnership with National Emergencies Trust (NET) which contributed £2.5 million to the initiative. In July 2020 Comic Relief confirmed £3.4 million of funding for 10 people-of-colour-led intermediary distribution partners to allocate funding to micro and small organisations, instead of using Comic Relief staff. As part of this, they have also launched a new Change Makers programme to provide sustainable funding to charities and have ring-fenced 20% (£1.8 million) of this funding for people-of-colour-led organisations.

What about the new wave of funder collaboratives that target power and privilege?

Democracy Frontlines Fund (US)

Galvanised by the national outcry resulting from the murder of George Floyd in May 2020, the Democracy Frontlines Fund is an important new collaborative for more than one reason.[138] To begin with, the decision making about grants is delegated to people in the best position to make choices: eight women of colour, mostly leaders from the US nonprofit sector, who were brought together to form a Brain Trust of accountable movement advisers. Their role was to determine the strategy and grant priorities for a pool of $36 million, contributed by 12 separate funding organisations. As the fund's website puts it with striking clarity, 'We are listening to the will and self-determined priorities of Black communities, supporting them, and getting out of the way.'

This partnership is interesting not just for its unusual degree of trust and delegation. The original idea for the collaboration was suggested by the Libra Foundation, a Californian funder that's been described as a 'movement-funding mainstay'.[139] Libra brought to the collaborative a group of foundations, some of which were experienced in funding the racial justice space and others for whom it was completely new. We think this is a very promising example of using a collaborative to get decisions made by the right people as well as to educate funders that are only just starting to think about privilege in their own grantmaking.

Resourcing Racial Justice (UK)

Launched in May 2020, the Resourcing Racial Justice fund is a coalition of people of colour, innovators, change makers, activists, artists and social leaders that is dedicated to social change.[140] As the name suggests, it was established to support individuals and communities working towards racial justice.

One notable innovation about this collaborative is that it refuses to work 'with funders who simply wanted to outsource their work on racial justice'.[141] Indeed, in a rare example of role reversal, it is the grantee that checks out the funder before helping them. Resourcing Racial Justice will take money only from funders that they believe are already part-way on the journey to thinking about racial justice.

To become a supporter, a funder has to go through an assessment process, in which senior leaders are questioned on their commitment and credentials. Resourcing Racial Justice then provides feedback to a prospective funder on areas for improvement. As one grantmaker told us, 'It's a great example of how to build a truly symbiotic relationship with a shared vision and shared goals.'

The Resourcing Racial Justice fund is currently 'redistributing £1 million to 52 different individuals, collectives and organisations across the UK'.

Diversity, Equity and Inclusion coalition (UK)

Thirteen foundations based in the UK came together in late 2019 to form a Diversity, Equity and Inclusion (DEI) coalition.[142] Scheduled to last for at least three years, it aims to 'provide a forum for the implementation of frameworks, processes and procedures within foundations and is focussed on building a body of practice for themselves and others in the UK sector to learn from'.

Fozia Irfan, the director of children and young people at BBC Children in Need, who helped instigate the initiative, noted that:

> We have seen DEI frameworks being implemented in foundations across the globe but it is an area which is new to the UK – what we hope to do is to critically analyse the way we work and how we distribute funding, to make sure that we are reaching the communities most in need.

How can I tell if my funding organisation is really acting on privilege and power?

> We went out to diversify our workforce. We went out to particular communities, we made ourselves open, and we succeeded in hiring new people. But a year later, when we analysed who had left the organisation, the leavers were disproportionately from those less traditional communities. Bringing people in without an inclusive culture is a recipe for disaster.[143]
>
> — ANONYMOUS GRANTMAKER

One sad and unacceptable phenomenon we have come across in the development of this book is grantmaking leaders 'faking it'.

What should I do about privilege?

What this means is that grantmakers – and especially grantmaking leaders – may make impassioned public commitments to change which are then followed by ... nothing, or at the very least no changes or actions that will result in the funder making different kinds of grants or employing different kinds of people.

This is the sibling of 'greenwashing' – celebrating environmental virtues while carrying on with life as normal. It is a particular problem because it can muddy the picture of what real change looks like. These two kinds of fakery have the same motivation: to look good and attract praise with the least effort possible. It's the lazy leadership version of having your cake and eating it.

One of the most common ways organisations fake it is by introducing new processes and procedures to make themselves feel they've done something, when that something doesn't result in any real change. As one anonymous nonprofit leader put it:

> Think of the buzzword phrase 'equity, diversity and inclusion', often called EDI. The acronym should be DIE – diversity and inclusion both leading to equity – but we changed the letters around to EDI to make it sound better. The way this whole approach has been co-opted as a tick-box exercise in some cases makes me think we should've stuck with DIE.[144]

The reason leaders in some funders fake it when it comes to power and privilege is because understanding and checking your power and privilege as a funder is difficult and uncomfortable. It is likely to unearth things that are challenging for individuals and organisations to accept initially and then to figure out how to act on these collectively. Consider this example, from one anonymous UK grantmaker:

> My proposal for investment in this important new anti-racism fund got rejected at the first go, partly because some board members, all of whom are white, had negative personal reactions to language used by an organisation about lots of philanthropic funds coming from 'exploitative structures'. It's as if they couldn't get that giving money away doesn't automatically put you on the side of the angels.[145]

We are familiar with this reaction: interpreting 'exploitative structures' as meaning 'You, personally, are terrible, exploitative people'. But this is in no way an excuse: funder staff and board members need to have enough of an understanding of their own privilege and historic injustices to accept this sort of language as being ordinary and not outrageous. This takes time, education and, fundamentally, a degree of humility.

Funding organisations need to accept that exploring these issues deeply and then making meaningful change is going to take quite a bit of time, money and energy. One or two training sessions delivered within an overall unreformed organisation are not going to cut it.[146] Joy Warmington, CEO of the UK nonprofit brap, sums up the overall problem starkly:

> Thinking about inequality demands that we confront some uncomfortable truths about the privileges we have and how some of us benefit from an unfair system. It's only natural that this makes some people feel guilty or defensive. But it's a necessary step if we are to become more responsive to the communities we serve.[147]

Instead of asking,

> 'why do we find it hard to engage minority groups when we fund projects aimed at those communities?', foundations need to wrestle with the harder question: 'Does our history, power, and privilege contribute to a legacy of distrust? What are we prepared to give up to combat this?'

Those questions are the key ones. What would you and your organisation give up to make the changes you need to make, to become both more impactful and more just? It won't be a comfortable journey, and as Gita Gulati-Partee and Maggie Potapchuk argue in a paper on foundations and systemic racism, 'any authentic process likely will increase conflict, at least in the short term'.[148]

We should also realise that the discomfort that comes from directly addressing inequalities and discrimination will not be felt primarily by highly educated, non-disabled white people who may be discombobulated by uncomfortable truths. The primary pain will always be felt by those who have lived experience of injustice and exclusion, so organisations need to invest adequately and to provide sufficient space and support to help people on this journey. For example, in his book *Decolonizing Wealth* Edgar Villanueva argues that 'Organizational designers now recommend that pain be publicly acknowledged and mourned. Sharing the grief destigmatized the feelings, validates them, and allows for healing.'[149]

The best place to address these organisational reform issues is in your funder's strategy. In the next chapter, we'll discuss what strategies are for and how to go about getting one that makes a difference.

Chapter 3 checklist

1. Do people in your organisation – at all levels (junior, senior and board) – feel comfortable talking about power and privilege?

   ....

2. Has your organisation taken substantive, impactful measures in response to its own consideration of the privilege of its staff and of the power relationship it has with grantees?

   ....

3. Has your organisation changed anything in its grantmaking rules or programmes in response to its consideration of power and privilege?

   ....

4. Has your organisation changed any of its internal processes (i.e. hiring or grant decision making) as a result of debate and consideration of these issues?

   ....

5. Does your organisation seek feedback from staff, grantees and partners about how diverse, equitable and inclusive it is?

   ....

6. Is your organisation involved in any action-oriented coalitions with other organisations working in this area?

   ....

7. Does your organisation have a plan in place to enable long-term discussion and action on power and privilege?

   ....

4
HOW DO I HELP MY FUNDER DEVELOP A GOOD STRATEGY?

> I want my organisation to have a purpose, not just think that giving money away is a good thing.[150]
>
> — ANONYMOUS CEO of a private foundation

'Strategy' is a fancy word. It's a word that inflates consultants' fees and helps to justify the big money paid to big bosses in every sector.

Part of what gives the word this wallet-opening power is that it is somewhat elusive and can be used to separate the workplace demi-gods who 'think strategically' from the mere working stiffs who get on with their jobs. Indeed, some of the definitions of 'strategy' are astonishingly hand-wavy, in a way that should make any reasonable person suspicious. For example, check out this humdinger:

> A strategy is a framework for making decisions about how you will play the game of business.[151]

When you see explanations of strategy like this, it can be tempting to assume that strategy may be just one big con – an excuse for management consultants in expensive suits to suck money out of organisations with weak leadership.

But for Modern Grantmakers developing and using a strategy is both extremely important and not that mysterious. In this chapter we'll explain what having a strategy even means, why it's so important and how you go about getting a good one.

What is a strategy and why would my organisation need one?

> I always used to joke that I was going to start a foundation called the Pendulum Foundation that would just swing from one approach to the other.[152]
>
> — RUTH LEVINE, former program director of global development and population at the William and Flora Hewlett Foundation

We can't give you a single definition of 'strategy' that everyone in your sector will agree with. It's just not a totally unambiguous idea. What we can do, however, is outline a definition of 'strategy' that we have found useful in our own working lives. Then in the second part of this chapter we'll talk you through a suggested approach to developing a strategy for your own organisation.

To acknowledge that very different approaches to strategy are possible, in the final part of the chapter we'll describe alternative ways to develop a strategy.

Let's start with our take. In our view, a strategy is nothing more mysterious than a highly useful document that explains the purpose for which an organisation exists and how it will go about its work. We apologise if you were hoping for something more transcendent than 'a highly useful document', but a strategy is essentially a set of words stretched over several pages, perhaps with some visual aids, that represent your mission and goals. There's no eureka moment when you develop a strategy: it's just an important document that helps an organisation to succeed.

What we think a strategy document should contain is also fairly simple:

1. A short, clear statement of what the organisation exists to do – its *mission*. This is the single most important thing in a strategy document.

2. A statement of *why* this mission needs to be achieved, i.e. the problem or opportunity that has driven the organisation to act.

How do I help my funder develop a good strategy?

3   A description of how the organisation plans to achieve the mission, often called a *theory of change*.

4   A set of objectives or *goals* which, successfully achieved, will fulfil the mission.

5   Some details on what steps the organisation can take to achieve those goals – often called *deliverables*.

So coming up with a strategy is really just the process of researching, debating and agreeing what to write down. It's tiring and challenging but it isn't magic.

Can you show me an example of a strategy for a funder?

Most funder strategy documents are a bit too long to fit into a chapter like this, so we've written a super-compressed strategy for the fictional ToyTown Foundation. You can see all the elements we described above in one page (overleaf), elements that we think should be in your strategy.

ToyTown Foundation's one-page strategy

Our mission

ToyTown Foundation exists to improve the life prospects of children from low-income households in ToyTown.

Why is this our mission?

Children from low-income families in Toytown are 53% less likely to graduate from high school and have worse employment prospects than children from higher-income households. This is unfair and economically harmful, and we wish to see it changed.

Our theory of change

We believe that children from low-income families have worse life prospects partly because they receive a lower quality of school education and lower-quality nutrition. We believe that we can improve outcomes for these young people by funding food and education initiatives in ToyTown.

Our goals

1. By the summer of 2022, we want to have contributed to reducing the exam results gap between the top and bottom decile households in ToyTown from 40% to under 10%.

2. By the end of 2024, we want to have contributed to reducing childhood obesity rates in ToyTown's low-income households from 50% to 20%.

Our deliverables

By the end of 2022 we will have:

- made grants to substantially strengthen the capacity of ToyTown's three biggest youth charities;

- launched a ToyTown Cares network of all organisations that focus on youth welfare to improve the circulation of knowledge and ideas;

- launched a campaign to replace the current ToyTown school-meal provider Gristle Corp, with a new provider, led by parents and carers, that supplies healthy, balanced meals to all students.

How can yet another document make any real difference?

One of the most famous quotes in business writing is 'Culture eats strategy for breakfast', which is often, though not always, attributed to Peter Drucker. It's a succinct observation of how organisations have cultures that often determine what happens in them, and how those cultures are often much stronger and more influential on decision making than the latest strategy document that floats down from the top level.

Drucker was right. Most organisations of any age are bursting with well-intentioned management documents that don't make a damned bit of difference to anything: target operating models, anyone?

So how can a strategy document actually make things happen? The answer is that a strategy makes a difference only if the leaders of a funding organisation use it in practical and visible ways every day. They have to use it regularly, not as a one-off but over a long period of time. Sticking with it is what will slowly shift cultures, even in older organisations.

But what does it mean to *use* a strategy? After all, it isn't a physical tool and you can't pick it up by its handle. There are four main ways to use a strategy document:

- *In leadership*: Strategy documents can change behaviour when leaders and managers regularly point to and cite them when making decisions. What this looks like in practice is leaders who talk like this: 'So you remember that our strategy says that our mission is X? And you remember that in order for us to realise our mission, we have to deliver these two big goals? Well, in order to get us closer to those goals, today we're going to …'

- *In day-to-day work*: Strategies also start to change behaviour when people who aren't the CEO actively choose to mention and refer to parts of the strategy as they do their jobs. This will happen only if they find it a useful tool, which is why designing a strategy with your colleagues' day-to-day use in mind is so important. When this is working, what it can look like is one colleague spontaneously saying to another, 'So I think we should work on this rather than that because it seems more likely to help us achieve our organisation's mission.'

- *In communications*: A good strategy can determine the way an organisation describes itself to the world. You know that a strategy has been effectively written and effectively communicated when you meet someone who doesn't work for the organisation but who can quickly and correctly identify what it does and why.

- *In impact research*: The final way in which strategy documents can lead to change in an organisation is when they are shared with research professionals. These individuals can seize on the clarity of a good strategy to work out new and valuable ways of studying the right things in the right ways. Without a clear strategy, researchers will be in danger of producing research on which decisions can't actually be based. There's lots more on this in Chapter 7.

A good strategy is a document that is regularly consulted by people trying to make good decisions, in the way that those trying to work out which horse to bet on consult the *Racing Post*. A strategy document may look like a short stack of paper to a casual observer, but it can be a powerful tool when it is deployed effectively.

Do we really need to go to the trouble of writing a strategy?

> There is plenty of grant-making still happening without a strategy, or indeed any kind of evidence or process to back it. Plenty of mistakes get made and the funds tend to go to a small network of people who fit the usual suspects, or whom the donor knows and trusts. That's the way minorities, women and other marginalised groups get shut out.[153]
>
> — JO ANDREWS, founder of Ariadne, a network for funders

Would it be so bad for funding organisations not to have a strategy? Organisations without good, clear strategies face a host of dangers.[154] Through our interviews and research, we identified the following as the main problems of opting out of the strategy development process:

- *Reduced impact*: Having an impact in a complicated world is difficult and requires lots of people pulling in roughly the same direction. Groups of people find it much easier to coordinate action if the goals and mission they share are clear and widely understood. Organisations without good strategies don't have such shared understandings, which leads to people pulling in different directions.

- *Inequity*: Biases in even the most well meaning of grantmaking staff, and badly designed and carelessly implemented funding processes, can lead to funders making grants that exclude some people and communities. A good strategy is one of the key levers you can use to change your organisation's behaviour so that it becomes a more inclusive and privilege-aware organisation that funds more equitably (see Chapter 3).

- *Sprawl*: Have you ever come across a funder that appears to work on every problem in the world at the same time while never focusing on anything? This is a classic sign that it doesn't have an effective strategy in place. To make a significant impact requires intense focus by funders and grantees, and sprawl is a sign that funders are trying to do too much all at once and are unlikely to make a significant impact on anything.

- *Inconsistent grant decisions*: If individual grantmakers don't have a crystal clear idea what they are trying to achieve, their lack of focus will be reflected in the total grants portfolio.

- *Wasted time from irrelevant applications*: Organisations with an ambiguous or missing strategy are much more likely to attract funding proposals that stand no chance of succeeding. A vague strategy or no strategy at all encourages inappropriate grantseekers to have a go at applying, which may waste their time as well as yours.

- *Greater difficulty in forming partnerships*: If potential partners, especially other funders, don't really understand what you're about or where you're going, or if they misunderstand your aims, they'll be less likely to team up with you. A clear strategy can help persuade other organisations that they want to work with you to realise common goals.

Will a clear strategy limit our ability to respond to every event?

Yes, absolutely. Setting goals and priorities inevitably means ruling some things out. But there is a simple solution to this problem that does not require you to completely abandon your previous plans whenever the wind blows in a different direction.

To cope with sudden events and short-notice opportunities, your funder should carve out a chunk of its budget that is *expressly for unanticipated events*. These are sometimes euphemistically called 'opportunity funds' or 'chair's funds', and they can allow you to move very quickly.

A good opportunity fund will have rules that allow lighter than usual governance, a higher appetite for risk and an intentionally broad remit. It will also have enough money set aside to make emergency grants that are meaningful. In some years you may not touch this sort of opportunity fund at all, while in others you may spend the whole pot in your first month.

A funder that made a formal provision for the unexpected in this way was Chuck Feeney's Atlantic Philanthropies, one of the world's biggest spend-down funds. According to Conor O'Clery's book *The Billionaire Who Wasn't: How Chuck Feeney Secretly Made and Gave Away a Fortune*:

> Funding big projects while maintaining a grant stream for worthy causes had always created difficulties in forward planning at Atlantic Philanthropies. When he was chief executive in 2003, John Healy had brought some order to Atlantic's giving by identifying four areas for grant-making – aging, children and youth, population health, and reconciliation and human rights – while maintaining a separate founding chairman's fund, or 'chairman's pot', for Feeney to pursue his initiatives.[155]

However, we also want to stress that, while flexibility is a good thing, making a U-turn every time something happens is not a good way to run a grantmaking organisation. The point of a strategy is to keep an organisation focused on going in one direction while it is being pulled in many different directions at the same time.

As Ben Harrison, a former executive at a large grantmaker, puts it: 'Things *will* go wrong, and when they go wrong, if you don't have a clear and well-understood purpose and strategy to guide you through that, you are more likely to make poor decisions.'[156]

Can I spend too much time on our strategy?

Here's one of our favourite grantmaking jokes:

> Knock, knock.
>
> Who's there?
>
> Look – I'd love to give you a punchline but I'm afraid we're going through a strategic punchline revision process right now. Could you give us a call next year?

We like this because it can sometimes seem that funding organisations are revising their strategies all the time, and while they're doing so the rest of the world has to stop what they're doing and hold their breath. One anonymous CEO of a large funder echoed this, telling us, 'One bad thing that you see funding organisations do is just constantly revisit their strategy and do so on a rolling basis.'[157]

We agree. While we think strategy is really important, if you have a revision process going on more than, say, 25% of your time over a period of a few years it means that something has gone wrong and you're in danger of navel gazing rather than making good choices.

Do you have real examples of funders with clear strategies?

Most strategy documents, even short ones, are too long to add to this book. If you wish to explore the topic on your own, you could start with the following (see endnotes for full details):

- The William and Flora Hewlett Foundation has sections on its website about how its grantmaking connects to its values.[158]

- Disability Rights Fund puts its vision and mission up front online.[159]

- The Joseph Rowntree Foundation, an organisation focused on solving poverty in the UK, outlines its mission and vision on its website and provides easy access to its strategic plan.[160]

- Malala Fund, 'working for a world where every girl can learn and lead', sets out its five-year strategic plan for anyone to download.[161]

How do I help my funder come up with a good strategy?

It is one thing to say that your funding organisation should have a good strategy but quite another to actually develop one. In this section we'll take you through some straightforward steps to craft a strategy document that will help your funder make more of an impact and enable potential grantees to understand your purpose and values.

The big caveat: What we can't help you with

Books about philanthropy and grantmaking often devote a lot of time and space to showing readers how to compare the relative impact of making grants in different spheres. They introduce helpful ways of thinking about very difficult choices, such as whether to fund primary education for girls in Bangladesh or to support scientists at the Massachusetts Institute of Technology.

Most grantmaking books focus on the skills required to make key funding decisions – whether to fund issue X or issue Y. However, in this

How do I help my funder develop a good strategy?

book we've deliberately chosen not to include several chapters explaining how we think grantmakers should weigh up different areas for investment, although we have included one chapter (7) on how to make use of research.

So why aren't we going to focus on it? In short, a fully rounded take on how such choices should be made warrants a book all of its own. Happily, such books have already been written by people who have skills and knowledge that we don't. If you want to boost your own skills in weighing up such tricky choices, we encourage you to seek out one of them:

- *Delusional Altruism: Why Philanthropists Fail to Achieve Change and What They Can Do to Transform Giving*, by Kris Putnam-Walkerly.

- *Giving Done Right: Effective Philanthropy and Making Every Dollar Count*, by Phil Buchanan.

- *It Ain't What You Give, It's The Way That You Give It*, by Caroline Fiennes.

- *Money Well Spent: A Strategic Plan for Smart Philanthropy*, second edition, by Paul Brest and Hal Harvey.[162]

Given that there is so much advice out there about deciding on your high-level grantmaking goals, we have chosen instead to focus on the practical side of successfully developing a good new strategy for your organisation. Then in the next chapter we'll introduce you to some of the questions that all funders should debate as they write or refresh their strategy.

How do we start the process of developing a useful new strategy?

Developing an organisational strategy is a bit like compiling a domestic shopping list. You have to work out what you want for dinner before you can start shopping.

For a funding organisation, working out what you want for dinner means taking the time and effort to produce good answers to a series of big questions, including:

- What is our mission?
- Why is this our mission rather than something else?
- What are the main goals we will pursue to achieve this mission?
- Why have we chosen these goals over other possible goals?
- How can we tell whether we're succeeding or failing?

These are massive questions and, as noted above, you probably won't have the authority as a grantmaker to answer most of them on your own. So what is a humble grantmaker supposed to do?

The answer is that you can be clear with your colleagues that good strategies come solely through good strategy development processes. Once you've explained that you need a multi-stage process, you can start introducing them to the steps.

What's the first step? A successful strategy development process, we would argue, starts with taking steps to ensure that the work gets done at all. This means that the first step is about people.

What sort of people do we want to lead our strategy development process?

The work involved in developing a strategy is considerable, and we strongly recommend allocating the task to a person or a small group of people who are ultimately responsible for making sure that it gets done – *and* that it gets done in a way that aligns with your organisation's purpose and values.

If your organisation can afford it, ideally it should appoint at least one full-time person to oversee and drive your strategy development process for its duration, which will probably be a few months. If your organisation

How do I help my funder develop a good strategy?

isn't big enough to sustain this, the next best option would be to form a small group of people, overseen by a senior leader, and give them the responsibility of running the process. Whatever approach you choose, there has to be an unambiguous strategy development leader, or there's a strong chance the whole thing will fall between the cracks.

Why do we suggest deploying someone full time if possible? Because having the right strategy is enormously important to your organisation's impact, and if the person running the strategy development process is being pulled in a dozen other directions, the strategy document they produce will almost certainly be much less good than it could have been. Your organisation will have saved some money on staff costs only to pay dearly for the false economy in subsequent grantmaking.

Not everyone can lead on developing a strategy for a funder. You really don't want to give this job to someone who will abuse the position, or simply use it as an opportunity to list their own personal hang-ups as top strategic priorities. The ideal person to lead on strategy development in a funder:

- *is blessed with a modest ego*: Modern Grantmaking is all about humility, and humility is definitely needed in strategy development;
- *is trusted* by communities that will be directly impacted by the grantmaking strategy;
- *has done it before or has been closely mentored by someone who has done it before*: ideally you want someone who has helped write at least one strategy before, to help avoid rookie mistakes;
- *is familiar with real grantmaking operations*: a strategy written without an understanding of what it's like to make real grants is likely to fall flat immediately;
- *is good at absorbing information*: this person needs to listen to dozens of voices and be able to extract themes without being overwhelmed or ignoring certain kinds of people;
- *is able to write clearly*: a boring strategy document that is hard to read won't influence anyone's behaviour, so this person has to know how to write engagingly;

Modern Grantmaking

- *is a well-respected and trusted collaborator*: it will help if the person running the process is widely liked and trusted.

Dan Paskins is the director of UK Impact at Save the Children, and a highly experienced grantmaker in his own right. He highlighted one of the most common mistakes made when funders carry out strategy processes in the wrong way:

> One division which happens too much is that you have one set of people who do the strategy and another set who implement, even in quite small grantmakers.
>
> And that's a missed opportunity. The people who are doing the strategy really need to know what the user journey is, what the decision making is, how this all plays out in practice, and the people who are preparing the papers for the board need to also be involved in the strategy.[163]

In short, do not entrust your strategy-writing process to someone who doesn't know how grants actually get made in your organisation – it will lead to grief.

When we've found the right people to lead our strategy development process, what should they do?

A worthwhile strategy development process has a few key phases. Your strategy lead should be the key person responsible for making sure that each phase is as well executed as possible. Here are some suggested phases:

Phase 1	Solicit views on what the funder should and should not be doing in future from people both inside and outside the organisation (note that this means more outreach than just speaking to grantmakers from other funders).
Phase 2	Synthesise these ideas into a single document and send it to a group of key staff and board members.
Phase 3	Hold a first strategy planning meeting with your strategy setting panel – a group of key staff and board members, at least some of whom will have final approval of the finished strategy. Ideally you'll also have some stakeholders from outside your organisation

	on your panel. We describe how to run this meeting below.
Phase 4	Write down the tentative strategy ideas that emerge from the first strategy planning meeting in a draft strategy document. Then circulate it (despite its rough and incomplete state) as widely as you can persuade your organisation to share it. Listen very carefully for feedback, write it down and share it with your strategy setting panel.
Phase 5	Hold a second strategic planning meeting in which you discuss the feedback, both supportive and critical. During this meeting the strategy setting panel should be challenged to make tough choices on the most important strategy questions, e.g. 'Are we definitely going to keep our current mission unchanged?'
Phase 6	Take the conclusions of the second meeting and turn them into a revised version of the strategy. At this point the strategy may be complete, or you may need to repeat phases 4, 5 and 6 before you get something good enough to be signed off.
Phase 7	Once it is finalised, start to use the strategy to actually change things (described in more detail below).

What substantial issues should we make sure our strategy addresses?

Large parts of this book contain issues that should be debated in a high-quality strategy session. To make your life easier we've condensed some of the key questions you should consider as a group into a list, with signposts for further reading:

- How will we know if we're taking enough risks? What do we do if it turns out that we're not? (Chapter 5)

- How transparent and accountable are we going to be? (Chapters 2 and 5)

- Does this strategy further equity? Have we made sure that it contributes positively to both the grants we make and the way the organisation is managed? (Chapters 3 and 8)

- Have we given decision-making power to the people who are most capable of making the right decisions?

- Are we planning to fund in perpetuity or to spend down an endowment? (Chapter 5)

- Is our funding strategy likely to create robust organisations that others can depend on or weak organisations that struggle from one grant to the next?

- If we're planning to support a movement rather than isolated proposals, do our goals and processes allow us to do that successfully or will they get in the way?

- Are we clear about our role in realising our vision in relation to the roles of other key organisations, including local and national government?

- What are we doing to make sure that our grantmaking processes are accessible? (Chapter 6)

- How do we study and measure the right things? (Chapter 7)

- Does this strategy mean that we're playing a responsible role in addressing the climate crisis? (Introduction)

How do we gather views on what should or shouldn't be in our strategy?

Every worthwhile funder strategy process involves lots of asking people from outside your organisation what they think it should do. This process of going outside is critical because the power and privilege of sitting inside a funder means that we live in bubbles of our own making, which cut us off from crucial information, feedback and opportunities. If your next strategy is going to be more than a collection of your own prejudices, you have to break out.

The problem is this: how are you supposed to work out who to talk to about your new strategy when the world has billions of people and you have finite time?

To help you out, here's a checklist of different types of people to talk to. You should try to talk to people from all these groups to ensure at least a modicum of balance in your inputs:

- *the people you support*: this should include a cross-section of grantees, grantseekers and ideally some of the people that those organisations serve – don't forget to follow up with these people once the process is over, for they deserve to know what happened to their input;

- *grantmaking collaborators*: people and organisations you work with to make aligned grants or investments;

- *experts*, who are in the business of helping people, e.g. aid workers, epidemiologists, social researchers;

- *your board members or trustees*;

- *other funders* who have attempted to do similar things as you but with whom you may not have worked yet;

- *your own colleagues*.

A checklist like this may leave you with too many people for one person to speak to. In such a situation you can call on the services of external consultants or specialists to help you research your strategy, especially if you have to talk to a lot of people. This can be very valuable, but the one key rule is: use consultants for advice but don't use them to make decisions for you.

So what should we ask these people?

While your context will determine the questions you should ask, there are some questions that will always yield useful responses to your strategy research process:

- What are the problems or opportunities that matter most to you, and what would it look like if things were going really well?
- What do you think is good or bad about the way in which this problem has been funded in the past?
- What should be a lower priority for us as a funder?
- Is there anything we should continue to do or that we should stop doing?

If you pose these questions, as well as others that are more specific to the area you work in, people will give you a lot of feedback. You may need to record meetings and have them transcribed – there are some great new AI transcription tools out there that lower the cost of this.[164] The information that people give you is precious: it is the raw material for your eventual strategy.

How do we analyse what people tell us?

On to phase 2. Once you have gathered a good amount of insight from within and outside your funding organisation, you should analyse what you've heard and start to pick out themes and patterns. Some of these themes will simply be observations about the world, while others will be suggestions, in particular recommendations that your organisation really should or shouldn't do something.

This is a large amount of analytical work, and you're going to need the time and space to work out the meaning and implications of your findings, such as whether your organisation needs to change. This means carving out decent amounts of time, probably over the course of a few weeks, to consider the ideas in detail. You may also want to use the skills of research specialists to examine and evaluate feedback (see Chapter 6 for more details on how to work with such experts).

Then you should write up the crispest, clearest summary of the different ideas that you can produce and share it with the individuals in your strategy setting panel. They'll need to be well briefed on the feedback before starting on the next phase.

How do we start discussing the new strategy?

You can't have a new strategy if you don't have a wide-ranging and searching conversation about what should be in it. In phase 3 you will need to convene a diverse strategy setting panel, which should ideally include some challenging outsiders as well as key staff or board members. All these people should have had plenty of time to consider the feedback collected, synthesised and shared by your strategy process lead.

This strategy setting panel will need to meet at least twice: once to develop a first draft and then to thrash out the inevitable sticking points. Note that professional facilitation can really help in these sessions.

Overleaf is a suggestion for how you can run the first planning day: phase 3 in our suggested seven steps.

Sample agenda for a strategy planning day

While you probably can squeeze this into a single day, it'll work a lot better over two days.

Session 1: What did our stakeholders tell us?

A summary of the ideas and themes that emerged from the conversations you've had in previous weeks. To keep it clear, it may be helpful to separate it into:

- important facts and context gained;
- what people told us they thought we should do differently.

If you have done desk research into various problems or opportunities, this is also the time to present it.

Session 2: What might our problem or opportunity statement be?

To be a really effective funder you need to be quite focused (otherwise the world is just too big for you to make a difference). So you need to be clear about the small number of problems or opportunities that primarily motivate your organisation.

You should debate this question as a group and try writing down your own version of what the key problems or opportunities are. When you put different people's versions of the problem statement side by side you are likely to see whether everyone is on the same page or whether there are more fundamental disagreements about what your organisation is trying to achieve.

Session 3: What might our vision statement be?

A vision statement normally sits alongside a mission statement. The vision statement says how the world would look if your organisation were successful, so you need to draft one of these together. Keeping this to no more than 50 words will help filter out otherwise invisible disagreements. To promote debate, write down lots of different versions emphasising different things.

Session 4: What is our mission statement?

Now you're really getting down to brass tacks. Does your current mission actually explain what you think the organisation should be doing? Can you express more clearly what you're trying to do and how you're planning to do it? Can you make it quotable? Again, having several people in the room writing numerous versions will help to bring out differences and common ideas.

Session 5: What are our key goals for achieving that mission?

So you've now agreed what the problem is (and ideally also identified the root causes and not just the symptoms of that problem) and you've agreed what your overall approach is going to be. But how are you going to break that down into more achievable goals? Are you just going to back established NGOs or are you also going to develop future leaders? Are you going to pay for services to be delivered *and* lobby for policy changes, or are you just going to focus on one of these? This is the point where the group has to debate and agree on which major areas of work are and are *not* going to happen.

Session 6: What are we not going to do?

This is a painful one, but critical for a good-quality strategy. What aren't we about? What are we ruling out? It's incredibly important to debate this and write down your conclusions. As Paul Brest and Hal Harvey say in their book *Money Well Spent*, 'The more things you do, the more you diffuse your resources, and the greater the likelihood becomes that you will not deploy them in the most effective way.'[165]

Session 7: What objectives can we aim for in the short to medium term, and how will we know we have achieved them?

So we've agreed that one of our goals is, say, 'to identify and nurture future leaders in field X'. That's terrific, but how will we know whether we've made a good start on it? How many people need to have achieved what milestone, and by what date, for us to say that we're making good progress? The process of setting objectives and key results is the very final part of the strategy, and it can sometimes seem like one of the least fun. However, if you want to make sure that your strategy document actually makes change happen, this bit is crucial because it determines what you do – and what you don't do – next.

Session 8: Where do we stand on a range of classic funder dilemmas?

In the next chapter we will lay out some of the strategic choices that all funders have to make: will we make restricted or unrestricted grants? How long will our grants last? These are key questions you have to tackle to develop a coherent strategy, but they can easily be kicked into the long grass. This is your chance to make sure this doesn't happen.

How do we produce a first draft strategy and then turn it into a better second draft?

Once the planning meeting is over, you should have all the materials required to write a rough first draft of a new strategy – this is phase 4. This probably means locking yourself away for a few days and trying to get the most important ideas down in a document. Top tip: use the following document framework to help your strategy avoid the terrible fate of shapeless sprawl (something that more or less guarantees it will never change anything):

- Section 1: What is this strategy document?
- Section 2: What is the *problem* or opportunity that motivates this organisation?
- Section 3: What is our *vision*, i.e. what does success look like?
- Section 4: What is our *mission* as an organisation?
- Section 5: What are the high-level *goals* that will help us to deliver our mission?
- Section 6: What are we not doing – what's *out of our scope*?
- Section 7: What are the *objectives and key results* that will help us measure progress towards our goals?
- Section 8: If we have a *problematic legacy*, how are we going to address that head-on?
- Section 9: What *type, size and duration of grants* will we make, and how will people get them?
- Section 10: What is our *timeline*?
- Section 11: What is our *budget*?
- Section 12: What are our *next steps*?

Once this is ready, it's time to share the draft with honest, critical readers from inside and outside your organisation. Some image-sensitive funders will, we know, worry about draft strategies circulating externally like this, but the value of doing this is immense, and you should try to

How do I help my funder develop a good strategy?

persuade doubters that not getting feedback is likely to lead to many more problems down the line.

When you do ask for feedback on your draft strategy document, don't forget that some organisations will be much more able to give feedback than others. To avoid the feedback being distorted, you may have to take steps to make sure that individuals who are under a lot of pressure and have less time also have an opportunity to respond. This could involve paying them for feedback, which some funders may find counter-cultural.

Once you've collected enough feedback you should have the second strategy meeting (phase 5 in our list) to discuss the draft document. Your main task will be to improve it during the meeting itself while responding to external and internal feedback. It would be enormously helpful if you could actually edit the document in real time (around a shared screen, for example). If you don't have much experience in this, a professional facilitator will, again, be very useful.

At the end of this session you should have a second version of the strategy. Your organisation now faces a decision as to whether to adopt the current draft of the strategy as official or to iterate it still further. The person you appointed to lead the whole strategy development process is critical here: it is their job to make sure that the process comes to an end and doesn't just go on for ever at the glacial pace of funder time.

Once you've got the final version of the document – probably called Strategy-Final.Final.Finalv102.docx – it's time to put it in a place where your team and stakeholders can easily and regularly access it. Your last task for now is to schedule a review at some point in 6 to 24 months' time to ask how things are going. Your strategy is always going to need revision, so you may as well plan for it in advance.

Now it's time to sit down with everyone in your organisation to talk about all the things they are currently doing that will now have to be boosted, altered, cancelled or otherwise re-prioritised so that their work is aligned with the new mission.

How do we actually make use of the new strategy to change things?

OK, so now you've got a good-quality strategy document, and it's all been signed off. How do you make use of it to change things? The most typical way a strategy is rolled out in a grantmaking organisation is probably that it's circulated as an email attachment to staff, who then largely shrug their shoulders and carry on doing what they were doing before.

What should you do if you want to deploy the strategy in such a way as to have more impact? Here are some suggestions:

- Whenever you make a decision, no matter how small, tie it clearly to the strategy. Do this in person, in email or via whatever channel you prefer: always explain your choices with reference to the relevant justification within the strategy. This will both help you achieve clarity and stop people from forgetting that it exists.

- Even the most motivated person can find a document without narrative hard to follow. You should develop stories, fictitious or real, that illustrate both what the new strategy is about and the motivation behind it.

- If you operate a budgeting process, formally change your budgets to reflect what's new. Then explain to everyone what has changed and why it aligns with the new strategy.

- If you are an organisational leader, and you have enough staff to have managers, make sure that they understand the connection between the new goals in the strategy and their own personal goals. Explain how you'll be looking for them to show progress against those goals in your catch-ups.

- Convene internal discussions with your colleagues about previous grants your organisation made that would still be supported under the new strategy and those that would no longer be the sort of thing you'd fund.

- If you have an online presence, don't just post the news. Consider rebuilding your online presence to make it fundamentally about your strategic priorities, so that they leap out at people when they first see you or visit your site.

- Make the strategy and its key ideas easy to find. Stick the key ideas on your walls, make the link easy to find on the website, and make stickers and put them on laptops. You could employ the skills of a professional designer to do this well.

- Most important of all, schedule 'progress against strategy' meetings regularly throughout the year. For example, your trustees board, if there is one, should talk about progress against strategy at each board meeting, and the whole organisation should see the results of this discussion too.

- Encourage colleagues to point out practices that are not aligned with the strategy. When they do this, celebrate their contribution in positive and visible ways to encourage others to do the same.

- Take the time to explain your strategy to key grantholders and other significant stakeholders such as other funders.

Is there anything else I should do?

Developing a new strategy for a funding organisation isn't a trivial thing, nor is it something with a simple right and wrong approach. Here are some further tips to make sure that it goes as well as possible:

- Set a sensible time frame for the entire process. Two to four months is a reasonable length of time to move from initial research to final approval. Slower than that and you're definitely into the decadence of funder time, where nothing is that urgent.

- Ensure that there are diverse voices and experiences both in the research phase and around the strategy-designing table. Nothing drives groupthink like everyone coming from the same perspective, so keep up the diversity to make sure the results are as good as they can be.

- If you work for a bigger organisation, don't do all your strategy planning in big rooms with lots of people. Use sub-groups to debate questions. This reduces the possibility of groupthink and tends to draw out people who are naturally quieter and less willing to speak in front of big audiences.

- Use 'red teaming' exercises, where one group of people is tasked with picking apart and finding flaws in another team's ideas.[166] In the writing of a grantmaker strategy, the key purpose of the red teaming exercise is to take draft versions of the final strategy document and really dig into the various ways in which the plan might backfire when it comes into contact with reality. Don't do red teaming too late in the process, though, or you may find that by that point people are emotionally committed to getting it out the door and won't change their minds.

Is this the only way of coming up with a useful strategy for my funding organisation?

As we explained at the start of this chapter, what we've set out is just one way of developing one kind of funder strategy. We're not saying that it's the only or best way of making something, as with any recipe – it's just a solid way to get started, especially if you've never done it before.

However, there are other approaches to coming up with a strategy. Here are a couple to spark your imagination.

Another approach to strategy no. 1: Support and enable a chosen community to set your strategy for you

From time to time leaders within funding organisations decide that they shouldn't be the people to set their funding strategy at all. In the following case study we show how one network of funders gave away a lot of power that funders would traditionally have kept to themselves.[167]

Prospera – International Network of Women's Funds is a nonprofit that calls itself 'the global hub of women's funds'. Women's funds are public institutions that raise money for women's, girls' and trans people's organisations to enable them to carry out their work. They give money to deeply political and often invisible work that supports gender justice by following the agendas of the movements they support rather than imposing their own agendas.

Prospera is the network that connects these funds to each other and to other funders, governments and corporations internationally. Its members give over 5,000 grants a year, totalling over $160 million, to women's funds operating at national, regional, sub-regional and multi-regional levels in over 178 countries.

It seeks to change traditional and current models of funding within private philanthropy, bilateral donor governments, corporations and individuals. To democratise decision making, it makes its funding participatory, inclusive, feminist, diverse and transformative.

One of its innovative models is the Women's Funds Collaborative (WFC), which was set up to support the members of Prospera with a $20 million investment by the Hewlett Foundation, Foundation for a Just Society, Open Society Foundations and Wellspring Philanthropic Fund.

These funders took a risk by creating an unusual governance model, and Prospera's executive director, Alexandra Garita, told us about just one of the ways in which the WFC differs from a traditional funder:

> Our steering committee made a solidarity grant to all 44 members of the Prospera Network. They were all eligible for $75k to strengthen their own funds. It was done as a way of showing that the committee trusts these organisations equally and that they can decide for themselves what strengthening capacity and infrastructure means for them.

Through the work of both supportive donors and Prospera over the past two years, the WFC is now a participatory funding collaborative whose steering committee includes four representatives of private foundations, four representatives of women's funds and a member of Prospera's secretariat. All decisions are made collectively by members on an equal footing, despite their coming from very different places. Thus the ability to set strategy is shared rather than being entirely owned by the private funders who have invested their resources in the mechanism.

What has been important to the WFC's success is a willingness to be uncomfortable at times and to work through the tensions that are inevitable in such a diverse group. The group has been forging ahead on the basis of its clarity of purpose, a commitment to feminist practices and good faith.

The WFC's governance structure and grantmaking is informed by feminist funding principles such as attention to equity, intersectionality and power dynamics at the centre. The grants it makes go to women's funds, specifically their core institutional and operational costs, with absolute flexibility as long as it serves their organisation's needs. In other words, the money is to be used for re-granting.

Given the success of the WFC, Prospera members are actively advocating for similar participatory governance and funding models to be adopted by corporate funders, other philanthropies and individual donor circles.

Feminist funding requires seismic shifts in traditional charitable and giving models towards transformative change. But as Alexandra Garita told us:

> If funders trust and fund the women, girls and trans activists and organisations that are at the forefront of justice; listen to, act with and resource community and movement-led solutions, we can reimagine feminist futures.

Another approach to strategy no. 2: Embrace randomness

That funding organisations have to carefully choose which organisations get money is one of the fundamentals on which our entire profession is based. But in the science funding universe there's growing interest in replacing the human selection of grantees with random choice.

A recent article from the journal *Research Integrity and Peer Review* sets out the argument:

> One alternative approach to allocating funding is to use lotteries or modified lotteries. In a modified lottery, short applications are screened for eligibility and/or to remove weak applications, and then applications are funded at random until the budget is exhausted. This reduces the burden on peer reviewers and administrators, which is a concern as funders often struggle to find well-qualified reviewers within tight timelines. This simplified approach also potentially reduces the burden on applicants, reviewers and funders if application forms can be simplified and if applicants reduce their preparation time because they recognise that funding is not guaranteed. This could return time and resources back to research given the large amount of time researchers spend on applications.
>
> By reducing the role of people in decision making, lotteries also minimise the problems of sexism, racism and ageism influencing who receives funding. Interestingly, lotteries may

also increase fairness and support more meritorious ideas. Lotteries also explicitly acknowledge the role of chance in winning funding, which occurs because the review process is somewhat random because of the selection and availability of peer reviewers.

Previous research found that amongst funded projects, the peer review score was a poor predictor of the subsequent number of research outputs. Related recent research found a low agreement amongst reviewers scoring the same application.[168]

So this isn't about randomly chucking money from helicopters. Indeed, this method has already been used for government grants in New Zealand and by the Volkswagen Foundation in Germany.

It is interesting to see an approach to grantmaking that calls into question the very notion of grant assessment. We shall probably be seeing a lot more experiments in random grantmaking in the years ahead, especially in scientific fields, where aggregate citations of papers can be used as a proxy for the ultimate impact of grants.

Another approach to strategy no. 3: Focus solely on righting wrongs the funder is party to

Some funding organisations, especially those that are many decades old, are based on money that was generated in ways we would now consider unacceptable. Addressing these historic wrongs may be the best – or the only – strategy for these organisations. For, as we were told by Jenny Oppenheimer, action inquiry manager at Lankelly Chase Foundation, 'Lots of funders in the UK have links to colonialism in that their wealth is built on slavery. For many, philanthropy was about buying their place in heaven.'[169]

If you discover that your organisation's money comes from shameful sources, your board should strongly consider embracing a strategy that seeks to use its money in ways that acknowledge and address these wrongs.[170] These could include directly funding anti-racist organisations and involving them in designing and deciding on any funding that, for example, supports the descendants of former slaves who still face inequality and discrimination today, or funding organisations that tackle modern slavery.

A very promising sign of an organisation taking its history seriously is John Ellerman Foundation in the UK. Its director, Sufina Ahmad, is leading a history project to review the origins of the foundation's money, which was generated by a shipowner and investor of great wealth who lived from 1862 to 1933, around the high point of the British empire. The foundation is making this enquiry to assess how its future activities should be shaped by its past.

Funders could go further. Edgar Villanueva in his book *Decolonizing Wealth* makes a case for individual US funders using 10% of their assets to establish trust funds to which Native Americans and African Americans can apply for grants for 'various asset-building projects, such as home ownership, further education or start up funds for businesses'.[171]

Having a problematic legacy should also affect your strategy planning in another significant way. We think that there is a case to be made that organisations with painful histories should consider spending down and closing up. In the next chapter we will address the question of whether private funding organisations should be permanent or should spend down and close.

Is that it?

There are innumerable ways of developing and deploying a strategy within a funding organisation. In this chapter we've set out one template approach in great detail, and three others briefly. We therefore want to admit that there are only three non-negotiable rules of funder strategy development:

Rule 1   Have a strategy – preferably one that makes it clear what's in your remit and what's outside it.

Rule 2   Make sure that the people who are affected by your strategy are given a say in its design and implementation. If possible, make sure they're in the decision-making room too and not merely 'consulted'.

Rule 3   Make sure that you review your strategy and your progress towards it, and that you share your progress with others.[172]

If that's all you can manage, you'll still have a strategy that's a great deal better than nothing.

In the next chapter we will look at some of the big questions that every funder needs to consider when developing a new strategy. It's time now to shift from the 'how' of a decent strategy to the 'what'.

Chapter 4 checklist

1. Does your organisation have a strategy?

....

2. Is it a strategy that everyone in the organisation can find in under two minutes and easily recall?

....

3. Is this strategy used and cited by teams at all levels when they make decisions?

....

4. Did your organisation consciously involve the people who are going to be affected by grantmaking in strategy development?

....

5. Does your strategy contain both a list of things you will do and a list of things you won't?

....

6. Can grantseekers and grantees find your strategy easily and can they understand it?

....

7. Does your organisation have a list of things it can do better for the next time it updates its strategy?

....

8. Does your organisation have a clear and transparent process for updating colleagues, grantseekers, grantees and other partners on how you are doing in relation to your strategy?

....

5

WHAT BIG QUESTIONS SHOULD ALL FUNDERS DEBATE FROM TIME TO TIME?

> There are these two young fish swimming along, and they happen to meet an older fish swimming the other way, who nods at them and says 'Morning, boys, how's the water?' And the two young fish swim on for a bit, and then eventually one of them looks over at the other and goes, 'What the hell is water?'[173]
>
> — DAVID FOSTER WALLACE, 'This Is Water'

In this chapter we look at a set of important strategic questions that are so fundamental that they are quite easy for funders to overlook altogether. We believe that it is only by making careful, conscious choices about these dilemmas that we, as grantmakers, can unshackle ourselves from the invisible constraints handed down to us as 'the way it's always been done'.

We call the subject of this chapter 'classic funder dilemmas'. They are classic because they are old familiar tunes that have been haunting thoughtful grantmakers for a long time. They are dilemmas because there's often no obvious right and wrong answer. If you're not in a mood for ambiguity, check out Chapter 2 on no-brainers instead – not everything in grantmaking is imponderable!

Before we get started, we should say that you don't have to be running a strategy development process right now to gain something from considering these dilemmas. Any board meeting or casual conversation with colleagues is an opportunity to discuss one or more of the dilemmas we outline below. Once they're on the table and people have had time to think about them, you may be surprised by the lack of consensus on issues that you might have thought so uncontroversial that they didn't require debate.

Dilemma no. 1: Should we be open to unsolicited proposals or be an invite-only funder?

One of the biggest strategic choices a funding organisation can make is whether or not to have a page on a website that says 'Apply here', such as this one:

When people are in the lead, communities thrive
The National Lottery Community Fund distributes <u>over £600m</u> a year to communities across the UK, raised by players of <u>The National Lottery</u>

Apply for funding under £10,000   Apply for funding over £10,000

Website excerpt showing that this funder is open to unsolicited proposals[174]

If you have an invitation like this on your website, it means that your organisation is open to considering funding proposals from anyone who successfully completes your form, including organisations that you would never fund in a million years. An organisation that chooses to accept applications must necessarily work very differently from one that receives applications only from organisations that it has actively invited to apply.

For convenience, we'll call organisations that accept proposals from anyone 'open' organisations and ones that don't 'invite only'. No moral judgement is intended by these terms. They are just a convenient way of clearly labelling the organisations.

There are pros and cons to both open and invite-only models, and there definitely isn't a simple right answer. Here are the main trade-offs you'll have to consider:

What big questions should all funders debate from time to time?

	Pros	Cons
Your funder is open to unsolicited proposals	You will receive funding proposals from organisations you would otherwise never know about and never hear from. It gives organisations that have no direct personal relationship with your staff or board a chance to get funded, which is especially valuable for social groups that are marginalised.	You will have to read and process many proposals, which will be more costly and time consuming than vetting fewer proposals. Grantseekers may waste their time writing and submitting applications that you would never consider funding. If you get a lot of applications, this could mean a lot of wasted time for organisations with few resources to waste.
Your funder is invite only	You will avoid having a backlog of unread applications. You will prevent organisations from wasting their time developing proposals you cannot fund. You can potentially use the time you save in not reading funding proposals to do other work, e.g. by forming more partnerships.	You are at much greater risk of funding organisations that are superb at schmoozing and networking but not necessarily the best at creating impact. You may perpetuate social inequalities by funding people mainly from groups that are well connected with the staff and board of your organisation.

So those are the trade-offs. But how should your organisation make this call between being open and being invite only? One interesting insight comes from a UK funder that has been unusually transparent in its thinking on this matter.

Reflecting on the time grantseekers spend writing and sending funding applications, the Indigo Trust shared the following analysis: 'In the last financial year [2017/18] … not a single unsolicited proposal was successful with all grants coming via referrals, meetings, desk research or they were simply previous grantees.'[175] Moreover, the Indigo Trust revealed that in the previous three years it had received 818 proposals, of which 104 were approved. This meant that seven out of every eight proposals it received were unsuccessful. Its team then calculated that grantseekers to this small foundation were putting in 'the equivalent of 2 years 9 months of effort for proposals that didn't receive funding'. These are startling figures, and without any further context they might lead you to conclude that every open funder should move to an invite-only model straightaway.

However, the choice to close off unsolicited applications is not at all easy or cost free. Soliciting funding applications in private means relying on research and social networks to find worthy applicants. As a result of the structures and biases within society at large, it is very likely that many prospective grantees will simply never be known to you because there is no mechanism that can connect your organisation with theirs.

For some causes, this problem of social distance doesn't matter. For example, if you are grantmaking to the only research laboratory that is trying to cure a specific cancer, this problem won't affect you. But if your focus is on issues that affect the most marginalised people in society, for example violence against sex workers, a closed, invite-only approach to unsolicited applications may make it harder for you to hear from many of the people you'd most like to help. The consequence may be that you end up having to invest even more time than you already do in building relationships one at a time.

As a funder you should think hard and do your research to find out whether closing yourself off to unsolicited applicants will lead to you under-serving the people you want to help most. As we note, the sectors and issues you focus on will largely determine whether an invite-only model will help you achieve your aims.

Scale is also an important factor at play here. Small funding organisations with one or two part-time staff obviously can't read more than a modest number of funding applications, so unsolicited proposals do risk grantseekers wasting their time. But the problem of being overwhelmed can also be real for medium-sized funders. The former CEO of one such funder told us:

> We worked very openly for some time. But it's totally exhausting. Every week you get hundreds of letters asking to be considered for money. Working in this way requires more people, even just to reply to these letters properly, let alone to consider requests in detail, and you still have to bear in mind the money is for social change, not your staff.[176]

We empathise with this and have personal experience of being overwhelmed by applications. It isn't a great feeling, especially when you know that you are going to have to say 'no' to a lot of people.

As funding institutions get bigger, it becomes more realistic to offer open funding channels. A funder that employs more than, say, 50 people is arguably big enough to accept at least some unsolicited proposals. Given that all funders should be taking steps to combat systemic inequalities, we think that all large funding organisations should offer some open grantmaking. It is only through an open application process that your funding organisation has any chance of receiving proposals from organisations with which you have no friend-of-a-friend personal connections.

What about smaller organisations that would like to accept unsolicited proposals?

For many smaller funding organisations the open or closed question is a no-brainer – they simply don't have the resources to read, let alone vet, a stream of unsolicited proposals. Even a modest number of unsolicited proposals would pile up unread, which would waste grantseekers' resources and be frustrating for grantmakers.

Nevertheless, in our research we came across smaller funding organisations that would like to accept some unsolicited applications if there was a way of doing so without being overwhelmed. So what can they do?

First, these organisations can piggyback on larger ones. Where a bigger organisation, which can afford to spend $10 million on funding a programme, is running an open call for proposals, a smaller funder can throw in $100,000 and increase the amount of funded work that gets delivered. Playing an arguably secondary role like this may not be compatible with the egos of some grantmakers and board members, but if this book is about anything it's about accepting this with humility.

Second, there is a new wave of crowdfunding websites where people and nonprofits can simply announce publicly that they are trying to raise money for a cause. Smaller funding organisations can visit these sites to look for attractive funding opportunities, or actively encourage potential applicants to consider posting on one of these websites (instead of sending a proposal directly to them). If you encourage people to apply, though, it is important to make it clear what their chances are, to avoid wasting their time writing an application.

Here are a few examples of websites where people and organisations post fundraising drives:

- Donors Choose (US): **donorschoose.org**
- The Good Exchange (UK): **thegoodexchange.com**

Modern Grantmaking

- GoFundMe (US and UK): **gofundme.com**
- Crowdfunder (UK): **crowdfunder.co.uk**
- Fundly (US): **fundly.com**
- Brevio (UK): **brevio.org**

Dilemma no. 2: Should we fund riskier projects with potentially higher pay-offs or less risky projects with lower pay-offs?

Whenever you as a funder make a grant, there's a chance that the money spent won't result in a positive impact or that it will make less of a positive impact than you had hoped. The chance that the money you give won't make a difference is what we call *risk*.

So our second classic funder dilemma is this: what should your organisation's attitude be to risk?

It might be assumed that our approach to risk as prudent grantmakers is straightforward – less risky projects are better than more risky ones. After all, who wants to throw away precious money for nothing? But the choice isn't so simple because some higher-risk projects – ones that aren't guaranteed to work – may turn out to have a much bigger social impact than safer, less risky investments.

Consider these two different $10 million grants that a funder could make:

- Option A (low risk): Donate the whole $10 million to a hospital so that it can treat 2,000 sick patients over a period of five years. The risk that the investment will fail and nobody will be helped is only 1%.

- Option B (high risk): Donate the £10 million to a medical research laboratory to fund the development of a vaccine for a disease that kills 2 million people a year. The risk that the research will fail is 90%.

Which organisation and project should your funder give its money to? There is no simple right answer – there are strong arguments for making each investment.

This is not a counsel of despair, however. Funders can do more than throw up their hands and say, 'It's all too hard!'

What big questions should all funders debate from time to time?

You should encourage your colleagues to think about risk as something that relates to your whole portfolio of risks, and not just one particular proposal. The advantage of this is that you can then meaningfully discuss, debate and agree your organisation's risk appetite in relation to a portfolio of higher- and lower-risk grants. This in turn makes individual grantmaking decisions more robust.

Here's a fictitious example of two organisations with different risk appetites, and thus two different portfolios of grants:

- The XTreme Foundation is run by a tech billionaire who loves base jumping and wrestling wild animals. This organisation has a high appetite for risk, so it decides that 80% of its grants will be higher risk, while 20% will go to lower-risk community projects.

- The Prudence Foundation is a branch of government and is nervous about being seen to have wasted taxpayers' money. Its board decides that 90% of its investments must count as low risk, with the remaining 10% being medium risk.

Deciding up front what proportion of your money you'll allocate to different kinds of risk is very common in the world of for-profit investments. If you have a pension or other investments you may have seen an explanation that '60% is held in shares and 40% in bonds'. This is just a way of saying, 'This portfolio of investments has a certain risk profile.'

It is unusual, however, to find funding organisations formally and publicly defining a risk appetite for their portfolio of grants or other social investments. But, happily, they do exist, and we were lucky enough that one anonymous UK director of a private foundation took the time to explain to us how they manage risk. This makes a really interesting case study, which we'd like to see discussed at every funder board:

> We're a funder with a single, clear social change goal, and we know that we can't succeed rapidly. So our board has backed a 20-year high-level strategy, which we revise every five years, and then set more precise annual objectives.
>
> Given the scale of the social change goal and the amount of capital we can deploy, we know that we won't succeed against our own mission if we only back 'safe' projects, such as those that predominantly involve service delivery, which

is important but won't lead to systemic change. At the same time we recognise that it's only human to want to continually lower grantmaking risk, and that if we don't take deliberate steps our grantmaking will tend to get more risk averse, and hence we will be less likely to achieve our mission.

To counterbalance this, we have incorporated some practices to encourage risk.

First, we have a default that we won't fund service delivery unless it is in pursuit of system change.

Second, we have a risk–reward discussion on each grant recommendation we make. For instance, does the hoped-for outcome represent real and significant change and is the path to achieving it plausible? Given our relatively modest grant awards (our average is £225,000 [about $250,000] over three years), our focus on reward leads us naturally to entertain supporting higher-risk projects, approaches and organisations.

Third, once a year we look at our entire portfolio of live grants, and we categorise them into higher- and lower-risk bets. We count the number of high- and low-risk projects, and we calculate what proportion of our grantmaking they represent. We usually subdivide them into programme areas and we often cross-reference with other data points, like organisational size. It's immediately obvious whether or not we as staff need to actively source more higher-risk grants in succeeding grant cycles or not, and in which programme areas. (On only one occasion have we actually dialled down risk in a following docket.) We do this to make sure that our grantmaking covers a smart mix of lower- and higher-risk projects, and to fight against the tendency for every new grant to be low risk.

Finally, our board regularly asks staff about grantmaking failures, with the expectation that failure is an inevitable consequence of taking risks. Staff don't usually elaborate on failures in board meetings but are given the clear message that there will be no performance repercussions for admitting and learning from experiments and investments that have not worked.[177]

We think there is a lot to be said for this sort of very conscious risk management structure becoming a normal part of grantmaking management practice. We encourage your organisation to debate and agree its risk appetite in terms of the kind of organisations and legal status, as well as projects, you're willing to support, and then to share your decision publicly so that others can understand the sorts of grants you do and don't make.

How do I run a session where we agree on our grantmaking risk appetite?

We recommend that funding organisations debate and agree their risk appetites in a formal way – and do so separately from the regularly scheduled meetings in which grant decisions are made. If you're debating your organisation's appetite for risk while holding a specific funding proposal in your hand, it probably means you've left the discussion too late.

We suggest that you hold a special *risk appetite session* with the key decision makers in your organisation. In this session you should present a few different scenarios about what it would mean to spend more money on higher- or lower-risk grants. To make it more real you could give real examples of grants that you perceive to be lower risk and lower impact, and contrast them with projects that may be higher risk and higher impact.

Before you go further in this crucial debate, remind your colleagues of the troubling connection between risk management and various kinds of institutional discrimination. Decision makers should consider their overall risk appetite explicitly through this lens to make sure that managing risk doesn't simply equate to discriminating against some people.

Case study: When risk management becomes discrimination

Here's a real-life example of this phenomenon from an unnamed funder in the UK.[178]

This funding organisation received a complaint from a nonprofit, claiming that Black-led organisations were disproportionately likely to fail the risk assessment process that the funder had had in place for many years. If this were true, it would mean that hundreds of organisations that served people of colour may not have had equal access to funding.

The risk assessment process in question consisted of a set of checks for all new applications that the funder used to reduce the potential for fraud. The checks looked for data characteristics that might signify that a proposal was not genuine and was just an attempt to steal money.

Upon receiving the complaint, the funding organisation's managers conducted an internal review. They privately concluded that the complainant had a point and quietly removed some of the checks that had been excluding some types of applicant.

As the funder made these changes, however, it failed to take advantage of a major opportunity for positive action. Instead of talking honestly and openly about bureaucratic mechanisms that can end up creating discrimination, it remained silent on the matter. It passed up the chance to be a leader in grantmaking by showing both other funders and grantseekers that discrimination is pervasive and that it requires energy and dedication to eliminate. In short, this funder showed through its actions that equity was less important than avoiding embarrassment.

What big questions should all funders debate from time to time?

Back to the business of clarifying your organisation's appetite for risk. If possible, you should find out about the risk appetites of other funders, especially those of comparable size and focus, before you meet. This may help your key decision makers to position themselves in relation to others.

Once you have met and formally debated your organisation's risk appetite, the meeting chair should ask everyone present to agree on a sentence or two to describe the organisation's risk appetite. They should push for this appetite to be quantified by agreement on a specific position such as '25% of our funding should be high risk'. This specificity will be enormously helpful down the line when comparing competing funding proposals. It will also help with measuring the performance and impact of your grants.

Articulating your funder's risk appetite clearly – and using numbers to do so – will also be very helpful to make sure that all the people in your organisation share an understanding that their grantmaking is going to be a mix of more risky and less risky bets. Without such a shared understanding, people working together as a group may become more risk averse, especially when things go wrong.[179]

Philanthropy should have a risk appetite

Most of the advice in this book is valid for any type of grantmaking, whether you are working for corporate, government or private grantmaking organisations. But there is one risk-related argument that applies specifically and uniquely to philanthropy.[180]

Put simply, philanthropic money should never be spent entirely on low-risk grantmaking. If you work for such an organisation, it's your duty to make sure that your employer is not making only totally safe bets. Here's why.

Government global spending dwarfs all philanthropy combined. Annual US government spending, for example, is about 10 times greater than all US charitable giving combined. This means that, for every dollar you can spend on an essential service like a nursery or a hospital, the government can spend way, way more (if it chooses to).

But there are various very important things that governments generally cannot fund. For example, governments cannot usually fund advocacy or campaigns to change social attitudes, corporate behaviours or the law itself. And many governments are not keen to fund various sorts of risky interventions that may have a high chance of failure for fear of being labelled as being reckless with taxpayers' money.

So philanthropic organisations have a specific and important social role to play in taking the risks that governments cannot take. If such funders choose to provide entirely safe and low-risk services, they're basically choosing to operate in a field where they will only ever be a drop in the ocean compared to government spending, while ignoring areas of spending where they — and they alone — can make a difference.

This doesn't mean that all philanthropic grantmaking should be high risk. But it does mean that all philanthropic risk portfolios should have at least some budget set aside for the types of risky spending that governments cannot engage in.

Dilemma no. 3: Should we focus on preventing harm or on helping people who have been harmed?

For those seeking to make the world a better place, there has always been one key question: do we try to prevent the bad things from happening or do we help clear up after they have happened? In other words, do we prevent or do we cure?

A lot of the most high-profile types of grantmaking are about fixing problems after they've hit, for example, giving money after a hurricane has destroyed a town. This is understandable because the sight of victims in distress has long opened purses and wallets. However, this strong emotional response means that worldwide a very large amount of grant money gets spent on things that are of value only when bad things have already happened, such as ambulances, homeless shelters and sacks of grain.

The problem with after-the-event giving is twofold. First, giving money only after a problem has revealed itself means that individuals, as well as animals and the wider environment, have to suffer before they are offered help.

Second, much evidence suggests that money spent on preventing problems is used much more efficiently than money spent on clearing up the mess afterwards. For example, a systematic review by a group of public health experts in the UK estimated that every £1 spent on preventative public health in the UK saves an average of £14 in costs associated with people getting sick.[181] A ratio of 14 to 1 is enormous, and it isn't hard to find similar ratios in other areas, such as the cost of preventing crime compared to the cost of locking people up.

But the moral calculus isn't as simple as 'prevention – good; mitigation – bad'. As Phil Buchanan, CEO of the Center for Effective Philanthropy put it in his book *Giving Done Right*:

> A focus on root causes isn't somehow superior to other forms of philanthropy. Nor is it the only type of philanthropy that can be considered strategic or results driven. Reducing car accidents and the injuries and deaths they cause is a great achievement, but so is improving the emergency room outcomes at hospitals where the victims of car crashes are rushed – even if that effort doesn't get to the root causes of the injuries.[182]

So funders who are serious about helping to reduce the impact of bad things need to ask themselves how much they care about stopping those things from happening compared to picking up the pieces when they do. Again, as with risk appetite, we feel that it is important for grantmakers and trustees to debate and decide their own ambitions in this regard separately and away from the room in which grant decisions are being made. And, as with risk again, there's a lot to be said for writing down and publishing your position on prevention versus cure to help keep your organisation committed to its conscious choices.

Funders who go big on prevention

Prevention-based grantmaking often focuses on certain areas where preventative approaches offer particularly good social returns, such as health, young people and education. Here are a few examples.

The *UK Prevention Research Partnership* is a £50 million multi-funder initiative in the UK that supports 'novel research into the primary prevention of non-communicable diseases to improve population health and reduce health inequalities'. This partnership supports large interdisciplinary collaborations funded to undertake research on a specific challenge. A typical example of their work is ActEarly, which aims to improve the life chances of children by focusing on improving the environments that influence their health.

The *Early Action Funders Alliance* supports UK funders 'to seek thoughtful and creative responses to the challenges of escalating needs and shrinking resources'. This way of thinking is being trialled by the Early Action Neighbourhood Fund, a five-year £5.3 million project that aims to reduce future demand for public services (e.g. children's services, mental health services and housing support) by providing innovative models of intensive preventative support now.[183]

What big questions should all funders debate from time to time?

Dilemma no. 4: Should we focus on helping in a specific place or on tackling a specific problem?

We call funders that focus on one area *place-based funders*, and those that focus more on issues *thematic funders*. So the Cripplegate Foundation, with its stated goal of 'giving grants and support to organisations working in Islington (a borough of London, UK) to benefit residents' is clearly place based.[184] The Stanton Foundation in the US, in contrast, is a thematic funder: its three chosen focus areas – 'international and nuclear security', 'informed citizens' and 'canine health and welfare' – mark it out as driven by issues, not places.

CANINE HEALTH AND WELFARE   INTERNATIONAL AND NUCLEAR SECURITY   INFORMED CITIZENS

Clear themes and a lack of geographical specificity show that this is the website of a thematic funder.[185]

Now there is obviously some overlap. Thematic funders will often specify countries or regions that they choose to work in, and place-based funders will usually have some themes on which they work. But their goals tend to be quite different in emphasis: one aims at making great neighbourhoods, and the other at solving specific problems around the world.

If you are rebuilding or creating a funding organisation's mission and strategy, you should decide whether you are more focused on a place or on a topic. Your grantmaking approach will be somewhat different, depending on your answer.

Place-based funders tend to fund quite a few different kinds of activities in the same area. For example, the same place-based funder may make grants that cover youth activities, reoffender rehabilitation, food banks, parks and local artists. Why such a broad range? Because the towns, cities and villages where people live are complex places and face many different problems. If a funder were to focus only on one kind of service in an area, they wouldn't help the community to improve overall, only in part.

Angel Shed Theatre Company

Angel Shed provides inclusive theatre workshops and performances for Islington's young people.

Organisation

Body & Soul

Body and Soul work with people of all ages who have experienced childhood adversity, including those affected by family disruption, suicidal behaviour and HIV.

Organisation

Centre 404

Centre 404 offers person centred support to people with a learning disability and their families in north London.

Organisation

Chance UK

Chance UK empowers children to develop their skills, confidence and life aspirations through a year-long mentoring programme.

A grants web page shows the wide range of issues supported by Cripplegate Foundation, a place-based funder, in one London borough.[186]

Thematic funders, in contrast, will tend to fund organisations that have similar or overlapping missions, and that are located in a wider range of places.

What big questions should all funders debate from time to time?

How do we choose to prioritise place or theme?

This choice is ultimately down to the motivations that underpin your organisation's mission. You should have deep, challenging conversations about place-based funding versus thematic funding as part of your strategy process. As noted earlier, it is important that these conversations are held away from the room in which you make decisions about specific funding proposals. You should make your strategic choices first and your grant assessments afterwards, not the other way around. Place versus theme is a big strategic choice.

Everyone thinking about this choice should be aware of the role played by trends in grantmaking. In the UK we saw thematic funding as the dominant model around the time of the Great Recession (late 2007 to mid-2009), and then over the next decade place-based funding rose in popularity and became the fashion in grantmaking.[187] Sometimes it felt as though this shift was based on nothing more than a reaction against the last big thing. If you find your organisation debating this choice, please be careful to make your decision based on more firm foundations than 'everyone else is doing it'.

Finally, we would like to note one thing about the choice of models: to make good grants to themes, as opposed to places, you need institutional capacity. Put simply, it takes more funder capacity to make good grants in particular places. This is because you have to understand what's going on in many sectors, not just one sector, and you can't lean as heavily on high-quality pre-existing research.

If you are a small funder that is thematically focused, you can usually lean on the research work of others to guide your spending. But, if you're a small funder that focuses on one locality, you'll have to survive with much less robust analysis and far more anecdotal evidence.

Dilemma no. 5: Who makes the final decision on who gets the money?

As a private citizen, you can make a personal choice about who to make a donation to. If you have money in your bank account and you want to give it away, you can. There are few legal restrictions on giving money away unless you plan to defraud the tax system or fund a political campaign.

Within funding organisations, however, the question of *who* actually decides to grant the money is more complicated. The most common model by far for grantmaker decision making is that of board members in a meeting deciding on whether or not to make a particular grant. This may involve lots of people in a grand corporate boardroom or it may take place between a couple sitting at their kitchen table.

So common is this model of 'the board decides' that it can hide the fact that there are quite a lot of other ways in which grantmaking decisions can be made.

> Option 1 *The board decides*: In this model the bigwigs, the people who have the most control over the money, make the grantmaking decisions. They could be a panel of senior government officials, the trustees of a private foundation or a single living philanthropist who is giving away their own money.
>
> Option 2 *A delegated staff committee decides*: In this model the people who ultimately control the money (i.e. the board or the private philanthropist) hand over grant decision-making power to a group of staff members who work for the board. They are formally told by the board, 'Within these limits, you can make the decisions.' This committee will normally be given a fixed budget and guidelines about acceptable and unacceptable uses of money. But the actual decision to grant lies with the staff members, not the board members.
>
> Option 3 *Individual staff members decide*: In this model individual staff members are told, 'You can make decisions to grant without consulting anyone else.' The advantage of this model is that it's very quick and flexible. The disadvantage is that poor-quality

What big questions should all funders debate from time to time?

or rogue grantmaking tends not to be discovered until the money has already been spent.

Option 4 *A group of people from the community you serve decides*: Also known as *participatory grantmaking*, this is where a funder agrees that a panel of people from a chosen community get to directly choose how an allocated grant budget is spent. (See the next section on participatory grantmaking for a lot more detail on this model.)

Option 5 *Matched funding*: In this model a funder agrees to match each donation to a certain cause from the public with money of its own. This decision is most often framed as: 'We'll match each dollar donated to this cause, up to a million dollars.' In this case a modicum of control is actually given over to people outside the organisation, who can 'decide' on how a funder spends money through the mechanism of making their own donation. This is, however, by far the most limited form of control over decision making on this list. Members of the public have very little control over what the funder does, and there's rarely a mechanism to make the funder pay up if it suddenly decides not to match the donations after all.

So what decision-making approach is right for your organisation? Again, there's no single right answer, but here are some things you should bear in mind when making your decision:

- The board pushing decisions down to groups or individuals is definitely an 'in' thing at the moment. As one senior executive at a large US foundation told us, 'We made a change to push our responsibility to the people in our organisation who are closest to the work. So each of the regional teams in our organisation has their own budget and the regional directors have the authority to make decisions, up to a certain dollar threshold.'[188] We also hear that Open Society Foundations have given a lot more grant decision-making power to individual programme officers in recent years.

- Do your board members and other critical grant decision makers actually have the time and the relevant skills to make good choices about individual grants? If there's a possibility that they don't, you should strongly consider getting the board to delegate most grant-making decisions to people who have both the resources and the skills to do a good job.

- Does your organisation's mission focus intensely on one place? If it does then there's a strong argument for having at least some of your grantmaking decisions made directly by people who live in that place.

- How important is speed? If you're in the sort of business where speed matters a lot (e.g. disaster response), giving individual grantmakers the power to decide unassisted may be very valuable. They can get money out faster than any committee.

- How important are democracy and legitimacy to you? For funders who worry that it may be wrong for them to have so much money and power in the first place, participatory grantmaking could be an appropriate way of letting go and handing over some power.

In summary, every funder should periodically spend some time asking the question, 'Should our board make all the funding decisions in our organisation?' In our experience there are many situations where this just isn't right, especially when board members are busy people with lots of other commitments.

What is participatory grantmaking and why should I care about it?

Participatory grantmaking is the term for a grantmaking process in which people in the communities that your funding organisation serves become direct decision makers about how grant monies are awarded. It is grantmaking where the key choices are made by people who aren't professional grantmakers.

There are several reasons why participatory grantmaking has passionate advocates:

- *Democracy*: By letting people in communities make decisions, you're showing that you value the sharing of power.

- *Decision quality*: Decisions made by people from communities directly impacted by grants will often contain knowledge and information that professional grantmakers couldn't possibly have.

- *Equity*: By allowing people from traditionally disenfranchised communities into the room where it happens, small steps are taken to give power to those who haven't had it.

- *Community engagement and strengthening*: Communities that engage in decision-making processes have opportunities to build their self-image, confidence, leadership and decision-making skills.

These positives are why high-profile funders like the Charles Stewart Mott Foundation, the Case Foundation, the Wikimedia Foundation and others have been deploying these methods to make some of their grants for over a decade, and why new funding organisations such as EDGE Funders Alliance started with a participatory model from their first day.

How do I get my organisation to experiment with participatory grantmaking?

First, study up. Participatory grantmaking isn't a new idea or practice, so there's plenty of material out there you can learn from, most of which is much more detailed than the brief overview in this chapter. Here are some suggestions:

- Ben Wrobel and Meg Massey published a book, *Letting Go: How Philanthropists and Impact Investors Can Do More Good by Giving Up Control*, which makes a strong case for the value of participatory grantmaking.

- Participation expert Cynthia Gibson has written two guides, *Participatory Grantmaking: Has Its Time Come?* and, with Jen Bokoff, *Deciding Together: Shifting Power and Resources through Participatory Grantmaking*.

- Older, but still useful, is *Facilitator's Guide to Participatory Decision-Making* by Sam Kaner et al., now in its third edition.[189]

Second, tactfully introduce the idea of participatory grantmaking to your board or senior management. You will probably need to explain the idea from the ground up, because you cannot assume that everyone has heard of it (and, even if they have, they may have a badly distorted understanding of it). If you can, bring in speakers who can explain what the process was like when they tried it.

Then, when your board or senior management are ready, help them to choose an area that aligns with your overall strategy in which to try participatory grantmaking. Make sure you pick an area that's covered by your current priorities and where you already have good relationships, to give yourself the best chance of success at what is essentially a new activity that will come with a steep learning curve.

Third, design a draft plan for how you might run your participatory grantmaking scheme, with close collaboration from people in your community and with veterans who have done this sort of thing before (i.e. check in with other funders). Get feedback on the plan from the people who will have to go through it, and from key decision makers within your organisation. Then develop a revised, iterated version of the plan, and try testing it with the actual community you'll be working with. This means organising a prototype run-through where a few people pretend to go through the full process but without real funding proposals or real money. This will reveal the parts of the process that are confusing or don't work, which will need fixing before you can go live.

Fourth, after getting and incorporating feedback into your plan, get your board to agree to a participatory grantmaking model for a certain budget and a specific remit. Just make sure that your planning allows you to flex, bend and change the rules as things go along. And make sure that the board has delegated the required powers to you, so you're not endlessly waiting for quarterly board meetings.

Congratulations! Having got to this point, you can actually start doing participatory grantmaking for real, either in its entirety or (perhaps more safely) in a pilot phase. Don't forget to make sure you have a high-quality independent evaluator working with you, if you can, so that you can learn as much as possible from the whole experiment.

We end our section on participatory grantmaking with the words of Hannah Paterson, a senior grantmaker and Churchill Fellow in the UK who undertook a programme of global research on embedding participatory approaches in funding. She shared the following recommendations:

- Understanding the blockers you are facing is the first step in changing tack. But be careful not to assume that people will be against this way of working. If you don't ask, you might end up creating barriers that don't necessarily exist.

- Embed evaluation into the design of your approach. Think about what success means and who gets to define it. Reflect on where the power sits with evaluation, and design an approach that supports and lifts communities rather than just ticking a box for your own records.

- Finally, support organisations that are already leading in this space, learn from them, fund them and pay them for their time and expertise![190]

Dilemma no. 6: Should we worry about the financial sustainability of the organisations we fund?

> Funders can be too simplistic when it comes to sustainability – asking for a 'sustainability plan' is more about a comfort blanket than it is about enabling organisations to improve what they do and become more resilient.[191]
>
> — LOUISA SYRETT, director of an international nonprofit

Most funding organisations are keen for the organisations they support to thrive. It is very disappointing to think that an organisation might simply shut up shop if we stop pouring money into it. It feels like a failure.

Consequently, it is quite common for funders to ask grantseekers to spell out their plans for how the organisation plans to achieve sustainability once the grant is over. This is a classic case of funders speaking in code. What it really means is 'Tell us how you'll keep making money after we stop giving you it'.

Achieving sustainability isn't, however, the unalloyed good it may seem to be at first or even second glance. For example, we don't want to encourage the continued existence of organisations that should be trying to put themselves out of business. A charity dedicated to eradicating a disease ought to be pushing for a world where it is no longer needed by eliminating the disease altogether. The permanent existence of such an organisation is a mark of failure!

Second, every time we as funders ask a grantseeker to explain how they will achieve sustainability we are nudging them towards adopting a commercial business model. This means encouraging nonprofits to charge for what they offer or to develop whole new products and services designed primarily to bring in revenue.

Now, in some areas of social impact work, this kind of social entrepreneurialism is a good thing – it brings fresh ideas and services to the table. We're all for that. But in other contexts the drive towards generating commercial income is a bad thing because it can distract organisations from doing work that cannot always or ever generate profits, and drive them into areas where a profit might be turned (e.g. consultancy or trading).

We especially enjoyed Phil Buchanan's acerbic take on this, in his book *Giving Done Right*:

What big questions should all funders debate from time to time?

> What's the alternative to a mix of philanthropic and government support for, say, Horizons for Homeless Children, which provides high-quality preschool for homeless kids in Massachusetts? Ask the four-year-olds to start a moneymaking 'social enterprise' and cover their own costs?[192]

As a Modern Grantmaker, you should make sure that your organisation's decision makers have a serious debate about the extent to which you do or do not want to encourage or demand that grantees develop non-grant income streams. In particular, you should have a clear-eyed conversation about the sorts of social impact activities that seem compatible with self-sustaining business models, and those where the drive for sustainability actually goes against your organisation's mission and goals.

Once you agree your position on financial sustainability, you should make sure that your application forms and guidance reflect that choice, so that grantseekers are not encouraged to tell you lies that you never needed to hear in the first place.

Dilemma no. 7: How should we approach our own savings and investments?

> Endowments, philanthropic and other, are of deep concern to us all. They are in many ways far more powerful instruments of change than grants.
>
> Here's one way to see it: the grants are the crumbs from the cake, but the endowment is the cake itself. Why focus on the crumbs when you can focus on the cake?[193]
>
> — JO ANDREWS, founder of Ariadne, a network for funders

This dilemma won't apply to you if you work for a government grantmaker or a corporate donor, but if you work for a private foundation – well – it's critical.

Most private funding organisations are themselves funded by investments in stocks, bonds and other assets. For a long time these investments seemed irrelevant to the business of grantmaking – they were for the finance professionals to worry about.

In recent times the view that foundation investments are disconnected from grantmaking goals has been much criticised. It is now widely appreciated that investments are made in companies and that those companies have impacts on the world around us. Those impacts can be very large and very bad, such as when a careless oil company dumps millions of barrels of crude oil into the sea. Buying shares in such companies, especially newly issued shares, is a way of putting money directly into such operations. Even worse, the sums injected into companies by funders tend to be much larger than those granted to nonprofits – because endowments are usually much larger than annual grant giving.

So all funders with investments must now ask themselves what their approach should be to funding businesses that cause social and environmental problems. This means making choices about whether they should avoid certain businesses or industries altogether. For example, in the last few years many asset managers have decided that they cannot justify continuing to invest in fossil fuel companies, and have withdrawn their funds.

But what exactly does it mean to review your endowments like this? One person who should know is Seb Ellsworth, chief executive of Access – The Foundation for Social Investment.[194] He says that it may take time to find an asset manager who can deliver an investment portfolio suitable for a mission-driven foundation, and he suggests taking the following steps to find the right person:

- ask them how they will measure and report performance in terms of both financial performance and mission alignment;

- agree on how you will hold them to account and how frequently;

- discuss how they will represent your organisation's interests, e.g. will they vote at company AGMs on topics that can help to enhance your mission?

What big questions should all funders debate from time to time?

For some funders the change that an endowment review could bring to their organisation may be very profound. Jake Hayman, founder of grantmaking reform initiative Ten Years' Time, asserts that, given the opportunity, he would 'disinvest every penny of philanthropic capital from every endowment and every investment portfolio, and only reinvest it if I thought it was aligned with our mission and fundamentally regenerative environmentally and redistributive socially, rather than tying myself in knots tinkering at the edges of the wholly inadequate prevailing approaches.'[195]

This is a demanding standard but clearly an idea that is now in circulation. For more information on this topic, you may want to check out:

- The Association of Charitable Foundation's guide on investments, published as part of its Stronger Foundations initiative;[196]
- Lankelly Chase's investment strategy, available on its website;[197]
- The Forum for Sustainable and Responsible Investment in the US.[198]

Dilemma no. 8: How transparent and accountable should we be?

> It's quite hard to judge grantmaking because there's not much accountability. You can make incredibly bad decisions across a very long period of time, indefinitely in some cases, and be sheltered from the impact of your actions.[199]
>
> — DAN PASKINS, director of UK Impact, Save the Children, and former senior grantmaker

In Chapter 2 we said that it was a basic rule of grantmaking to be transparent about what you fund and what you don't fund. We stand by this, but there are many different things about which funding organisations can choose to be transparent or private. For example, they can choose to be transparent or private about:

- what grants are made to which people or organisations;
- how decisions are made;
- research findings about grant impact;
- feedback from grantseekers, grantees and other partners;
- process questions, including information about eligibility, success rates and turnaround times (see the next chapter for more on this);
- who sits on the boards and on the leadership teams;
- any equity, diversity and inclusion data and plans, including workforce data and data concerning any pay gaps;
- data relating to impact on the environment such as the carbon impact of the organisation and its grants;
- data relating to how any endowments are invested.

All these issues are worth debating fully and frankly, even if your organisation doesn't change its position on any of them.

For what it's worth, grantseekers love transparency, and will generally support any moves you make to be more transparent. You'll pretty much never hear a funder criticised by a nonprofit for being too transparent, unless they do something spectacularly irresponsible.

While almost all nonprofits value funder transparency, it is disproportionately valuable to nonprofits from marginalised communities, who benefit from the knowledge that would otherwise flow solely through networks of more privileged people. Furthermore, transparency can be useful in revealing whether some funders simply don't work with some communities. For more on this, see Chapter 3 on power and privilege.

However, funders have other stakeholders, for whom transparency may not be so desirable. They include:

- private philanthropists who may not want the hassle that comes with a reputation for giving away money;
- professional grantmaking staff who may be uneasy about attracting criticism by publishing details on grants.

What big questions should all funders debate from time to time?

Our general advice on this dilemma is to be as transparent as your organisation can stand – and no less.

Transparency is great for people who are interested in your money and for other funders who want to know what you're doing, and it's an encouragement to positive behaviour. If you're worried that your organisation appears to resort to a list of usual suspects for its grantees, make your grantmaking more transparent and soon enough the pressure will grow to drive you to do better.

Rachel Rank, former CEO of grantmaking data experts 360Giving, suggests that funders ask themselves these questions before deciding what they should do to improve general transparency:

1   Who are you being transparent for and why?

2   Do you know what information people would find useful about you?

3   Why wouldn't you make some information available?

4   Do you have a duty to be open about where your money comes from as well as what you're funding?

5   Could you be more open about what you think rather than just what you do?[200]

If you want to talk to an organisation that specialises in helping funders to become more transparent, we suggest that you connect with 360Giving (in the UK) or GlassPockets (in the US). Both organisations are highly experienced and will not judge you if your organisation is just taking its first steps in this direction.

In a similar vein, GrantAdvisor is a website that allows grantees of US-based funders to post anonymous online reviews of funding organisations, in the spirit of TripAdvisor or Yelp.[201] Such services have a chance of working only if funding organisations actively direct their grantees and grantseekers towards them, so if you are ambitious for your transparency and accountability goals you should definitely check it out.

One final observation about transparency and accountability: most transparency efforts are based on historical data. This means that people are supposed to consider information about what an organisation has done and compare that to what it said it was going to do.

Jayne Engle, director of the Cities & Places Portfolio at the McConnell Foundation, suggests that funders are in a unique position to push themselves beyond this retrospective model and to make efforts to be accountable to the future:

> Grantmakers should set ourselves to a much higher standard when it comes to accountability. Accountability is not just about our being responsible to the partners we work with and the communities they serve *now*; it should be about how, through the work we do, we are being accountable to future generations and to the Earth.[202]

So, if your organisation decides it is time to examine its transparency and accountability practices, why not try the following:

1. Discuss the first-order questions recommended by Rachel Rank (see above).

2. Consider these questions in relation to the list of things (at the start of this section) you could decide to be more or less transparent about.

3. Ask yourselves how you would like your organisation to be known in the future, and whether you would need to change anything now so that people could meaningfully hold it to account for its choices in 10, 20 or even 30 years' time.

Speaking of the future, let's dive into the final dilemma in this chapter.

What big questions should all funders debate from time to time?

Dilemma no. 9: Should our funding organisation be permanent or should it spend down and close?

> 2020 has given us a global pandemic and multi-system failures: economy, climate chaos, politics and society. If this year isn't jarring enough for people sitting on huge endowments saving for a rainy day, I don't know what would be.[203]
>
> — PIA INFANTE, co-director at the Whitman Institute

Many funding organisations, especially private foundations, are fundamentally piles of cash with people on top. Not every funder works like this – government funders, for example, tend to be given a budget to spend each year – but many funders are essentially just an endowment with some staff and trustees orbiting around it.

If you work for an organisation with an endowment, one of the most fundamental strategic questions you need to consciously address is 'Do we preserve our endowment for ever, or do we spend it down until it is all gone?' Or, translated into the jargon used by many grantmakers, the key question is 'Is your organisation perpetual or are you spending down?'

In some cases the staff or board of a funder will have no say in this question: the money may have been left in someone's will with this decision already made. But in other cases board members do have the leeway to decide.

There's an enormous difference between how much a spend-down funder can spend compared to a perpetual funder. Even a spend-down funder that spends down slowly, over a decade, say, can normally make annual grants 10 times the size of a perpetual funder.

Despite this, by far the most common model for trusts and foundations based on endowments is the perpetual fund. The endowment may go up or down a bit with changes in economic conditions, but fundamentally it's always there, throwing out cash every year.

When people defend perpetual funders, their argument is often simple: there are social ills that will never go away, so we shouldn't either. This is true – for example, we will never live free from the fear of a new disease – but of course there are some social ills (such as legally enforced race discrimination under apartheid) that should not last for ever and that can be ended by decisive action.

Whether your funder is perpetual or spend down should ultimately be determined primarily by your mission. If you are focused on the type of problem that requires one big heave, such as climate change, you should strongly consider a rapid spend-down model to concentrate the maximum firepower within a given moment. But if you are in it for the long term – for example, promoting racial justice – the perpetual model has a lot to be said for it.

Perhaps the most important thing that a foundation can do in relation to the perpetual versus spend down debate is to remember to debate the issue regularly in the first place. We think that trustees should discuss this issue at least every two years or so, as social and market conditions may change in a way that makes the previous decision no longer the best one. One easy way of ensuring you do this is to make it part of your strategic review process. While you're asking lots of key questions about your activities, why not ask the biggest one of all: should your organisation exist for ever?

For more research and information on funders who have made the decision to spend down, we suggest accessing the treasure trove of publicly available reports and articles on GrantCraft.[204]

Case study: Increasing impact by spending down

In 2011 the Whitman Institute (TWI), a small US foundation with modest assets, found itself at a crossroads.[205] Having consistently given above the legal minimum foundation payout of 5%, its leaders realised that this level of giving could not be sustained indefinitely. At the same time, they could not justify reducing their grants budget when resources were so scarce and their grantees were doing important work.

Things had come to a head for TWI and its leaders had to make a decision: they could either stretch their resources by cutting yearly expenditure or they could sustain their higher payout rate, possibly even raise grant amounts, at the inevitable cost of running out of money. Ultimately, the board made the decision to spend down and to close by 2022. They made this huge decision in a conscious attempt to sharpen their focus and exercise greater influence in the field of philanthropy.

The choice to spend down strengthened TWI's partnerships, expanded its possibilities and enabled it to live out its aspirations and to better support its grantees. It also increased the visibility of the trust-based philanthropy principles TWI had pioneered.

The larger multi-year and annual grants enabled the foundation to better meet community needs over time. And, as the foundation looked towards its 2022 spend-out, it turned outwards to connect and communicate with its peers in philanthropy. Informed by its grantee partners, TWI focused on seeding its story, partnering with other funders to launch the Trust-Based Philanthropy Project (see Chapters 3 and 10) and encouraging wider networks of investors and funders to question the idea of funding in perpetuity.

Reflecting on its work, Pia Infante, co-director of the Whitman Institute, said:

> We encourage our peers to question perpetuity, and if that reflection sharpens purpose, creates opportunities to align values with financial stewardship and program strategies, and increases an institution's accountability to the communities and constituencies it is intended to serve, then we are moving in the right direction.

Once you've worked out whether your funding organisation should even exist, it's time to work on something that seems infinitely more prosaic, but that will be of much greater importance to almost every grantseeker and grantee you'll ever meet. The question for the next chapter is simple: does applying for money from your organisation just suck?

Chapter 5 checklist

1. Has your organisation thoroughly debated whether to accept unsolicited funding proposals or to operate as an invite-only funder?

2. Has your organisation debated its appetite for risk and set a clear risk profile for its grant portfolio?

3. Has your organisation debated whether it is more focused on preventing harms or on mitigating them after they have happened?

4. Has your organisation debated whether it will focus mainly on helping in a specific place or on tackling a certain kind of problem?

5. Has your organisation debated who is going to make the final decisions on who gets grants and who doesn't?

6. Has your organisation debated what kind of sustainability plans it expects or does not expect from different grantseekers?

7. Has your organisation debated its approach towards its own savings and endowments?

8. Has your organisation debated how transparent and accountable it should be and on what fronts?

9. Has your organisation debated whether it should continue for ever, or spend down in some predetermined time frame?

6

HOW CAN I IMPROVE THE EXPERIENCE OF GRANTSEEKERS AND GRANTEES?

> As a funder you have a very interesting power dynamic because you can provide a really poor service and a terrible user experience and people will still come back, because they need the money.[206]
>
> — ANGELA MURRAY, experienced designer of funding programmes and grant management systems

We've all been there. It's mid-morning on a warm summer's day, and you should really be getting on with your job. But not today. Today you're sitting with an increasingly sweaty mobile phone glued to your ear, listening time and time again to the message that 'Your call is important to us'. You've been on for over 30 glacial minutes, and your will to live is sapping away as Slade sing 'Here it is, Merry Christmas' on repeat.

You'd love to just slam the phone down, but this call really matters. If you don't stick with it, something is going to go very wrong. Without this call you're not going to have any heating, or an airline ticket, or perhaps the right toy for a highly unpredictable two-year-old. In fact you'd absolutely love to not be on the phone at all, but when you were using the website to solve your problem, something went wrong – your credit card kept getting rejected or maybe your login wouldn't work. So here you are on the support line.

Eventually a real human picks up the call – a nice one if a bit hard to hear down a crackly phone line. They ask you a number of questions before transferring you to another department. But as they hit the transfer button the call simply hangs up. Your heart sinks. You're back to square one.

If this story sounds familiar to you, you know what it is like to suffer from a poor-quality customer experience. This chapter is about trying not to cause this kind of suffering to some of the world's most hard-working and inspiring people.

Why should we invest time and energy in offering grantseekers and grantees a good experience?

One of the shadiest secrets of the grantmaking profession is that utterly miserable applicant experiences are the norm, not the exception. Here are a few anonymous quotes from grantseekers about their experience of applying to different funders:

- 'It was worse than dying.'

- 'This proposal has ruined me. It's taken probably 20 full days of work by five people with no indication of whether it will be successful.'

- 'It made me want to leave my organisation and change careers.'[207]

Nor are really awful experiences in grantmaking limited to people trying to get money – they happen to grantees too. If the process of agreeing contracts with funders, securing payments, filing reports and doing the work of measurement and evaluation is badly designed and thoughtlessly delivered by the funder, it can also cause misery.

It doesn't have to be this way, and with a bit of knowledge, courage and diligence you can make sure that your organisation doesn't make your grantseekers feel like the people above.

What causes bad applicant and grantee experiences?

> The challenge in foundations is that very often they are set up to serve the needs of the board so they can make decisions about how to allocate money rather than the needs of a 'secondary' user group, that is people that are after that money.[208]
>
> — DAN SUTCH, director of the Centre for the Acceleration of Social Technology

It is quite common for some funders to provide a very good service to their boards but not such a great service to their grantseekers and grantees. In these cases, it is usually because grantmakers regard their boards – rather than their grantseekers and grantees – as the main people they serve. This can result in funders putting time and effort into trying to understand and meet the needs of board members instead of the needs of grantseekers.

Another cause of problems is that it is generally quicker and cheaper for institutions to offer a bad customer experience, and generally more time consuming and expensive for them to offer a good one. Funding organisations, in particular, can be guilty of offering poor experiences because they aren't under any market or political pressure to offer good ones. There's nothing to counterbalance the bureaucratic tendency to put in place yet more questions, attachments, surveys, letters of support, accounts, incorporation documents, budgets, inside leg measurements and so on.

As Sufina Ahmad, director of John Ellerman Foundation, told us, 'In the funders I've worked for previously, I've seen time and again a layering or adding of more complexity to processes rather than reviewing wholesale and figuring out what should be removed to make our offer better.'[209] Sadly, we aren't surprised.

So, given that there's a lack of incentive to offer a good experience, why should a grantmaking organisation such as yours bother to improve things? Why go to the trouble?

For many grantmaking institutions this will be a novel question – one that has never come up before in internal discussions or board meetings. That's because an organisation will analyse and assess the quality of service it offers only if it sees itself as offering a service in the first place.

Modern Grantmaking

Some traditional funders don't see grantmaking as a service. They see the activity of grantmaking as an act of munificence – the bestowing of gifts on lucky individuals whose only conceivable reaction is delight and gratitude. Just as it would be very rude and ungrateful to complain about your birthday presents, it would be unthinkable to criticise the nature of grants or the way they are handed out. This, we believe, is not an uncommon view of customer service in funders: *they ain't customers and we ain't providing no freakin' service.*

Attitude-wise, Modern Grantmakers come from a totally different place. As set out in Chapter 1, one of the five key values of Modern Grantmaking is service. This means that Modern Grantmakers see themselves as serving grantseekers and grantees, not as a monarch tossing coins from the window of their gilded coach.

Ultimately, there are three reasons why grantmakers should be motivated by a service mindset:

- out of a basic sense of decency and a desire not to cause pain to others;
- out of a sense of equity and a desire to eliminate discriminatory barriers;
- out of a desire to have the greatest possible impact.

Let's dive in to see how these relate to the seemingly prosaic business of customer experience.

What's the connection between a funder's service quality and discrimination?

To see how a funder's quality of service is connected with discrimination, consider the two following stories, which contain elements drawn from several real-world experiences.

> A grantseeker from a disability charity comes up with a project idea that is in line with what your funding organisation has said it wants to fund. This being the 21st century, the grantseeker visits your website to start the online application process.
>
> The applicant has a visual impairment, which makes it challenging to use your not particularly accessible website.

How can I improve the experience of grantseekers and grantees?

However, they persevere for a couple of days, slowly and painstakingly cutting and pasting answers into a form that they can't quite see properly and that isn't working very well in the highly magnified view they have to use. It's draining, but they persist.

Eventually, exhausted by the experience, they get to the final page of questions in the application form. And there's a problem – right at the end, there are several additional eligibility questions they hadn't been told about before. They realise with horror that their organisation is not actually eligible for funding, and that all the time they've spent copying and pasting has been for nothing.

The despairing grantseeker slams shut their laptop and then phones a colleague to complain bitterly about how horrible the whole experience has been. Following this complaint the word slowly spreads through the whole community of disability charities that your funder 'doesn't care about people like us'. Gradually your funder receives fewer and fewer applications from disability groups without ever being aware of what's caused this change.

A year later your funder convenes an internal meeting, in which your colleagues agonise over the fall in applications from disability organisations. Nobody connects the problem to the application process (because nobody has done any research into user experience), and the problem remains unacknowledged and unresolved.

In the second story you work for a grantmaker that is invite only – it doesn't accept unsolicited applications. It finds prospective grantees through research and recommendations.

Checking your emails one day, you find an email introduction from a friend of yours. They're connecting you with an asylum-seeker-led project that they think you should consider. You're not terribly enthused – it doesn't sound like the sort of thing your organisation supports – but you and the correspondent go back a long way and you don't want to jeopardise your friendship. So you arrange a call with the leader of the project quite far in the future, as this isn't a hot prospect.

A few weeks later it's time for the call. By this time you are feeling a bit resentful of your friend – you've been so busy preparing for a board meeting – but you go ahead with the meeting. The project leader on the other end of the line is obviously quite nervous and inexperienced – their English isn't so great and they take forever to describe what they're interested in.

Your head is so full of other stuff that you don't really take in fully what the grantseeker is saying, so you quickly end the call, while saying, 'Look, I can't promise you anything, but please could you send me something in writing.' The next morning a funding proposal from this grantseeker drops into your inbox, but you don't read it because there's a board meeting starting in five minutes. The email completely slips your mind for three months – until you do a post-summer-vacation check of your inbox and find it lurking there unread.

With a pang of guilt, you open the mail, read the proposal and find that it definitely isn't eligible at all. You tap out a vaguely apologetic 'sorry, no' email and hit send. Moments later you've forgotten about the whole thing.

But for the applicant, on the other side, the whole picture looks very different. They've never made a funding application to any organisation before. They're living apart from their family in an unfamiliar country, and they've been enormously stressed about the whole thing from start to finish. They have no real idea how to find other funders, or even that there *are* other funders, so they don't make any attempt to find funds elsewhere.

Every night for three months, before going to bed, they discuss with their partner over WhatsApp what your silence might mean, and what the word 'interesting' meant when you used it in the phone call. They worry about whether racism will impact on their chances. Their mental health and self-esteem suffer terribly, not helped by the lack of sleep, money and security. When your rejection finally arrives, it's the last straw. Crushed, they abandon their idea for good.

How can I improve the experience of grantseekers and grantees?

What are the problems demonstrated by these stories?

These two stories, while different, show some common problems that result from funders not taking the time and effort to make grantseekers' and grantees' experiences better. These include:

- The time and energy of people who deserve kindness and respect is sapped and wasted for no justifiable reason.

- Bad news about mistreatment by funders can spread through communities, and a funding organisation can end up suppressing applications from people that it may actually very much want to support.

- Poor service quality can lead to people concluding that funders, overall, are part of the problem of discrimination and marginalisation in society at large, not part of the solution.

- Better connected, more expensively educated and more self-confident grantseekers can overcome almost any application hurdles. This then contributes to an overall skew of funding away from more needy groups and towards organisations run by more privileged people.

When you add these up, bad customer service leads directly to grants that are made to groups that actually need them less. Rubbish application processes lead to inequitable outcomes. This in turn then leads to an overall lower impact (see Chapter 3 for more on inequity, discrimination and reduced impact in grantmaking).

Put together, these consequences are the exact opposite of why most funders get up and start work in the morning – to help great organisations make big impacts. As Helen Turvey, executive director at the Shuttleworth Foundation, says, 'When it comes to being a nonprofit, necessity is *absolutely not* the mother of invention. When nonprofit leaders have time and space to think, they just do better work.'[210] Bad, frustrating applicant experiences rob nonprofit leaders of exactly that time and space.

Finally, good-quality customer experiences aren't just about prospective grantseekers. Grantees' quality of life and ability to focus on the things that matter are hugely shaped by the demands placed on them by funders. Just because you've awarded someone free money it doesn't mean that you are not still at risk of wasting their time or of making them feel belittled and worthless. The most common cause of miserable experiences for grantees is progress reporting requirements – especially writing different reports for every funder, in a never-ending cycle of grind (see Chapter 7 for more on this).

OK, so what does a Modern Grantmaking customer experience look like?

> Modern Grantmakers design funding services that meet the end users' needs and create the kind of flexibility that means people don't have to jump through arbitrary hoops. This requires cultural change and training across everything to empower and support grantmakers with the right skills to become enablers and facilitators versus blockers and gatekeepers.[211]
>
> — NGOZI LYN COLE, experienced senior UK grantmaking executive and board member

Applying for a grant, or managing a current grant, isn't exactly an everyday activity like buying something from a supermarket. However, despite being a somewhat niche activity that only a minority of people will ever engage in, the factors that make it a good or a bad experience are actually very similar to good-quality experiences in other areas of life.

For example, a good shopping experience in a store and a good grant application experience with a funder both have the following characteristics in common:

- They're easy to find.

- You can achieve what you want to quickly and without unnecessary steps.

- It's easy to understand what the whole process is going to look like right from the start.

- While you don't have to speak to a person to achieve your goal, you can do so easily if you need to.

- They're welcoming and accessible to people with different abilities.

How can I improve the experience of grantseekers and grantees?

If this all sounds like quite a bit of work, we have some good news. First, there are a lot of helpful books and online information out there waiting to be used by you, which we'll dive into in a minute. And, even better, there's a small cadre of people out there who specialise in helping funders to develop application processes that are easy and inclusive. One of these is Angela Murray, a former staffer at multiple funders who now works for Hyphen8, a company that builds highly accessible grantmaking systems for lots of clients. She summarises the whole situation thus:

> A good user experience in grantmaking is when the people applying for funding find it easy to communicate their idea to you and even if they don't get funding they understand why. It's grantmaking where there's a transparent process, where applicants know what's going to happen, when it's going to happen and who's going to make the decision.[212]

Is any of this relevant to an invite-only funder that doesn't accept unsolicited applications?

Sorry, but you shouldn't skip this bit. This stuff is really important for you too – not least because most invite-only funders still ask applicants to write proposals, make presentations, complete monitoring forms, sign contracts and so on. Each of these activities can be done in a way that is accessible and inclusive, or the opposite.

Even if you are an invite-only funder, you should still make time and space to explore what it feels like to be a grantee or prospective grantee, and then to improve their experience with you.

How can I improve my organisation's user experience?

> We always tried to treat applicants with respect, but it's only been in the last few years that we've begun to develop and implement systems to promote the idea of customer service for our grantees.[213]
>
> — ANONYMOUS VICE PRESIDENT FOR PROGRAMMES at US foundation

Eternal optimists that we are, we are going to assume that you have accepted our argument that offering a high-quality applicant and grantee experience is not a luxury but an essential requirement when you are running a grantmaking organisation that wants to be as inclusive and as impactful as it can be.

That means it is time to move from the *why* to the *what* and the *how* of a good applicant and grantee experience.

What do I need to understand before I can offer a good service to grantseekers and grantees?

First, designing a good service for grantseekers and grantees can be really tough. There are many, many ways in which you can offer a service that will confuse and let people down, and it takes skill and effort to offer a service that's genuinely easy for everyone to use. Every time you've experienced poor service as a citizen or a consumer you've seen just how much easier it is to offer a bad service than a good one.

So how can you overcome this challenge? Well, you will need to familiarise yourself with two new ways of working. Then you will need to work with colleagues to incorporate these into your organisation's normal way of doing business. The way you incorporate these new ways of working will differ according to the size of your organisation. But, whatever the size, the key concepts are the same, and that's where we're going to start. The most important key concept you need to become comfortable with is *human-centred design*.

How can I improve the experience of grantseekers and grantees?

What is human-centred design?

When you hear the word 'design' you may think of shiny coffee machines, fancy handbags or futuristic buildings made of glass, but design is so much more than this. 'Design' refers to any process in which people work on how an object or a service should be created or improved. If you've ever planned a holiday or chosen the paint colour for a wall, you've been doing design.

When funders choose what questions to ask in an application form, they are doing design. When they write a boilerplate rejection letter, they're doing design. When they develop and publish a call for proposals, they're doing design.

The term 'human-centred design' – or HCD – refers to a set of practices for deciding how objects or processes should be. As the term itself suggests, it is a set of practices that do design by paying extremely close attention to the users of a service. It is a design process that seeks to understand what it is like to be a user, to 'walk a mile in their shoes', in the words of Harper Lee.

Human-centred design was previously a specialist skill that has increasingly become one of those things everyone should know about. As one anonymous chief executive of a forward-looking grantmaking foundation told us: 'Not having any concept of human-centred design – that's a huge hole in any funder's skill set now.'[214]

What does human-centred design mean in practice?

Human-centred design is not some grand, airy philosophy – it's a set of working practices that any organisation can adopt and learn.

We're going to focus on just two of these practices, although there are plenty more if you decide to go deeper. For that, we recommend checking out IDEO.org's *The Field Guide to Human-Centered Design*.[215]

The two areas we are going to explore in this chapter are:

- iteration;
- user experience research.

We think they represent the absolute minimum you should understand if you're going to use HCD to help improve your funding organisation and make it more welcoming.

What is iteration?

> Modern Grantmaking respects that, in order to find out what works and what can make change happen, you need to fund in iterative cycles and allow people to be wrong.[216]
>
> — SARAH DRUMMOND, co-founder and CEO of Snook design studio

Iteration is one of the crucial central practices underpinning human-centred design. But what is it?

Iteration means continually improving a service that you offer in response to feedback from users. It means seeing the service you offer grantseekers and grantees as something you have to keep improving every day: it is the opposite of doing a job once and then ticking it off as 'done'.

To make this easier to wrap your head around, consider two people with different jobs: a chef and an architect.

The chef works hard every day to make each meal as good as or better than the last. It doesn't matter how good their cooking was yesterday: those meals are history. The only thing that matters is that they cook really well tonight, and if possible better than yesterday. The chef is continually receiving feedback from diners, constantly trying to improve their menu – this is what iteration means.

By contrast, the architect works intensively for a year on designing a new building. At the end of this time the building is completed, and the architect moves on to the next job. They are not called back to change or to improve the building after people move in, because that's not their job. Architects may iterate their plans as they make them, but they can't really iterate the buildings once they've been built.

Traditional grantmakers – especially senior leaders – often saw their job as being like that of the architect and not that of the chef: building and launching a grand scheme, and then moving on to the next thing. But we want to encourage Modern Grantmakers to see their work much more like that of the chef. The work of making our grant services as good as possible is never done, and every day we have to ask, 'Can this be done better than yesterday?'

How can I improve the experience of grantseekers and grantees?

What is an iterative design process?

Iterative design processes are often visualised as a simple loop, like this one:

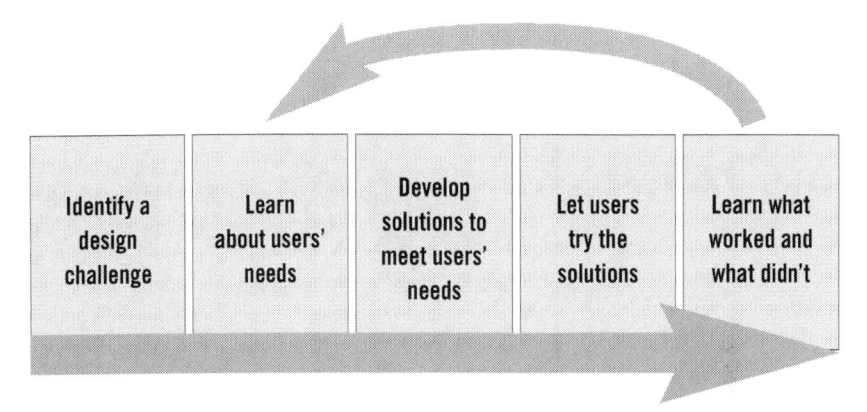

| Identify a design challenge | Learn about users' needs | Develop solutions to meet users' needs | Let users try the solutions | Learn what worked and what didn't |

People carrying out an iterative, human-centred design process normally start by being assigned a task by a client or a manager. In our occupation this might mean a foundation CEO saying to their team, 'Please rebuild our funding application process.'

The people charged with delivering the project will usually start by studying prospective users to find out what they need from this product or service – in this case a funding application system. Because we're talking about grantmaking, this means that the designers will seek to learn as much as they can about the needs of prospective grantseekers and grantees by talking to them.

Once the design team has gained a measure of information about their users, they will develop quick, rough and ready, prototype solutions that they will then share with real people. In grantmaking this might be a prototype website or even a prototype phone call.

The users who have agreed to be studied by the design team will then try making use of the prototypes – for example, by writing and submitting a test funding proposal. Their reactions to the prototype will normally be mixed: 'I love this bit, but I hate that bit.' The designers watch and listen to the users carefully, learn what didn't work and go away to develop further prototype solutions, which are again tested with real users. This repeated cycle of learning, building and testing is what iteration means in the real world, and it is at the heart of human-centred design.

To find out whether you currently work in an iterative organisation, ask yourself when the last time was that you had a meeting specifically about whether the service you're offering is working as well as it could for all its users. If you can't remember having such a meeting on a regular basis over an extended period of time, the chances are that your organisation isn't working in an iterative way. Instead, it has probably been treating the design of its grantmaking services as something that can be marked off as 'done', and to be replaced in colleagues' minds by 'more important things'.

Case study: An example of design iteration in a large funder

A funding organisation in the UK was in the process of replacing all its application forms and application guidance so as to offer grantseekers and grantees a better and more inclusive experience. It had just launched a new online form to a small number of grantseekers and was keen to improve its service as quickly as possible.

When these grantseekers had finished applying through the new form, they were given the opportunity to write short, anonymous feedback directly on the website. Many users took the chance to comment. The feedback immediately showed that the users were confused about whether or not the application system was automatically saving partially complete applications. Some people complained that they had lost text that they'd spent a lot of time writing.

A quick analysis of the feedback showed that users had not understood that pressing 'next' on each part of the application form would save what they had filled in on the form so far. Some of them had lost part of their application because they had closed a tab without pressing 'next', and ended up feeling very frustrated with the process.

In a quick iterative response to this feedback, the design team revised the explanatory text on the form and animated the 'next' button to make it clearer how users could save their form in progress.

The problem was identified and the solution implemented within a couple of days, because the team was already set up to respond rapidly to feedback. After the improved version of the form went live, the negative feedback about lost work stopped, and the team moved on to improving other aspects of the grantseeker experience.[217]

How can I improve the experience of grantseekers and grantees?

What is user experience research?

We said above that there were two working practices that grantmakers need to know about if they are going to offer a great service. The first was iteration, and the second is user experience research (often abbreviated to 'UX research'). 'User experience research' refers to research into the people who use your services and learning what it feels like to be one of your own customers.

Successful user research will reveal what different kinds of users need from your organisation and whether those needs are being met painlessly or painfully or are not being met at all. (Note that UX research is definitely not the only type of research grantmakers need to know about – see Chapter 7 for a broader overview.)

Funding organisations have quite a few different types of users, more than may be obvious at first glance. They include:

- current grantees;
- historic grantees;
- prospective grantees who haven't decided to apply to you;
- actual grantseekers who are trying to get money from you;
- other grantmakers at other funding organisations;
- prospective employees or suppliers;
- academic researchers;
- journalists;
- public servants and elected representatives.

So, before you start planning to improve the user experience that your organisation offers, you first need to work out the kind of users you want to find out more about. Few organisations have the resources to do user research on all the types of users on the above list, so you may have to have some tricky conversations about competing priorities. A good organisational strategy (see Chapter 4) will help you work out what is most urgent to work on and what isn't.

Once you've identified who your highest-priority users are, it's time to construct a user research plan. If you've got the resources, this is a good moment to bring in a user experience research professional either as a contractor or, if your organisation is big enough, as a permanent staff member.

Modern Grantmaking

This specialist will consider your user research challenge carefully and present you with a research plan that will almost certainly contain a mix of user research activities. They may suggest quite a few different methods, but some of the most likely activities will be:

- interviewing people about their lives and their experience of being a user;
- watching users as they try to solve problems relating to your service (i.e. work out how to apply for funding);
- analysing user feedback submitted through feedback channels that your organisation may already operate.

Once you have written and discussed your plan, your main task is to carry out the work: learning as much as possible about your users, and then analysing and synthesising the findings so that your organisation can work out which aspects of your grantmaking service need fixing most urgently.

Whatever approach you deploy to research your users, it's extremely important to remember that they are people who deserve dignity and respect. Moreover, they are your crucial partners, without whom your funder won't make any difference at all. For more on treating the people you research with respect and dignity, read the discussion on research ethics in Chapter 7.

Does the size of my funder change how we should use human-centred design?

> Size doesn't cut it for funders, in terms of an excuse, about not being able to be human centred and agile.[218]
> — ANONYMOUS GRANTMAKER

In an ideal world every funder would have the resources to offer a great grantmaking service, deploying human-centred design to succeed. But in the real world funders vary enormously in size and capacity. This means that our advice on building better services would be quite different depending on the size of your employer.

To keep things simple, we've split our advice into two parts in the following two sections to address:

How can I improve the experience of grantseekers and grantees?

- small funders: funding organisations that can't afford to spend more than $50,000 a year on the design and delivery of their funding systems;
- larger funders: funding organisations that can afford to spend over $50,000 a year on their funding systems.

How do I improve our service quality if I work for a small funder?

Smaller funding organisations cannot build big teams of design experts as if they were Apple designing the latest iPhone. They need to borrow techniques from the world of human-centred design while acknowledging that they'll never be able to carry them out in quite the way the design textbooks recommend.

If you work for a smaller funder, here are a few specific recommendations for investing in a way that is most likely to make a difference.

Small funder tip no. 1: Pre-schedule several 'How do we improve our service?' meetings a year

Iteration and user research won't happen if there's no time carved out of your shared diaries to ask 'How are we doing?' Funders are busy places and it's extremely easy to conclude that there are more important things to do than analyse feedback and discuss how to improve a funding service.

One tip you should try is to pre-schedule regular service-quality conversations with your colleagues, either once a month (ambitious) or once a quarter (probably more realistic). In these meetings you can debate what your grantseeker feedback is saying about how your grantmaking service could be improved, and you can assign specific improvements to people. At these meetings you should also carve out time to discuss how you're treating your current grantees. They're under a lot of social pressure to be flattering about funders, so you need to take steps to ensure they'll feel safe sharing their feedback honestly.

Small funder tip no. 2: Commission an accessibility review of your website, guidance and forms

If you are a non-disabled person you may well have no idea of the problems that badly designed web pages, forms, PDFs, emails or Word documents can cause for people with visual impairments and other conditions.

Thankfully, there are now a large number of specialist nonprofits and companies that can check your services for accessibility, so that you can make sure you're not excluding people. Getting accessibility right isn't optional, and in some countries it is a legal requirement. We suggest paying disabled-led organisations to provide this service for you, so you can take into account all aspects of what makes a service truly accessible.

Small funder tip no. 3: Watch videos of your website users

If your organisation operates a website (which it should – see Chapter 2), you should install a tool that lets you watch videos of your – totally anonymous – users as they use the site. Just to be clear: you won't see people in their pyjamas but you will just see where they click or scroll.

There are now various tools on the market that can produce a video showing what users look at and do when they visit your site. These videos make it very obvious how and where people are getting lost or confused, even though you never actually hear anyone say anything. We have used the tool HotJar to do this, but there are several similar services available at modest cost.[219]

Small funder tip no. 4: Implement website microsurveys

If your organisation operates a website, add microsurveys to your pages. A microsurvey is a tiny set of buttons and forms that sits somewhere on your web pages. They often look like this:

Was this helpful? Yes No

While most people will never click on these links, some will – and the people who do are most likely to be those who are really lost and frustrated. The surveys that appear when you hit 'yes' or 'no' are

How can I improve the experience of grantseekers and grantees?

extremely short (usually just one question), and conspicuously anonymous, which reassures people that they can be honest. Using these sorts of tools, user-focused funders have acquired a lot of useful feedback on which parts of their website might be confusing users.

While microsurveys will tend to be answered by more people than longer surveys, they won't produce as much detail as more in-depth surveys. Some funders host slightly longer surveys on their websites to try to gain additional information on what their users are thinking and feeling. Here are some excerpts from an anonymous feedback survey used by the UK private foundation the Dulverton Trust.[220]

Dulverton Trust Anonymous Feedback Survey

The Dulverton Trust is seeking initial feedback to improve our processes for applicants and grantees.

This is a deliberately short survey – we don't want to take lots of your time! We hope answers will lead to more in-depth research in the future. Please answer as much as you wish below. Not all questions will be applicable.

The final question is open for any comments on aspects that are not covered by the questions.

We appreciate your responses and suggestions for improvement, thank you. Please note that your answers are anonymous.

The Dulverton Trust

1. Are you...
◯ a prospective applicant
◯ an applicant (not funded)
◯ an applicant (decision pending)
◯ a grantee (current or former)
◯ Other

2. Information on the Trust's website was clear and helped me to decide whether my organisation should apply or not
◯ Strongly agree
◯ Agree
◯ Somewhat agree
◯ Disagree
◯ Strongly agree
◯ Other

An excerpt from the Dulverton Trust's anonymous survey, requesting feedback on whether its website is clear and helpful.

Collecting feedback is of no value, however, if you don't actually analyse and act on it. Some of the best smaller funders, such as the Blagrave Trust in the UK, also share examples of feedback they receive on their grantmaking via their website, and report progress over time.

Small funder tip no. 5: Run user testing sessions

Here is a technique you can use even if your organisation is purely invite only and doesn't operate a website. You could arrange user testing sessions where you watch someone trying to use your application form or application guidance to apply for funding at your organisation. Ideally that someone would be a real prospective grantee but, if you can't manage that, try to find someone who doesn't know much about your organisation or how it works. If you can, try to find test users who aren't super-confident people with several PhDs. You should also strongly consider paying the people who do testing for you, especially if they come from smaller organisations.

As you sit there during the test, try to resist the overwhelming temptation to help the person doing the test to use the guidance, to explain or to support. Try to act as though you're not there (because you won't be there when most real applicants read your guidance).

Encourage the person doing the test to share what they're thinking as they go along. We guarantee that, in a shockingly short space of time, you will uncover an immense number of problems that you never realised existed with your guidance or application forms. You'll find it a squirm-inducing experience!

User testing sessions were traditionally done by sitting by people and looking over their shoulders. But, even before the COVID-19 pandemic, such tests were increasingly conducted through remote screen sharing with participants who had consented to be so studied and were fully aware of the purpose of the test.

These remotely conducted sessions probably offer the best value of any user research you can do. Each session will take a few hours to arrange, conduct and then analyse for useful findings. If you are a smaller organisation, try to do half a dozen or so of these tests a year. We are confident that you will find it of immense value and that your view of how your organisation is perceived will shift in ways you never expected.

Small funder tip no. 6: Run Q&A webinars to reveal and overcome any problems in your guidance

One of the upsides of living in the video-conferencing era is that you can arrange online Q&A events, to which quite a lot of people can come, to explain your grantmaking processes.

We interviewed the CEO of one small foundation who explained that such webinars were doubly valuable for them. First, they help ensure that less confident applicants have a chance to ask questions in an environment that is quite safe and fairly anonymous. Second, as the questions trickle in from the guests, points where the funder's guidance or application process may be confusing to grantseekers rapidly become clear. Such events, which are quick and cheap to organise and fairly easy to run, can also become a valuable means of gaining knowledge about bad or confusing service experiences. They're well worth a go.

Case study: How a smaller funder rebuilt its grantmaking model around listening

> COVID-19 really made us think about whether what we were doing was the best way of helping us to achieve our mission. When we decided to create proximity to young people ourselves outside of a mediated relationship through charities, what we heard was so different. It was mind-blowing all the things we were missing.
>
> — JO WELLS, director at the Blagrave Trust

The Blagrave Trust has been practising and promoting trust-based philanthropy for years. It provides mostly unrestricted, multi-year grants, and made a splash in the UK grantmaking sector for its innovative Listening Fund. This started as a £900,000 pooled fund focused exclusively on making sure that the voices of young people were listened to more – an unusual focus for a grantmaking programme. The initiative, now in its second phase, will dedicate another £1.25m to this work, supported by ten Young Advisers.

The impact of the pandemic in 2020, in the context of youth activism energised by injustices such as racism, the climate emergency and rising youth unemployment, made the trust question whether this model was right for such extraordinary times. After considering its options, the Blagrave Trust made a concerted effort to focus more on listening directly to young people across the UK, and not just to the nonprofits that claimed to serve them.

Working with the Centre for Knowledge Equity, Blagrave co-designed a new Challenge and Change Fund with young people. What was so different about this fund was that, instead of encouraging ideas from nonprofits, whether or not these were led by young people, it was aimed directly at young social activists themselves.

By doing user research and listening carefully, Blagrave had heard very clearly that many young people wanted the opportunity and more support to advocate for and make change directly themselves. For some, the concept of charity didn't seem relevant to or the most effective way of getting things done.

Using £95,000 in seed capital and a further £105,000 provided by two other funders (ZING and Ellis Campbell Charitable Foundation) Blagrave began to test a new grantmaking concept that emerged from its design process. This included committing itself to a delegated decision-making model where young advisers – not professional grantmakers – made all the final decisions on a set of awards.

This summary makes Blagrave's human centred design transition sound easy, but it wasn't. Reflecting on the Challenge and Change Fund so far, its director Jo Wells is clear that seeking to develop a truly fair grantmaking process – even one co-designed with a range of young people and equitable evaluation experts – will involve greater introspection. As she told us, 'You have to be open constantly to figuring out how to improve and make what you do more inclusive, in our case, of more young people, especially people we don't already have a connection to.'

That's why Blagrave has six Young Advisers now working on their regional grant programmes directly, and it's this commitment to continuous improvement that makes the Blagrave Trust stand out to us, and that shows they really get what the iterative part of human centred design is all about. With the support of specialists at the Centre for Knowledge Equity, Blagrave is moving towards equity-centred design that meaningfully includes the voice of young people from marginalised communities.[221]

How do I improve our service quality if I work for a larger funder?

If you work for an organisation that spends or could spend over $50,000 a year on its grantmaking systems, you are in a fundamentally different position from smaller organisations. This is because, with a larger budget, you can afford to contract or employ people whose only job is to improve service quality. These specialists are likely to do a better job than even the most motivated grantmaker because they won't be juggling dozens of other responsibilities at the same time.

The availability of greater resources to throw at this problem also means that the actions you need to take are rather different from those of smaller funders. Rather than implementing user research techniques yourself, you need to focus on acquiring and using specialist staff to do it for you.

Here are our top tips for Modern Grantmakers working in larger organisations.

Larger funder tip no. 1: Appoint a service owner

Good services, whether in the private or the public sector, invariably have an owner whose main job is to make sure that they're providing customers or users with a great service. This person will often have had their skills honed in professional customer service or product management, and they will be highly motivated to understand how customers feel and how their experience can be improved. If you have only a modest budget, contracting someone a couple of days a week to do this will still be very valuable. Trying to improve services without someone in this position at your funder is likely to turn out to be an expensive false economy.

Larger funder tip no. 2: Empower your service owner to acquire a team, agency or contractors

High-quality service delivery, especially through digital interfaces like websites, is too complex for one person to be able to do on their own. For example, user research is usually done well only by professional user researchers, and web design is done well only by professional web designers.

How big this team is will depend a lot on your budget, which can range from about $50,000 a year for someone using part-time freelancers through to easily $500,000 a year for an industry-standard service design team employing half a dozen full-time experts . This is undoubtedly a lot of money, but we think that if you are making over $50 million of grants a year, you should definitely have a dedicated team working to offer grantseekers and grantees a great, accessible funding experience. Anything less than that means inflicting painful, time-wasting and most probably inequitable experiences on grantseekers that have far fewer resources than you. It's very hard to defend this as an acceptable choice for funders with a lot of money.

Larger funder tip no. 3: Show user testing videos regularly to your board members and top team

Those at the top of larger funding organisations are apt to think that 'operations' isn't really that interesting or important – at least not compared to huge investment decisions. Showing them videos of real people struggling to understand guidance or to fill in application forms will drive home to them how critical this work is rather than just some nice-to-have.

Larger funder tip no. 4: Develop success metrics that are human-centred

Most funders operate some degree of metrics, but these rarely capture whether a funder's services are making grantseekers miserable or leading to their wasting large amounts of time and money. You should try to record data on whether grantees find it pleasant – or not so pleasant – dealing with you. Example questions used by the Center for Effective Philanthropy's Grantee and Applicant Perception Report to capture this sort of knowledge include:

- 'Overall, how fairly did the Foundation treat you?'
- 'How comfortable do you feel approaching the Foundation if a problem arises?'
- 'Overall, how responsive was the Foundation staff?'[222]

Answers to each of these questions are scored on a seven-point scale from 'not at all' to 'extremely'. They make for fascinating reading, especially when the answers are broken down by demographics, which will often show markedly different levels of comfort and satisfaction with funding processes between different groups of grantseekers and grantees.

If you make sure your organisation asks its users at least a few questions like these regularly and anonymously, you will rapidly acquire information that will give you the collateral to push for experience-improving reforms that may not otherwise be forthcoming.

What are the barriers that prevent my funder offering grantseekers and grantees a great experience?

Making your organisation's experience better for its users isn't always a walk in the park. Here are some of the problems you may encounter along the way:

- There may be a technical or contractual barrier to improving the experience you offer, such as a web agency contract that limits how many changes can be made to an application form.

- Despite saying that they are committed to serving grantseekers and grantees better, leaders in your organisation may not actually be willing to support the changes this would require, preferring the status quo over potentially uncomfortable change.

- Outdated accounting, project management and general governance practices can make iteration impossible because of the baked-in assumption that grantmaking services will be improved every couple of years rather than every single day. For more ideas on what this type of reform involves, we recommend checking out the UK government's Service Manual at **gov.uk/service-manual**.[223]

- Leaders who like to preside over their own internal fiefdoms can stymie the collaboration that is required to rebuild your funding service.

- You have too many other duties yourself and cannot make the time to lead the changes for a better service experience.

If you're lucky you won't encounter any of these problems, but in reality you will almost certainly run up against one or two of them. Here are a couple of tips for overcoming them.

The first is to build relationships with reforming grantmakers at other funding organisations who are also battling to offer a better service themselves. See Chapter 10 for ways to find other Modern Grantmakers. The whole struggle will feel easier if you have allies and are part of something bigger.

Second, make liberal use of the authority of eminent external voices. When you are trying to make a case for human-centred design, we suggest referring to respected authorities in the design world such as Lou Downe, former director of design for the UK government, and Tim Brown, former CEO of the design firm IDEO. Such figures have big institution credibility and show that you're not just obsessing over some hobby-horse. Both have written books on service design: Lou Downe, *Good Services: How to Design Services that Work*, and Tim Brown, *Change by Design: How Design Thinking Transforms Organizations and Inspires Innovation*.[224] They have also spoken and written on various other platforms that are publicly available to share with your colleagues. Their voices and stories may help you to convince others to start or to continue to improve your organisation's user experience.

Can we help grantees to focus more on the experience of the people who use their services?

This is a delicate area. On the one hand, you as a grantmaker want the organisations you support to offer great services to the people they aim to support. But, on the other hand, it's against the core values of Modern Grantmaking to tell competent grantees how to do their job – it's not a position of humility.

So how do you square this circle? Well, there are a few things you could consider doing.

- *You can run or sponsor events that introduce your grantees to the practices of human-centred design.* There are a growing number of service design experts who specialise in nonprofits and other social impact organisations. If you give them a platform, you can help grantseekers and grantees to learn without forcing anyone to do anything.

- *You can celebrate nonprofits and other grantees that invest in human-centred design.* It is easier for you, from your vantage point as a funder, to identify which organisations have tried to make use of design practices and which haven't. Using this knowledge, and the attention that is accorded to you as a funder, you can highlight, celebrate and draw attention to good uses of design practice.

- *You can make it clear that you will fund grants that improve service experiences.* One reason many nonprofits don't use human-centred design as much as they could is that they simply can't afford to do it. If your organisation is clear about your eligibility criteria, including your interest in supporting this kind of work, you will inevitably find organisations asking for help with this that didn't think they could before.

- *You can subsidise design infrastructure and support services.* While directly granting to a nonprofit is undoubtedly the most direct way you can help them embrace design, another thing you can do is to pay for shared assets and services that can help multiple nonprofits get better at design.

What do you mean by design infrastructure?

While every human-centred design process focuses on understanding the users of a particular service and seeing things from their perspective, this work can be speeded up and made easier if you can make use of shared design assets. In the following box we lay out a real-life example.

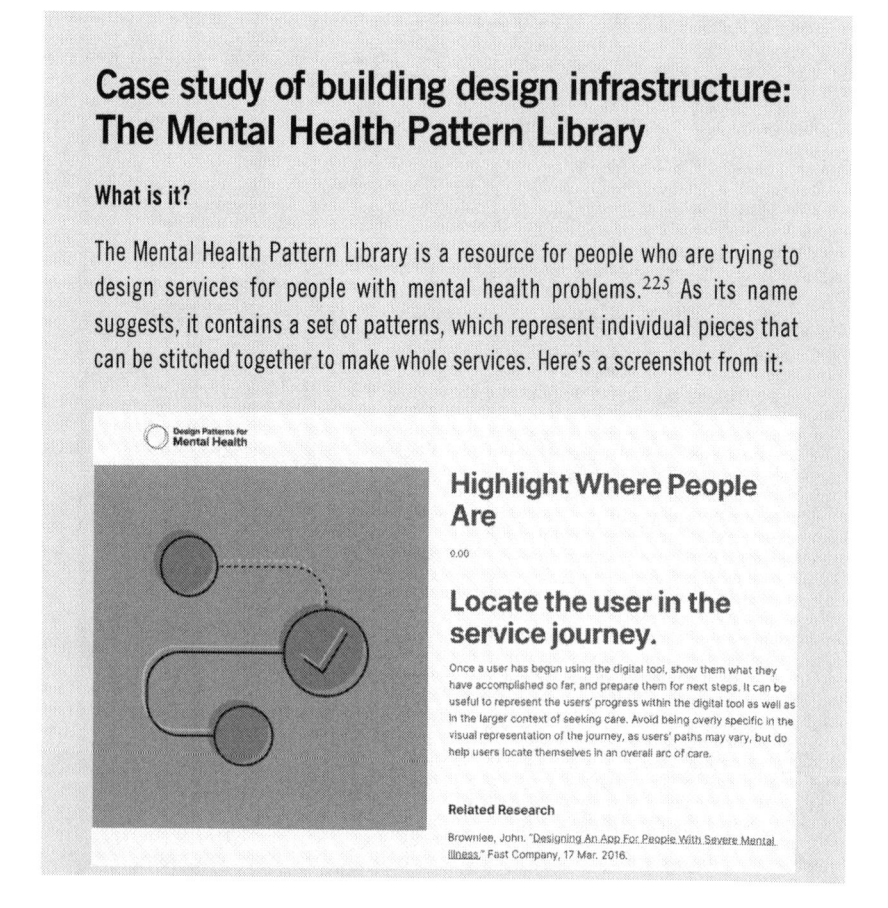

Case study of building design infrastructure: The Mental Health Pattern Library

What is it?

The Mental Health Pattern Library is a resource for people who are trying to design services for people with mental health problems.[225] As its name suggests, it contains a set of patterns, which represent individual pieces that can be stitched together to make whole services. Here's a screenshot from it:

Highlight Where People Are

0.00

Locate the user in the service journey.

Once a user has begun using the digital tool, show them what they have accomplished so far, and prepare them for next steps. It can be useful to represent the users' progress within the digital tool as well as in the larger context of seeking care. Avoid being overly specific in the visual representation of the journey, as users' paths may vary, but do help users locate themselves in an overall arc of care.

Related Research

Brownlee, John. "Designing An App For People With Severe Mental Illness," Fast Company, 17 Mar. 2016.

How did it come about?

As awareness of mental health issues grows, more and more digital products and services, ranging from meditation apps to online therapy courses, have appeared in the last five years.

In 2017 the design agency Snook recognised the huge potential of taking a step back and reviewing what had been learned during a period of feverish innovation. By studying what sorts of design patterns work or don't work in a mental health context, Snook believed that it could be possible to design and build better tools to support people.

Working alongside the Public Policy Lab in New York, Snook set out to connect the dots. Its designers conducted desk research, spoke to government and nonprofit experts, academics and front-line staff.

Over time a range of common, repeated design patterns started to emerge. Design patterns are familiar features that pop up again and again, for example when you sign in on a website or enable a location service on an app. They exist to solve common problems and to make services more accessible. In the case of this library, the services that needed making better and more accessible were ones directly aimed at people managing their mental health.

This work led to the first *minimum viable product* for the library. It involved putting four patterns online and maintaining a suite of around 35 others in an open Google document to which over 100 people from around the world could contribute.

Before going live with the next stage of the library, the partnership tested the content design to make sure that it was in a language that people could understand and use. It also held cross-sector workshops to develop further patterns and review the content to date.

Fast-forward two years and Snook is now in a partnership with Barnardos, a large children's charity in the UK, and securing funding to focus on a suite of patterns for young people to ensure that more services use inclusive and proven best practice to support their mental health.

Most importantly for Snook, the pattern library has influenced the design of services in the real world. In the words of their CEO Sarah Drummond, 'We're confident in the feedback we've had from developers, designers, CEOs, service owners outlining that the library made them consider features they had never thought of before.'

So, if you get bitten by the human-centred design bug, it would be well worth talking to both nonprofits and designers within the sectors you support to find out whether there are any opportunities to fund shared design infrastructure that can help everyone to succeed.

Is there anything else I can do if I don't have the power to put in place human-centred design in my organisation?

We fully understand that many of our readers won't have the individual power to hire people, build teams or choose to overhaul a funding programme or a website. So in this last section we've put together a list of things you can do if the only thing you can change is some of the wording on your website or on your Word or PDF guidance documents.

- Make it easy for grantseekers to understand your eligibility criteria up front so that they can make an informed decision about whether or not to apply to your organisation. It's an act of cruelty to hide key assessment criteria from grantseekers, so work to make sure there's nothing hidden from them.

- Make it easy for a grantseeker to either talk to your organisation directly before they apply, or submit a short, quick pre-application so they can get feedback on whether they have any chance of success, before they invest a lot of time in a full application. Don't ask for more information in advance than you need.

- Answer all queries you receive quickly and clearly, even if all you have to say to the applicant is: 'You will have to wait until March for a decision.'

- Be transparent about any service standards you operate, such as turnaround times for specific funding programmes and the historic success rates of people applying to this programme (or similar ones). This helps those who are considering applying to you to figure out whether it's worth their time and effort to do so. It also enables your organisation to be held (informally) to some degree of account.

How can I improve the experience of grantseekers and grantees?

- Be clear in written guidance about your organisation's strategy, priorities, budgets and any impending changes to these. As the former Hewlett Foundation funding director Ruth Levine told us, 'You should share as much information as possible about your funding, like the total amount of funding; about timelines; and whether there are going to be pending shifts in strategy.'[226]

- If you ask grantseekers to fill in an application form, make it as short as possible; ensure that it asks clear, comprehensible questions; and test it with real users to make sure it is accessible to people who may have very different needs.

- Remove any questions from your application form that are not truly necessary. Don't let your organisation ask lots of questions only because 'it's always been done this way' or 'someone might need it'. As one of our interviewees told us, 'I think a lot of funders ask questions and go through checklists because they think they're supposed to prove their value.'[227] Ask grantseekers questions that really matter and scrap the rest.

- Let grantseekers know as soon as possible whether or not they have been successful. Remember, a quick and clear 'no' is second only to a 'yes'. And never ever go totally silent on a grantseeker. As one foundation senior executive told us, 'Some funders don't always get back to applicants and you only hear from them if you get funding. That's bullshit.'[228]

- Remember it's not just about the application process. To give nonprofits a really good service, you'll need to review your whole funding cycle, including contracting, monitoring, evaluation and ultimately winding up a grant.

And with that we wind up our chapter on user experience and user research.

In the next chapter we'll zoom out to look at the wider world of research, and explain why grantmakers should have an informed view of what research is for and when to bring in the specialists.

Chapter 6 checklist

1. Has your organisation taken credible steps to acquire honest, anonymised feedback on what it is like to be a grantseeker or a grantee with you?

   ....

2. Do your colleagues talk and act as if they see themselves as providing a service to grantseekers and grantees?

   ....

3. Have you been in a meeting dedicated to the question 'Are we offering a good enough service?' at any point in the last year?

   ....

4. Can you quickly find data on what grantees think is good and bad about your service?

   ....

5. If you have a website or a Word/PDF application form, has it been tested for accessibility by independent specialists?

   ....

6. Does your funder regularly iterate services so that you provide a better experience for grantseekers or grantees?

   ....

7. Have you ever taken part in or witnessed any user experience research in your current role?

   ....

8. Does your funder employ or contract one or more people whose job is to improve grantseeker or grantee experiences?

   ....

7

HOW SHOULD I MAKE USE OF RESEARCH?

> For funders, using research means doing the due diligence required to make sure you're not re-inventing the flat tyre.[229]
>
> — Dr TIAGO PEIXOTO, The World Bank

Modern Grantmakers value evidence and research because they know there's simply no other way to find out whether the money being spent is making the world better or worse. This is such an important idea that we made evidence one of the five values that underpin Modern Grantmaking back in Chapter 1.

In this chapter we'll set out some of the most fundamental research concepts that all grantmakers should be familiar with and some of the day-to-day practices that should be part of your working life.

Before we dive in, we must add a major caveat: this chapter is aimed at people without university degrees in research-intensive subjects. If you have a master's or a doctorate in a highly technical field, you will probably find what we're about to say somewhat elementary.

This chapter's intended audience is grantmakers who are not at all confident about their mastery of research concepts and practices. This includes readers who encountered research methods and professional researchers only after they started working for funding organisations.

In this chapter we will explain what we mean by research, and we will describe when grantmakers typically need to engage with research. We will also explore some common mistakes that funding organisations make when producing or using it. We'll then give some practical advice about how you can have a relationship with research that's fruitful, responsible and a rewarding part of your job. All this advice is given with the full understanding that most readers will not be in a position to change their whole organisation's approach to evidence and research.

Sadly, what we cannot do in a couple of dozen pages is give you a full education in how to be a researcher, or explain the deep history and philosophy of the scientific method. We do not, for example, include a list of different research methods, even though an understanding of which methods are required for which kinds of research is very important. So, more than any other chapter in this book, this is a taster and contains signposts to help you learn more elsewhere.

What does 'research' even mean?

Let's start with the fundamentals. What is this thing we're talking about? It's a bit of a cliche, but we may as well start by looking in the dictionary, in this case Merriam-Webster:

> *research*: studious inquiry or examination; especially: investigation or experimentation aimed at the discovery and interpretation of facts, revision of accepted theories or laws in the light of new facts, or practical application of such new or revised theories or laws.[230]

This is a helpful definition because it covers both what research looks like – 'studious inquiry' – as well as what it is for. It tells us that research is worth doing because it enables the 'practical application' of 'new or revised theories' about the way the world works. In our occupation 'practical application' most often means choosing between different possible grants, but it can also mean choosing between different strategies, different ways of giving and different ways of running our organisation.

What the dictionary doesn't tell you is that research is fundamentally about trying to produce knowledge that is more useful and more reliable than the kinds of information that pervade most of our lives – news, opinion, rumour, gossip, hunches and prejudices. Research is really about using greater rigour than we would apply to most activities in our daily lives to uncover useful knowledge.

The great thing about deploying research is that we get to stand on the shoulders of giants. Humanity has spent much of the last 500 years coming up with different ways of making sure that we can have a reasonable degree of confidence in important pieces of information. These different ways of producing knowledge are now called *research methods*, and the great majority of people who deploy them are called *professional researchers*. Many of them work in universities but many others work for companies and nonprofits.

How should I make use of research?

Research methods sometimes involve collecting new information, for example by conducting interviews or surveys, or by deploying sensors to measure data like air quality. Other methods can involve reading and analysing pre-existing research findings or data to identify new findings. Whatever research methods are deployed, the goal is always the same – to reveal knowledge that is more robust and trustworthy than people's unverified hunches or opinions.

When do grantmakers need to think about research?

While both grantmaking and research are complex professions full of infinite nuances and wrinkles, the question of when grantmakers need to think about research actually has a clear answer.

There are five moments in our jobs as grantmakers when we need to pause and consider the role of research. These are:

1 *Renewing a funder strategy*: When you are designing or revising your organisation's strategy, your colleagues and your board need to engage with research to work out both what to do and whether the new strategy is working (we cover this in detail in Chapter 4).

2 *Designing funding programmes or services*: If you are designing or redesigning a funding programme and are serious about wanting it to be both effective and inclusive, you'll need to engage with research in several ways. For starters, you can use pre-existing research from science, medicine and the social sciences to work out what opportunities exist that can make a difference. Then, as you build a new programme or product, you should use user research to make sure that the types of organisations you want to support can understand what you're offering and can write successful proposals (see Chapter 6). Finally, you'll need to study evaluations and impact research to find out if your whole programme is likely to be a success.

3 *Analysing funding proposals*: When you are deciding whether or not to award a grant, you will need to engage with pre-existing research to help you make a good decision. This is the case for all funders, not just those – such as medical funders – with an explicit focus on funding

the production of research. It is also likely to require an open and honest conversation with any potential grantee or group of partners about what you and they believe constitutes 'effective performance' in relation to any proposal. For more on this, we recommend reading Chapter 6 of Phil Buchanan's *Giving Done Right*, 'No Easy Answers: Assessing Performance'.[231]

4 *Before committing your organisation to a grant*: When you are discussing a funding proposal with an applicant you need to have a clear conversation about how the grant is going to be successfully evaluated, and whether or not that's even possible. This is where you'll need to think hard about what is going to be studied, why it's going to be studied and whether the findings will make any meaningful difference to anyone. You'll find a lot more on this in the second part of this chapter.

5 *After a grant has been made*: Once grant money has been handed over, the chance to develop and share new knowledge really begins, especially knowledge about impact.

While these are all examples of using research as a grantmaker, they're actually quite diverse activities.

For example, when you are deciding on a grant, you will need to know how to find the appropriate research or the relevant researchers that will shed light on the proposal, and how to interpret it. That's one set of skills. When you are discussing evaluation with a prospective grantee, you're in the business of designing and producing useful research, not consuming it. And, if you are trying to make your funding application process more accessible, you'll need to engage in user research, which we explored in Chapter 6.

This chapter aims to help you understand both how to consume research and how to commission it to be produced by specialists. The main thing you have to remember is that, as a grantmaker, you need to engage with both consumption and commissioning.

What is the connection between research and monitoring and evaluation?

Many funding organisations don't use the word 'research' at all, and instead favour the phrase 'monitoring and evaluation' (M&E). So how are these related?

In a nutshell, M&E refers to tracking the progress of a grant by doing two very different types of work. *Evaluation* refers to carrying out research to discover whether or not a project has been successful. Evaluation involves choosing and implementing appropriate research methods, and then diligently collecting, analysing and writing up findings, while taking steps at every stage to avoid bias. Evaluation considers important questions such as:

- Did anyone benefit from this grant?
- Who benefited?
- What sorts of benefits did they get?

Monitoring, by contrast, consists primarily of collecting and counting key bits of data, usually data that help a person be sure that progress is being made on the way towards a goal. Monitoring doesn't require research skills to do successfully. The sorts of questions monitoring covers include:

- How many bags of concrete have been delivered?
- How many teachers have signed employment contracts?
- What proportion of contracted teachers have been showing up to teach classes?

The skills and resources required to do monitoring are quite different from those required to produce evaluations. Designing and delivering evaluation properly is a specialist skill that usually requires training in research methods, as well as a considerable investment of time to generate any meaningful results.

Monitoring is generally easier and quicker than evaluation – although, as with most things in life, there are exceptions. For the most part, it involves collecting accurate data and sending factual updates. Monitoring may produce new data every day, whereas evaluation might produce an important result once a year.

When you consider funding proposals, you should probe whether monitoring and evaluation will be done by people with the appropriate skills or have just been lumped together in a vaguely defined budget line. Monitoring is often essential for an evaluation to take place, but that doesn't mean they should be treated as identical tasks.

Before moving on, it is worth noting that evaluation isn't a single, monolithic concept. There are several quite different kinds of evaluation that can be commissioned, and they're not all the same. For example, a formative evaluation assesses whether a start-up initiative is coming together properly, at quite an early stage, whereas an impact evaluation will look at the extent to which a programme meets its ultimate goal. For a simple guide to these different sorts of evaluation, we suggest checking out the Centers for Disease Control and Prevention's cornucopia of resources.[232]

Do grantmakers need to make use of research other than monitoring and evaluation reports about grantees?

Yes, absolutely. Monitoring and evaluation reports about grantees represent only a fraction of all the research carried out by professional researchers worldwide, and only a subset of the information that may be valuable to grantmakers. Other forms of research that may be enormously important to funders include:

- books and papers revealing new findings about the way the world works, which can therefore influence a grantmaker's view about what is worth funding and what isn't;

- research specifically commissioned by funding organisations to answer a grantmaker's strategic question, such as 'Which anti-malaria intervention is the best value for money?' or 'Which reoffending programme is most likely to help people into secure long-term employment?';

- data publications from governments that directly reveal trends in society, such as changes to unemployment rates or educational attainment;

- user research into the people and organisations who apply for money (see Chapter 6 for more on this);

- scientific, medical, social and cultural research which, while it may not be used directly by grantmakers, creates value for the world.

How should I make use of research?

It's important that Modern Grantmakers are aware that much of the research that will be most valuable to them might very well not arrive in their inbox marked 'grantee report'.

Do I always need to read loads of research before I make day-to-day decisions?

The life of a grantmaker is generally a busy one, with too many meetings, too many people to speak to and not enough hours in the day. So to be told that there's another time-consuming thing to do is probably not what you want to hear. It's especially annoying if it seems obvious that the funding proposal in front of you is a good one.

We really empathise with you – we've been there! But putting effort into engaging with relevant research really does matter. As the director of Giving Evidence, Caroline Fiennes, puts it:

> You can't just rely on your judgement because you might fund something that is harmful or just pointless. For instance, some grant-funded programmes to reduce ex-prisoner reoffending appear to actually increase it. In other words: your common sense may simply not be very sensible.[233]

As humans, we approach every decision through the lens of our own personal experience and thus our own personal biases. Your decision to pick up and eat a snack is based on your previous experience of eating similar ones. You do not consider this choice to be an experience-based decision but that's exactly what it is: your previous consumption of similar snacks causes you to eat this one rather than, say, the pencil lying next to it. Because we use our own experience a thousand times a day to make a thousand mostly successful decisions, it can be difficult to accept that our own experience is not always enough to make a good grant decision.

There is now a vast psychology literature on humans' tendency to make mistakes that stem from semi-predictable self-delusions. Back in the 1970s the scholars Amos Tversky and Daniel Kahneman gave a name to these types of errors: they called them *cognitive biases*.[234] More than a hundred such cognitive biases have now been identified and named, although not all of them are supported by equally robust research.

Grantmakers are human, so they have cognitive biases too. To give just one example of why this is a problem, consider the phenomenon known as *confirmation bias*.[235] Confirmation bias is the involuntary tendency of humans to select and recall information that supports their views and to ignore and forget non-supportive information.

This means that, if you are a grantmaker who firmly believes that a particular education programme boosts the attainment of young people, you are highly likely to dismiss or even forget negative comments suggesting that it doesn't work or that it actually harms students. A robust, well-researched evaluation report showing that this educational intervention has negative consequences for students may not be enough to change your mind: stubbornness is part of being human. But, if a funding organisation were to at least take the time and expense to acquire and consider such research, it is much more likely that someone will eventually say 'stop'. This, in a nutshell, is the value of research to grantmakers: it saves us from ourselves and helps us to make better choices than we otherwise could.

Admitting and coming to terms with the fact that our flawed brains and limited experiences can lead us to make bad decisions is fundamentally an exercise in humility. Many people find it very hard to accept because it challenges their identities as capable, reasonable individuals. The only way to cope with the bad news of our own fallibility is to be humble.

Once we admit that our thinking and reasoning are flawed and that we must therefore be humble, the importance of using research before we make choices becomes crystal clear. We need research to compensate for our weaknesses and biases, and to stop us from making harmful choices.

As Geeta Gopalan, an experienced board member of multiple funding organisations told us, 'Modern Grantmaking is about understanding what is working and what's not working because we have to learn and do better. The simple act of giving is not enough.'[236]

What are the most common problems with the ways grantmakers use research today?

> It's all too complicated – I don't do numbers.[237]
> — ANONYMOUS GRANTMAKER

Research problem no. 1: Everyone is marking their own homework and giving themselves A+

Here's a quick exercise for you. Find the nearest grantee or grantseeker budget document you can grab and open it up. It can be old or new, but try to pick something that's at least five figures in total grant value.

Skim through the line items, i.e. budgeting costs for staff or equipment, and in due course you're very likely to hit a line for 'evaluation' or 'impact research', or perhaps just 'reporting'. Very often this will represent 5% or 10% of the total budget, although there's no hard and fast rule.

Now pause for a moment to consider what this line item means. It means that you as the grantmaker are being asked, or have been asked, to give the grantee some money so that they can report back to you, and possibly to others, what has happened as a consequence of being given this grant money.

On the surface this looks like an entirely reasonable idea – indeed a praiseworthy one. But in truth it is a sign of something deeply problematic: by giving money to a grantee to commission evaluation research, a funder is ensuring that the people who produce the evaluation report will be working for the grantee.

Any contractual relationship between a grantee and commissioned researchers includes an unfortunate incentive. Because most grantseekers' greatest concern is staying afloat and not having to fire all their staff, it is generally undesirable for them to collect and share research findings that will show their funder that there has been some kind of failure or underperformance.

The people commissioning the research within grantees know this, and the people conducting the research know it too. This leads predictably to final reports concluding that an initiative has been a smashing success, regardless of what actually transpired.

This problem was pointed out to us by more than one interviewee. Stephen Tall, who works for the Education Endowment Foundation in the UK, a charity focused on getting schools to use research, explained the problem very clearly: 'Too many funders get their own grantees to mark their homework. This is both a conflict of interest, and gives grantees a task they're mostly not set up to do.'[238]

An anonymous story from a former senior grantmaker at a large funding organisation paints a memorable picture of what happens when marking your own homework is the norm:

> When I first started in this role I asked to read a broad cross-section of evaluation reports about grants we'd made in the past. As I read through, I realised to my enormous scepticism that my new employer had literally never made a grant that was anything less than a triumph. I knew what it meant – it meant I couldn't trust the vast majority of the research that had been commissioned previously.[239]

So evaluation reports produced by grantees themselves need to be treated with considerable scepticism. The preferable option – which you've probably already worked out – is for funders to commission independent researchers to evaluate projects, while making sure that grantees still have enough money to work with those researchers.

You may already be working for a funder that does this routinely, in which case you should count your blessings. Unfortunately, in our research we didn't come across many funding organisations where independent evaluation was the norm. If your organisation doesn't regularly commission independent evaluation, it's time to open up that conversation with your colleagues or your board.

Research problem no. 2: Too much reporting given to funders is about outputs, not outcomes

The *output* of a typical grantee is a certain amount of stuff or activity. It could be two new hospitals, a thousand youth counselling sessions or a single new virus vaccine. An *outcome* is how the world has changed as a result of some outputs. An outcome is a million lives saved by that new vaccine, a thousand families reunited or a dozen unemployed people who secured decently paid, fulfilling jobs.

Outputs are usually much easier and cheaper to measure than outcomes: you just count the people, the boxes, the training sessions delivered and note them in a monitoring report. In a resource-strapped sector this means that outputs are far more often counted than outcomes. But the purpose of all grantmaking is to make a difference in the world, not just to produce a certain amount of stuff. This means that outcome measurement is much more likely to tell you whether an organisation or a project has really been successful.

As a Modern Grantmaker you should be keenly aware of the difference between outcomes and outputs. Most of grantmaking is about making some kind of real impact on people or the environment. Output measures can conceal a lack of impact behind a barrage of numbers: 10,000 textbooks have been delivered and 25 classrooms built, but has anyone actually learned anything useful or enlightening?

Outcomes are what most grantmakers really care about: lives saved, people employed, self-confidence grown, artistic and cultural joy experienced. But grants are often signed off with reporting requirements that will never produce knowledge about outcomes. Outcomes are generally (not always, but often) slower and more expensive to capture than outputs. In a world of finite resources this means that a funding organisation that wants to understand the outcomes of its grantmaking choices will not be able to make as many grants as an organisation that doesn't understand or care about outcome measurement. This is because the funder will have to spend more money on evaluating each grant. The costs can drive some grantmakers to be sceptical about outcomes research because they think it means wasting money on researchers that could be given to grantees.

But this is an extremely narrow way to think about grantmaking bang per buck, if only because it fails to acknowledge that the biggest funder in the world is the government. And, as we'll show in case studies below, high-quality, outcomes-based impact evaluations can persuade governments to pour more resources into an area than any grant funder ever can. Cutting corners on outcome measurement can mean forfeiting access to the scale of spending that only governments are capable of.

A good funding organisation will ultimately acknowledge that outcomes measurement is what is needed to understand whether a grant has had any impact. However, it will also understand that this can be costly and that in some situations (such as long-term social change campaigns) it may be difficult or even impossible to achieve.

In the end, good choices about using and producing research start with everyone within a funder being clear about the difference between outcomes and outputs in the first place. Now that you've read this section, you can help make sure that all your colleagues understand the difference too.

Research problem no. 3: There's a systematic lack of honesty about grants and grantees that fail

Nobody likes failing. Even Silicon Valley management gurus who encourage others to 'fail fast, fail often' don't get out of bed seeking to fail, especially not in front of their bosses or clients.

Grantmakers and grantseekers have a dislike of failure that, if anything, is even stronger than that in the private sector. This is because they feel they have embarked on an important social mission, and any failure could mean something precious being undermined. As we were told by the experienced senior grantmaking executive Ngozi Lyn Cole:

> Although we're now seeing some green shoots of change, funders have as much a fear of failure as those they fund. And they translate this fear to those they fund so that people stagnate and don't feel brave or courageous as they're too worried about what the funder will think and do all the time.[240]

This dislike of failure has an unfortunate side effect. It means that neither grantees nor grantseekers clearly and regularly share knowledge about when projects or grants don't work out.

Here's a quick exercise: try to recall a time when a funder proactively shared information on a programme that didn't work out, and set out what went wrong. Nothing comes quickly to mind? It is not surprising, unfortunately. Examples are rare enough to be noteworthy events, such as the Hewlett Foundation's bracingly honest report *Hard Lessons about Philanthropy & Community Change from the Neighborhood Improvement Initiative* (2007).[241] The Bill and Melinda Gates Foundation also deserves some credit for permitting publication of an evaluation of a large education initiative they funded that 'did not achieve its goals for student achievement or graduation', even though they must have known that this would lead to personal attacks on Bill and Melinda French Gates themselves (as it indeed it did).[242]

The general atmosphere of failure denial that permeates too much of almost all of grantmaking has a deeply negative effect on the wider nonprofit and social impact sectors. It means that nonprofits may continue with grant-funded activities that have been shown to not work or to do actual harm.

For example, the juvenile awareness programme Scared Straight gained fame in the 1970s, after a documentary about it showed young people meeting prisoners, who were supposedly deterring them from a life of crime. Scared Straight was copied and implemented in many places. Unfortunately, despite the intuitively appealing notion that fear could drive youngsters to behave better, an authoritative report stated that 'Meta analyses of seven studies show the intervention to be more harmful than doing nothing.'[243] Young people who had gone through the programme were more likely to offend than those who had not. The money spent on this programme made the world worse, not better.

Ultimately, as with so much else in this book, being honest about failure in grantmaking is all about humility. If you can learn to put your ego aside, or at least in second place to the impact your organisation can make, you will find it easier to admit and discuss problems and are more likely to make bigger and more positive impacts in the future.

Research problem no. 4: Funders burden grantees with heavy reporting that is too often a waste of time

> Often you have to retrofit the way you do evaluation for what a funder wants. It's a pain in the butt and not productive for anyone. In my career, I've had very few programme officers who have read the full report and then come back to me with questions. For the most part, you just get a generic 'great, thanks', 'box ticked' and you have no idea whether anyone really cares.[244]
>
> — JEN BOKOFF, director of development at Disability Rights Fund

Once a funding organisation has given an organisation some money, it usually expects to be sent reports on how the money is being spent and generally what's going on. Depending on the size and nature of the grant, this reporting can vary from a few paragraphs in a quick email to many documents and datasets.

It is an open secret in the grantmaking universe that the burden this reporting can place on organisations is often substantial, and in many cases too extensive to be justified. In the words of one experienced senior grantmaker working in the US, 'One problem that grantmakers unintentionally create for grantees is the organizational strain and resource drain caused by detailed reporting requirements, which are often bespoke for each funding entity. Organizations could be using that time, effort and money to do the work, rather than reporting on it.'[245]

There have been various attempts to collect data on how much time is spent on reporting. One investigation of UK charities by the research consultancy Time to Spare found, via a survey, that a rough average of reporting time on one grant was 40 hours. When they multiplied this by the total number of grants in the UK, they observed: 'we find that charities spend 15.8m hours every single year just filling out reports for funders. That's ~£204m of staff time.'[246]

In the US, a RAND report found, via a deep dive investigation, that a single anonymous nonprofit devoted 11% of its budget and 44% of its time to 'compliance'.[247] In their now famous article *The Nonprofit Starvation Cycle*, Ann Goggins Gregory and Don Howard reported that 'when one Bridgespan client added up the hours that staff members spent on reporting requirements for a particular government grant, the organization found that it was spending about 31 percent of the value of the grant on its administration'.[248]

A successful small-to-medium grantee with five or six funders will routinely find itself with five or six grantee reports that need to be conducted, analysed, written up and sent. This cycle never ends, is enormously burdensome and takes away considerable time from doing the real work of actually delivering impact. Worse still, it consumes time while producing the kind of deeply conflicted 'Everything is fine and dandy!' reports that we criticised earlier in the chapter.

Finally, as a cherry on top of the cake of failure, we know from our own experiences that reports very often pile up in the inboxes of grantmakers and are simply never read because those individuals are too busy and have few strong incentives to open them.

It doesn't take much to realise that it would be far better for both grantees and funders if each grantee were to produce a very small number of higher-quality reports (perhaps just one a year), in conjunction with independent researchers who do not have problematic conflicts of interest. This would be more similar to the way in which private sector investors read the same annual or financial reports from businesses, rather than each shareholder demanding their own custom report.

Furthermore, a grantee that produces just one or two high-quality reports a year will end up with far better, more actionable intelligence on which to base key decisions, as well as with solid research that it can use to persuade funders to support it.

So, the next time you talk to a funder who co-funds an organisation with you, see if you can have a conversation with them about just asking for one shared grantee report. As well as being less burdensome on your grantee, it will also mean that you can discuss the findings with another organisation to help you avoid the classic problem of commissioning a report that is never actually read or used.

What steps should I take to make better use of research?

> If you're a funder that wants to follow your heart and hope it's doing good, you're welcome to do so. But if you're a funder who wants to know if you're actually having impact, you need to get serious about research.[249]
>
> — STEPHEN TALL, Education Endowment Foundation

We've spent quite enough time talking about the woes and difficulties that can make the production and use of research in the grantmaking world difficult. It's time to turn positive and talk about how you can overcome those problems and start to benefit from what research can offer grantmakers and the people they serve.

Research tip no. 1: Remember to seek out research in the first place

Let's start with an easy one: the next time you assess a new grant proposal or design a new grantmaking programme, don't forget to look for helpful research that will enable you to make better decisions. With dozens of funding proposals piling up on your desk and nagging calls coming from every direction, we are aware that one of the easiest ways to make time as a grantmaker is to simply skip the whole business of seeking out and analysing potentially valuable research.

Choosing to opt out of any engagement with research can be even more tempting if you work for the type of funding organisation that will never question or criticise you for failing to study existing research. We have both seen funder processes where the 'official' way of vetting grants simply doesn't involve any encouragement, or even permission, to seek out and use research.

This means that, unless you work for a highly research-centric funder (such as a science funder), you will very likely need to seek out and use relevant research without anyone pushing you to do so. This can be tough and may even feel subversive. But it's absolutely critical if you're to live up to the values of Modern Grantmaking, which prizes both humility, and evidence (see Chapter 1 for more on these values).

Lastly, don't forget that you need to turn to research not just when you are making individual grants, but especially when your organisation is developing a new strategy or grants programme. Again, if you don't bring relevant research to the table to bear on these debates, it's entirely possible that major strategic choices will be made solely on the basis of habit, hunch and a vague sense of what's cool. That doesn't sound like Modern Grantmaking to us.

Research tip no. 2: Lobby your leadership to make sure that your grantmakers have access to professional researchers

Most grantmakers are not professional researchers, but virtually all grantmakers need the help of research specialists to do their jobs as well as possible.

For some funders this isn't a problem. If you work for the Wellcome Trust (UK) or the National Science Foundation (US) you'll be able to just throw a stone and probably hit a research expert (although they might be unwilling to answer your questions afterwards). But most funders, being both smaller and less scientifically focused than these behemoths, don't necessarily have a lot of researchers just hanging around, waiting to be pulled into planning conversations.

This is a real problem because professional researchers offer capabilities that are essential for funders that want to maximise their impact. They can analyse the existing research and comment on its quality in ways that people without their skills and experience cannot. This capability can help grantmakers to know whether or not their decision making should be influenced by a particular piece of data, study or report. As Ruth Levine, a former programme director at the William and Flora Hewlett Foundation, told us, 'Not all research is born equal – some methods are better than others to answer a given question and it's often not easy for people without research training to know what quality research is.'[250]

Also, and of great value for funders, professional researchers can design and implement approaches to studying the grants we make which will produce robust findings that may be useful for future decisions.

Without these skills on tap, funding organisations are likely to make

How should I make use of research?

poor grantmaking and strategy decisions, not just once but again and again. Even worse, they are likely to end up paying for lots of research and reporting to be done that simply isn't useful: findings that either cannot be trusted because of research quality failings or findings that aren't actually useful to anyone.

The only way to ward off this threat is to do one of three things:

- employ your in-house researcher(s) as staff members;
- contract researchers or research companies;
- partner with universities so that their researchers can study your prospective grants.

As one anonymous interviewee put it to us: 'you either need to hire someone who can do [research] or you need to bring someone in.'[251] There really aren't many other options.

Now, we absolutely understand that you may be working for an organisation that doesn't currently provide its grantmakers with regular, good-quality support from research professionals. If that's so, it is incumbent on you to start making the case for change and investment. This may take time, and lobbying your own bosses can be intimidating, but here are a few simple tips:

- *Look for allies*: You may well not be the only person in your organisation who thinks that better research capabilities are required or that your funder has worrying knowledge gaps on critical issues. Try to search them out by raising your own concerns over coffee.

- *Circulate stories about the harms caused by funders who don't study their impacts properly*: We mentioned Scared Straight earlier, but there's a whole (if politically slanted) book on this called *Great Philanthropic Mistakes* by Martin Morse Wooster, if you're in a mood to wallow in funding disasters.[252]

- *Celebrate positive achievements in research-enabled social impact*, such as the work on poverty done by the Nobel Prize winners Esther Duflo and Abhijit Banerjee.[253]

- *Warn colleagues of the danger that current research and monitoring might be unethical.* It can be easy to harm people by designing research projects thoughtlessly, as we discuss below. It is legitimate to worry that, without good access to researchers, monitoring and evaluations currently taking place right now may cause harms that should be avoided.

- *Explain to colleagues that research may not be as expensive as they think* because external researchers often want access to data collected by grantmakers and grantees, which opens up the prospect of mutually beneficial agreements that don't involve much money.

- *Read Chapter 9*, in which we have a section about the general skills required to manage upwards in a funding organisation.

Research tip no. 3: Use this cheat-sheet to help you find pre-existing research that could help you make better choices

So, you have a funding proposal or a new strategy sitting in front of you. It is time to find some research that might shed light on the matter at hand. Where do you start?

How to find useful research: a cheat-sheet for busy grantmakers

1 Ask your colleagues if they have previously seen a grant or a government programme that resembles the one you are currently considering. If they have, ask them how you might go about getting your hands on any independent studies, evaluations or even just progress reports that exist for it.

2 Ask grantmakers who work for other funders if they know of evaluations or research papers that might help you. It may not be appropriate to ask such questions in public, so consider writing to people via private channels or going into private funder communities where questions are freely shared in trusted spaces. Some examples of private funder communities for sharing questions include Ariadne: European Funders for Social Change and Human Rights (Europe), The Funders Network (US), Environmental Funders Network / greenfunders.org (UK) or any of the many US regional funding networks.[254]

3 Visit a research repository website within a domain that relates to the grant you are considering (see more on these below). Search within its website for evidence relating to work similar to that which you're currently considering.

4 Approach other nonprofits that carry out work comparable with the application that you are considering. Ask them (privately) if they have any research on the effectiveness of these projects that they would be willing to share. Many nonprofits have evidence on the effectiveness (or otherwise) of projects that they never publish.

5 Use a public grant search database to find similar-seeming projects. There are now various public databases of grants made by funders, and even more directly within funder websites. By using a site like Candid's database of over 16 million US grants[255] or GrantNav's website for UK grants,[256] you can quickly find grants that may be similar to the one you're considering. Then you can write to the parties involved to see if they can share any evaluations or other research findings with you.

6 Visit Google Scholar, the online journal search tool, and search.[257] This may be a tougher experience because the volume of results will be more overwhelming and the target audience is not funders. Be aware that this may lead you to papers that sit behind paywalls, and you may need to make the case to your board or leadership that this kind of spending is a good investment.

If you draw a blank after all the above steps, consider contracting a professional researcher for a specific investigation. Their skills and experience often mean that they can quickly find studies that you may not be able to find yourself.

The main effect of following our cheat-sheet will be to help you put your hands on some actual research reports, data or individual experts that may be potentially relevant to the grantmaking decision you've got to make. But obtaining research reports or findings is only the first step. Next you have to read them and work out whether or not you should trust them enough to let them inform your decision. Skip forward to research tip no. 7 if you want some help with this.

What are research repositories and why should I care?

One of the most fantastic resources for grantmakers in recent years has been the growth of institutions that share research findings about what happened when money was spent to pursue a desired social impact. These repositories don't just contain lots of research about the impacts of different kinds of funding, they also make the information easy to find and use for overworked grantmakers. Here are some of the big ones that are currently out there.

J-PAL: The J-PAL evaluations database, containing nearly a thousand evaluations of different programmes aiming at reducing poverty in a range of nations: **povertyactionlab.org/research-resources**.

Early Intervention Foundation: The Early Intervention Foundation's Guidebook contains studies 'about early intervention programmes that have been evaluated and shown to improve outcomes for children and young people': **guidebook.eif.org.uk**.

Access to Justice Lab: The Access to Justice Lab at Harvard University is compiling rigorous studies about which interventions help people to use the legal system successfully and which don't: **a2jlab.org**.

Arts and Health: The Repository for Arts and Health Resources contains over 300 studies on the relationship between arts and health: **artshealthresources.org.uk**.

How should I make use of research?

> **International Development**: The repository of the International Initiative for Impact Evaluation contains records on 'development interventions': **developmentevidence.3ieimpact.org**.
>
> **College of Policing**: The Police Knowledge Fund Catalogue from the College of Policing is full of studies into the effectiveness of crime reduction: **whatworks.college.police.uk**.
>
> **GSDRC**: The Governance and Social Development Resource Centre's research helpdesk has lots of studies into the promotion of good government: **gsdrc.org/research-helpdesk**.
>
> **Blueprints for Healthy Youth Development**: 'a comprehensive, trusted registry of evidence-based interventions (programs, practices and policies) that are effective in reducing antisocial behaviour and promoting a healthy course of youth development and adult maturity': **blueprintsprograms.org**.
>
> **Campbell Collaboration**: The Campbell Collaboration produces systematic reviews on a host of areas, from crime and policing to the nutrition of adolescents: **campbellcollaboration.org**.
>
> In addition, the UK government subsidises **What Works Centres**, which fulfil similar functions across youth employment, homelessness, well-being and more: **gov.uk/guidance/what-works-network**.

Research tip no. 4: Commission independent research to avoid grantees marking their own homework

In the first part of this chapter we criticised the practice of asking grantees to evaluate themselves. So what should a Modern Grantmaker do instead?

Put simply, you need to commission independent evaluations of any significant grants that you make. More specifically, you need to commission evaluations of the work that you care about, which should be carried out by research specialists who can choose and apply the relevant research methods. And you need to commission evaluations that ask the *right* questions – questions whose answers may contain the sort of information that real people can use to make real decisions that have real consequences.

Now you might be thinking, 'But I just can't – my organisation doesn't do this, and I don't have the authority.' We do understand if you are in this position. Take a look at research tip no. 2 above or Chapter 9, in which we talk about persuading your colleagues.

If you do eventually get permission and the budget to commission this sort of evaluative research, here's what we suggest you do:

1 Be clear with new grantseekers that independent evaluation is how your organisation does research. It isn't fair or polite to spring something this significant on a grantee after you've made a funding offer. Your guidance will need to be revised to explain clearly that you prefer and will pay for independent evaluations, and why you don't do the kind of self-evaluation they might be more familiar with.

2 Find and contract a suitable researcher or research team that has the right skills to evaluate the work of a grantee. If you are new to this, one of the best things you can do here is to approach funding organisations that are already heavily research-centric. As your peers, they are likely to listen to you and to point you to people they trust. This may also be a good moment to talk to people from the research repositories named above, who often have considerable experience of vetting prospective researchers and who will probably leap at the chance to do a prospective funder a favour.

3 Finally, after you have built a relationship with a reliable research contractor, you need to introduce them to the grantees. They need to build relationships so that they can jointly design a research project that doesn't destroy the grantee's ability to do their normal work, while also producing meaningful results. This will be a process of negotiation and mutual learning: it may take some time.

Conducting research in this way is more bureaucratically complicated for funders than just dumping the work of monitoring and evaluation entirely on the grantee. It will be a learning curve, and there are likely to be some bumps in the road.

For grantees, working with an independent evaluator will be more of a mixed bag – sometimes the presence of a researcher will increase their workload, and sometimes it will decrease it as some of the reporting burden is shared.

As always, when you are trying something new and tricky, one of the oldest pieces of advice is still best: reach out to other grantmakers and grantees who have been there before and ask them to talk to you about their experiences.

> ## The value of cultivating a network of friendly researchers
>
> We've talked a lot in this chapter about the need to contract or employ professional researchers. But this sort of formal relationship with research professionals isn't the only kind of interaction you should aim to have with academics and other research specialists.
>
> Grantmakers work in many areas where there will be researchers who are already specialists in that domain. These individuals will often be surprised or delighted to find that you are investing in their area, and that you'd like to read their research or get their views on issues related to funding proposals.
>
> You should, of course, be careful not to use your aura of funder power to intimidate researchers into working for you for nothing. But often research professionals will be excited to know that they can help inform funding decisions.

Research tip no. 5: Agree rules of thumb for when grantmakers at your organisation should and shouldn't commission research

It may seem strange that we would ever advocate for grantmakers to not commission useful research, but there are a few situations in which engaging in research is actually not such a great idea:

- where grants are very small and the cost of doing research is disproportionately high ($500 for a community street party probably does not justify $10,000 in researcher fees);
- where the output is entirely artistic, such as a book, film or play;
- where the impact of an initiative is almost impossible to disentangle from other causes, for example the impact of a single grant on a mass social movement.

In the last case (giving money to influence social change) it is probably still worth doing a little monitoring, simply to see if the money is being spent at all. However, as we explained in the first part of the chapter, monitoring of this sort will not help you to really understand the impact of a grant. But, in the case of a $2,000 grant made to support a century-long social struggle, asking for evidence of impact is simply unrealistic, and you shouldn't waste the time of busy campaigners to ask for something they cannot possibly deliver.

In general, you may want to hold off commissioning new research when you think there's a chance that the findings simply won't matter to anyone and won't be used to make any better decisions in future. As we were told by Mary Ann Bates, an executive director at the anti-poverty research goliath J-PAL:

> You should do a rigorous causal impact evaluation when you're going to learn something new. Very often you're not working at a size or in a context where you will learn anything. So instead of producing a not-useful study, you should step back and ask 'Where can I learn what I need to know?'[258]

This is a great piece of advice, and one that you should think about whenever you see signs that your employer is about to pay for research to be produced that might not actually be of any use to anyone.

Research tip no. 6: Ensure that your research practices are ethical and inclusive

To find out whether a grantee has succeeded in meeting a goal or ambition, it is often necessary to talk to or to study the people served by that organisation. So, for example, to find out whether a youth employment nonprofit is helping young people get jobs, you need to learn about the young people it serves. This means that, as you work with grantees and professional researchers to figure out how grants will be evaluated, you will be engaged in the design of research activities that will impact on people's lives. Research that impacts on people's lives can both harm and benefit those people.

As a Modern Grantmaker you need to know when and how to consider the ethical implications of research that you may be about to commission. The best way to develop these skills is not by reading this book – it's much too big a topic to fit into a few pages. But, happily, there are lots of good and often free courses out there, such as 'Introduction to Research Ethics: Working with People' from the University of Leeds, offered via the FutureLearn website.[259]

There is no bar exam that will tell you that someone is qualified as an ethical researcher, but the signs that a researcher is familiar with research ethics include a proven record of engagement with institutional review boards (IRBs) or independent ethics committees, an understanding of the Common Rule (a US baseline standard of ethics in research) and evidence of having taken specific research ethics modules or courses. If you have taken a course or read a book on research ethics, you'll be better placed to ask probing questions when the time comes to appoint a researcher.

Ultimately, an experienced researcher with ethics training will be able to identify ethically problematic research ideas or practices that you probably wouldn't be able to spot without their help. This is just another reason why it is so important to push your organisational leadership to give you access to researchers if you don't already have it. Specialists will also be able to suggest measures you can take to ensure that the research you fund complies with appropriate ethical standards, such as putting in place a formal ethics panel in situations where that is appropriate.

But there are some research ethics problems for which you should be on the lookout yourself and be able to spot without extensive training. Here are a few:

- Be aware of commissioning impact evaluations that may require non-trivial amounts of time from participants who simply do not have the time to give you. In such cases you should strongly consider paying people for their time instead of expecting them to give you their time for nothing.

- Consider carefully whether any data being gathered may be sensitive and, if it is, triple check that it is really necessary to ask such questions.

- Check to see if the people being studied might feel that they have to answer questions or share information in order to receive some kind of important service (e.g. health care). If this is their perception, think carefully about whether it is ethical to impose this kind of transactional relationship on the people being served by the grantee.

Research ethics isn't just about preventing direct harms to the people being studied. There's also a category of problems relating to systematic bias and inequality. In his book *Decolonizing Wealth* Edgar Villanueva shares one example, quoting an anonymous grantmaker:

> We had to hire a consulting firm the last six months just to do a full scan of [the field], just to bring it back to my boss and to his boss to say everything that I've been saying for the last year. Literally the report is verbatim all of the stuff I had brought up, but no one heard it, or it wasn't given the same weight without having some sort of outside external person who was paid a lot of money to say it and put it nice and neatly down on paper. That's the game we're forced to play.[260]

This is an example of research methods being inconsistently applied to scrutinise the words of some groups of people while the testimony of other groups is simply presumed to be true. In a non-discriminatory funder, every person's testimony, whoever they are, should be treated with respect, as well as meriting scrutiny and verification.

Another related ethical problem is *extractive research*. This is what happens when researchers study a community, extract knowledge from it and then disappear to claim their PhDs and grants, leaving the people who gave them the knowledge with nothing much in return.

How should I make use of research?

It is possible to do better. One way of doing better is by helping communities to make use of research to understand the strengths and weaknesses of their own key social institutions – schools, nonprofits and so on. You can do this by helping organisations and groups that have not previously had the capacity to study or measure the work they do to benefit from the illumination that real research can provide. Funders can help here by providing both money and access to respectful and open-minded researchers with whom a community can work.

This type of participatory research into the effectiveness of key institutions is useful. It can help communities to focus their efforts on what's working and to stop doing what isn't working. Perhaps even more significantly, the production of such research may persuade governments to make policy changes or spend money that they simply wouldn't do without evidence. This kind of research can be genuinely empowering.

However, it won't be of any value at all if it isn't truly co-produced by the people and the organisations being studied. Research won't solve real problems if the people who are supposed to benefit from it aren't involved in working out what is to be studied and why. And if research is done *to* a community it just looks like more extractive research under a new guise. So if you, as a funder, want to gift this kind of research to a community, make sure it's research that the recipients are fully aware of and have bought into.

Finally, we think that research should never be seen as being in tension with equity. Ethically conducted and inclusive research into questions that really matter to communities can be an asset for people pushing for a more equitable world.

While the choice of research methods deployed in a particular research project should always ultimately be endorsed by a trained researcher, we think it is helpful to share one model of research practice that embodies the principles set out in the last few pages.

The Equitable Evaluation Framework

Imagine for a moment that you are a grantmaker who is worried that your organisation's current way of evaluating grantees is problematic, or even discriminatory. For example, you may suspect that current ways of commissioning or using research aren't fair or don't bring the right voices into the conversation.

What can you actually do?

This problem has been tackled head-on by the Equitable Evaluation Initiative (**equitableeval.org**).[261] It was founded by people from different parts of the US nonprofit sector to 'explore the ways in which foundations were both conceptualizing and using evaluation to advance equity'.

Together they developed three clear principles that can inform anyone working on a nonprofit evaluation:

> *Evaluation work is in service of and contributes to equity*: Production, consumption, and management of evaluation and evaluative work should hold at its core a responsibility to advance progress towards equity.

> *Evaluative work should be designed and implemented in a way that is commensurate with the values underlying equity work*: It should be multi-culturally valid and oriented toward participant ownership.

> *Evaluative work can and should answer critical questions* about the effect of a strategy on different populations and on the underlying systemic drivers of inequity, and the ways in which history and cultural context are tangled up in the structural conditions and the change initiative itself.

A focused conversation with colleagues or grantees, working through these points, will almost certainly help to identify weaknesses in current evaluations, or be of value in the design of new and forthcoming evaluations.

How should I make use of research?

Research tip no. 7: Develop your dodgy research detection skills and learn when to call in the experts

Let's imagine that you've done some digging and you've found a research study that looks like it will help you to decide on a funding proposal. To be more precise, let's imagine that the proposal you're considering is to fund family planning clinics, using a particular intervention, in the city where your organisation makes most of its grants.

The research report you have found says that the type of intervention outlined in the funding proposal is effective in helping prevent underage pregnancies. So, at first glance, things are looking promising. At this point the key question for you as a grantmaker is whether you should trust the study you have found. And, even if the intervention worked in one place at one time, how will you know if it will work in the place you care about now?

In an ideal world you would just trust the research you have found. But you can't. Some research is excellent and robust, and you'd be a fool to ignore what it tells you. Some research is valid for certain but not all circumstances. And some research is just of low quality and irredeemably untrustworthy.

So what can a busy grantmaker who isn't also a full-time researcher do? Well, if we all had infinite time and resources, we'd become deep research experts in the areas where we make grants. We'd spend years poring over the evidence, gathering data that's missing and refining our understanding of research methods to a point where we can understand what every piece of data or evidence really means.

But in the real world we can't do this. By the time most of us become grantmakers, we will have left school or university and we're not going back full time. We've got dozens of other commitments, not just this one funding proposal. We have to learn on the job and we can't drop everything for months or years to become subject experts.

So, as we've said before, this is the moment to turn to your research colleague or research contractor – assuming that you have one (if not, see above) – and ask for their help.

However, while you will benefit enormously from the help of a professional, it doesn't mean that you can't do some crude quality assessment on your own. Here's a checklist you can deploy the next time you're staring at a piece of research, wondering if you should believe it.

Basic research quality detection skills 101

Welcome, students! In this extremely brief course, we're going to introduce you to some of the key concepts that will help you to become an amateur research quality detector.

These tips are aimed primarily at a grantmaker who is considering an outcome evaluation, typically of a social or medical intervention of some sort.

Quality test 1: Does the research study outcomes or outputs or neither?

The first thing to look for in a piece of research that you plan to really lean on is that it analyses and discusses what actually matters. As grantmakers we want our money to be useful and not wasted. We talk to each other about our desire to make a difference, to have an impact or perhaps to 'move the needle'. We want to get good stuff done.

An impact evaluation is useful when it tells us that someone somewhere has spent some money and created an impact of the kind we care about. It's also very useful when it tells us that someone has spent money pursuing a goal but has failed. Don't be negative or down at heart about a piece of research describing a grant or intervention that has failed – it's a great gift to the world as long as the knowledge is shared with people who can use it.

The problem with a lot of research produced within the grantmaking sector is that it doesn't tell us anything about the impact as a result of the money being spent. This is primarily because a lot of studies and 'reports' within the research field measure outputs rather than outcomes.

We explained the difference between these two similar-sounding words earlier in this chapter. Outputs are quantities of stuff and services, while outcomes are how the world has been changed. Your job in reading a piece of research is to ask yourself whether the study even tries to measure how the world has been changed or if it is just counting stuff and ticking boxes. If it is mainly a record of outputs, not outcomes, you can safely assume that you're not actually going to learn a lot about the true impact of a grant from reading this document.

Quality test 2: If the study is quantitative, was it big enough to draw meaningful conclusions from?

This test applies only to quantitative studies, ones that claim that a numerical analysis of data provides useful information.

Most quantitative impact evaluations study a number of intended beneficiaries of an initiative to see how they have been affected by a grant. Beneficiaries are not the people who work for or volunteer for a nonprofit, they're the people that a nonprofit serves. Because the social impact sector is so huge, beneficiaries could be almost anyone: a specific group of ex-offenders from a prison, a set of older people living alone or even a set of small businesses that have been the target of assistance. They are normally studied to answer some variant of the question 'Did the work being studied make a positive difference to these people?'

If a quantitative researcher gathers data on a small number of people or organisations, their findings are liable to distortion by outliers, people whose reported experiences are extreme – either very, very good or very, very bad. Responsible researchers try to study enough people so that they can determine who is representative of a typical beneficiary and who is an outlier.

Various statistical techniques are deployed to work out exactly how many people have to be studied so as to get clarity about what constitutes an outlier or a representative answer. This isn't the place to dive into those, but for the purposes of this test we suggest something very simple. If an analysis studied many tens of thousands of people it is likely to be more statistically robust than a study of just 10 people.

In contrast, qualitative research – which focuses on words and meanings rather than numbers – can be extremely valuable even when only a handful of people are studied. A deep qualitative study of just 10 people that is rich in stories and has been conducted by a sensitive researcher can create great value too. It just won't ever count as impact assessment.

The question of whether a study is big enough or of high enough quality is one that you will need some expert help to answer.

Quality test 3: Do you have any reason to suspect that the key data in the research study is skewed or biased?

Consider for a moment the simple research question 'How much are you enjoying this book right now?' The answer that just flashed through your mind is probably quite honest. After all, there's no pressure from any direction to think one thing or another.

Now imagine that we are standing in front of you with manic grins on our faces. 'DO YOU LIKE THE BOOK?', we cackle menacingly. The odds are that your answer will be distorted by this change of context.

While this thought experiment is obviously silly, you should always look at studies and ask the question, 'Is the evidence in this study biased or unrepresentative in some way?' You'll be surprised by how often it is quite easy to see reasons why the answers given by participants might not be truthful or might not represent the whole story.

In particular, one really common cause of bias in research studies is questions that ask people to assent to positive conclusions: 'Did you find service X helpful?' There's quite a lot of social pressure on people being asked this question to say yes, which will tend to bias the data and lead to false conclusions. We've seen this many times in many grantee reports to funders.

So you should look at any study you've been presented with for signs of skew or bias in the data. This is particularly important because the people commissioning studies into grant effectiveness are frequently not neutral. They very often face very strong incentives to commission research that will show that a programme has been a success. The chief source of bias in grantee research is, sadly, the need to look good to funders.

Stronger, better-quality studies will often tackle the issue of biased data head-on, often in the opening sections of their reporting. They will also detail the various steps they have taken to avoid bias. If you spot this kind of discussion in a report, it suggests that the authors did at least make some attempt to avoid ending up with distorted conclusions.

Quality test 4: Has the research been peer reviewed?

Peer review is a process academic journals use to ensure that papers are good quality by exposing them to analysis and criticism before they are selected for publication. In peer review a group of anonymous experts are asked to analyse and critique a paper that has been submitted to a journal. The purpose of this process is to try to ensure that research that is published in journals is robust and is not full of elementary mistakes.

Very few pieces of research directly produced by foundations or nonprofits will have been peer reviewed, so this is not something to look for in every paper. But if the research does say it is peer reviewed, it is a positive sign that should generally increase your trust in it. However, a huge number of retracted or subsequently disproven papers have also been peer reviewed, so do not mistake a modest plus for a cast-iron guarantee.

Quality test 5: Are there many other pieces of research that come to the same conclusion?

A crowd can be wrong, but if 20 papers all say that the same intervention has similar effects on the same kinds of people your confidence in the work can be higher than if just a single paper reports this finding.

Final caveat

This brief cheat-sheet contains the only roughest of rules of thumb for spotting poor-quality research. Doing research well is really hard, and even reports that look incredibly robust, are filled with data, have been written by eminent experts and have been peer reviewed can still be completely wrong.

The real lesson to take away from this cheat-sheet is that you can't and shouldn't cheat when it comes to using and producing research. You absolutely have to work with people who have real research skills and real research experience. Your goal is to be an informed consumer, not a pretend professor.

Research tip no. 8: Include the production of useful research in your overall grantmaking strategy

As you may well have found yourself, there are often significant gaps in the existing research literature that leave funders unable to base their decisions fully on solid evidence.

Funders have a duty to fill in these knowledge gaps. We use the big word 'duty' because, if we have the means to answer key questions and choose not to do so, we're actively choosing to be ignorant about really important matters. As the evidence-based grantmaking expert and director of Giving Evidence, Caroline Fiennes, told us, 'Where there are important gaps in the research then somebody needs to fill them. A necessary component of that is funding.'[262]

This isn't an absolute duty with no exceptions, of course: no funder has a duty to carry out a national census to compensate for the lack of official statistics. But, as a general rule, all funders should support the production of research that will help better grants to be made in future.

If you need any further convincing as to why funding key research is a smart and moral thing for grantmakers to do, check out the two case studies below.

Two stories about how funder-commissioned research influenced government spending

Magic Breakfast

The Education Endowment Foundation (EEF) is a UK-based foundation with a mission 'dedicated to breaking the link between family income and educational achievement'. It supports teachers and school leaders to use evidence of what works – and what doesn't – to improve educational outcomes, especially for disadvantaged children and young people. It is a significant funder of primary research and synthesis which it seeks to make understandable and useful to non-researchers.

As part of its work, the EEF funded the largest and most robust study, covering 106 schools, of school breakfast clubs in the UK. It tested the impact of a programme called Magic Breakfast, which was designed to ensure that children from lower-income families do not start the school day hungry.[263]

How should I make use of research?

The independent evaluation concluded that Magic Breakfast appeared to have clear benefits for pupils and made a positive, measurable difference to outcomes in their learning, attendance and behaviour. The findings were taken up by the UK government which, in response, dedicated £26 million to scaling up a national school breakfast programme to deliver morning clubs to 1,775 schools across the country, particularly in disadvantaged areas. This funding was far more than the EEF itself would have been able to allocate to expanding the service, and is a textbook example of a relatively modest funder investment unlocking a lot more public money.

Not Too Late

The Abdul Latif Jameel Poverty Action Lab (J-PAL) is a global research centre based in the US that works to reduce poverty by ensuring that policy is informed by scientific evidence. J-PAL-affiliated professors at the University of Chicago Urban Labs were funded by the Laura and John Arnold Foundation (now known as Arnold Ventures) to study an important question: if a child has fallen behind academically by middle school, is it possible for them to catch up again? For a long time there had been a grim consensus that it was too late by this point in a child's life, and that early schooling problems could never be compensated for.

The creators of the Not Too Late programme hypothesised that this might not be so.[264] They designed and carried out a randomised controlled trial in conjunction with Saga Education, an educational nonprofit. Through careful study, it showed that individualized math tutoring for 9th- and 10th-grade boys had profound effects on their academic achievement. Students on the programme learned an extra one to two years' worth of math in addition to what their peers learned in an academic year. Tutoring raised participants' average national percentile rank on 9th- and 10th-grade math exams by more than 20%, and their failure rates in math fell by more than 50%.

These positive and exciting findings led directly to significant grants from the Chan Zuckerberg Initiative, AmeriCorps, the Bill & Melinda Gates Foundation and others. Furthermore, they came to government attention: the New York City Mayor's Office decided to allocate $6 million over three years to implement the program in New York City public high schools and middle schools. All this funding – over $20 million in total – was unlocked as a direct consequence of the Laura and John Arnold Foundation's decision to take the risk in supporting the initial study.

Further reading

This book cannot give you a full grounding in research methods, but the following books will give you much more detail:

- *The Goldilocks Challenge: Right-Fit Evidence for the Social Sector* by Mary Kay Gugerty and Dean Karlan.

- *Research Ethics in the Real World: Euro-Western and Indigenous Perspectives* by Helen Kara.

- *It Ain't What You Give, It's the Way that You Give It: Making Charitable Donations that Get Results* by Caroline Fiennes.[265]

We also recommend checking out Candid (**candid.org**) and GrantCraft (**grantcraft.org**). Both websites have lots of publicly available information about funders commissioning and using research.

Next you'll find the checklist for this chapter to help you go over the main points.

Chapter 7 checklist

1. Does your organisation seek out relevant prior research whenever it faces grantmaking decisions or strategic choices?

....

2. Do you advocate internally for grantmakers at your organisation to have access to professional researchers?

....

3. Does your organisation help grantees to develop independent evaluations of their work, or does it ask grantees to essentially mark their own homework?

....

4. Do you check the research practices used in evaluations to make sure they're not unethical?

....

5. Are you familiar with a few basic research quality detection skills?

....

6. Does your organisation include the funding of useful research as part of your overall grantmaking strategy?

....

7. Do you feel that you personally have a network of research specialists in the domains where you make grants, with whom you can discuss key questions and the challenges you encounter?

....

8

HOW DO I MANAGE WELL BOTH UPWARDS AND DOWNWARDS?

> So much of what we call management consists in making it difficult for people to work.[266]
>
> — PETER DRUCKER, *The Practice of Management*

In this chapter we will share ideas on how to be a good manager and leader within a funding organisation. We'll also talk about how to manage upwards in terms of your board, and how to recruit new grantmakers into your organisation.

Wait? What was that? Did a little yawn just escape from your lips? Not in the mood for a meditation on the finer points of management theory?

We get it. Most people become grantmakers because they believe that getting money into the hands of important causes is a crucial and rewarding job. Very few people come into grantmaking because they are passionate about perfecting the art of people management.

For a lot of people who are driven by the goal of social impact, the very word 'management' is actively off-putting. The mere word itself can conjure up memories of feeling trapped in boring management meetings in soulless beige rooms, wondering when we can get back to doing our real jobs.

Good management – the kind that inclusively enables people to work to the best of their ability – often isn't greatly valued in funding organisations. Just take a moment to consider how often your board asks tough questions about staff welfare compared to tough questions about grant proposals. Ponder this question for a moment and you'll probably see where management skills sit in your organisational priorities.

This really isn't surprising since the penalty for being a bad manager in grantmaking is very small compared to other kinds of professional organisations. The traditional costs of bad management in most businesses are poor-quality work, wasted money, staff complaints and industrial action, but all of these are *way* less likely to emerge as clearly identified problems in a funding organisation. The most likely consequence of really bad management within funders is talented staff quietly leaving to find other jobs, and the silent tragedy of brilliant, impactful grants that 'coulda been, shoulda been' but never were.

We don't blame most grantmakers who struggle with being good managers at the same time. As in many other aspects of their jobs, grantmakers are too often expected to somehow figure out how to be a good manager while vetting a never-ending stack of funding proposals and monitoring reports.

Yet the difference between a funding organisation with bad managers and one with skilled managers is night and day. A poorly managed funder has a much lower potential social impact than a well managed funder. As we have made clear throughout this book, good grantmaking is really hard, and nobody is likely to succeed if their working life is being made a misery by their own boss or if processes are just badly designed and carelessly run.

One thing that makes the current generation of grantmaking reformers different from waves of reform in the past is that they care more about how professionally and inclusively funders are run, and not just which organisations ultimately get given the money.

Bad management in funders also takes a human toll. Back in Chapter 3 we cited a 2018 survey undertaken by the Grant Givers' Movement in the UK which recorded more than 95 instances of prejudice or discrimination in trusts and foundations from only 130 respondents.[267] As well as being morally unacceptable, this sort of behaviour will lead to skilled staff with career options leaving and generally drive down the capacity of a funder to make the best possible choices.

There aren't many people who have written honestly about bad management in funders, so we want to give particular kudos to Edgar Villanueva for his book. As well as containing lots of immensely constructive advice, Villanueva frankly tells the stories of problematic and deeply hurtful management at more than one foundation. They are his own personal stories, so we're not going to quote them here – instead we suggest you read his account directly. But we did both nod in sympathy when he concluded, 'I am far from alone in having had these kinds of terrible experiences with the very people I would most have hoped to be supported by.'[268]

A quick word on 'management' and 'leadership'

The two words 'management' and 'leadership' are often used interchangeably to mean 'being a boss'. In this chapter we've tried to be a bit more specific.

We use 'manager' to refer to a person who is responsible for individuals within a group or team that is responsible for performing a specific function within an organisation.

We use 'leader' to mean someone who inspires others to act or think differently. The leader may or may not also be a manager.

Got it? Great! Let's press on.

Can I skip this bit if I don't manage anyone else?

There are all sorts of good reasons why you may feel that you personally don't need to develop your management skills. It may be because you work for a small funder where you are the only paid staff member or you hold a position that doesn't involve having line management responsibility for anyone else. Even in such cases – where you don't have people reporting directly to you – there are still a host of reasons why it would be helpful for you to know the basics of good management, for example:

- To be effective at your own job as a professional grantmaker, you need to know whether or not you or your colleagues are being well managed or led. If you can't perceive or analyse weak management, you won't be able to help your organisation to improve, and you're in danger of repeating bad habits when you assume management responsibilities at a later date.

- Life is unpredictable, and you could easily find yourself working in a new job for a new funder where you will have management responsibilities. If you are given such a role, the people you manage will be less than sympathetic and forgiving if they find out that you're only beginning to learn the basics of people management on their watch.

- Every grantmaker needs to be good at managing upwards, i.e. managing their bosses or their board, or perhaps even managing the principal donors themselves. This is a kind of management, even if it doesn't immediately seem like it! (See below for our specific guidance on this.)

So that's why we think it is worthwhile to learn more about good and bad management, even if you're not anyone else's boss today.

What does a good manager look like in a funding organisation?

First, we need to present a trio of Everest-sized caveats about what we're about to tell you. Teaching management techniques isn't like teaching mathematics. Nearly every piece of advice about management can be hedged or even contradicted by some other piece of advice. That's because management is fundamentally about working with and getting the most out of people, and people are gloriously, infuriatingly unpredictable. As the philosopher Immanuel Kant put it, 'Out of the crooked timber of humanity, no straight thing was ever made.'[269]

Second, a lot of management advice that can be picked up in airport bookstores isn't necessarily helpful. Classic macho, alpha 'leading from the front' can be problematic in grantmaking.[270] As John Palfrey, President of the John D. and Catherine T. MacArthur Foundation, told us, 'It is super-important to approach the work with a humility that might not serve, say, the leader of a big city, or the CEO of a big company.'[271]

Third, we are aware that all management advice is very much culturally situated. So, for example, management norms in countries and communities with consensus-based cultures are going to be very different from those in countries where more individualistic behaviour is rewarded.

So, with these caveats in mind, let's actually set out some good practice. We interviewed a large number of grantmakers and asked them what they thought good managers within funding organisations should do, and they told us that good managers should:

- *Encourage awareness of the power problem within teams*: Managers of grantmakers should regularly remind their team members of the power imbalance that exists between them and grantseekers. As one foundation CEO told us, 'As a manager you have a responsibility to make sure people manage their own egos and remember they're in the service business.'[272]

- *Show trust*: The very structure of a traditional funder can perpetuate mistrust between junior staff, who source funding proposals, and those at senior or board level, who approve them. A good grantmaking manager compensates for this by showing real trust in the grantmakers they support.[273] As one interviewee put it, 'A good manager shows an active interest in the work of her direct reports but defers to them as subject-matter experts.'[274]

- *Demonstrate an active commitment to equity, diversity and inclusion:*[275] As one experienced grantmaker put it, 'What is it to be a good leader in grantmaking these days? Maybe the primary thing I would say is to pursue a commitment to diversifying the staff.'[276] Good managers will treat equity, diversity and inclusion as a long-term project and will not accept tokenistic gestures. For a useful perspective on equity and funding organisations, we recommend Kris Putnam-Walkerly and Elizabeth Russell's article, 'What the Heck Does "Equity" Mean?' in *Stanford Social Innovation Review*, October 2020.[277]

- *Encourage learning and the evolving of beliefs*: A good grantmaking manager will be constantly seeking to learn the ways in which they were previously wrong or misguided. They will then bring that desire to learn and improve to their teams, actively encouraging colleagues to share mistakes in a safe environment rather than sweep them under the carpet. A good grantmaking manager will also often say things such as 'I used to believe that, but then the evidence showed me I was wrong', as a way of modelling good practice in front of their teams.

- *Be a critical friend*: You can fail as a manager of grantmakers by giving too much negative feedback or by giving none at all. The perfect balance is being the critical friend, who, in the words of one senior foundation manager, 'balances being really supportive and enthusiastic about the underlying work with not shying away from the difficult conversations about what's going well and what's not'.[278]

- *Be a coach, not a micromanager*: One thing that can challenge grantmakers who are promoted to management positions is the tension between the new skills they need to deploy and the skills they were originally hired for. In the words of one anonymous grantmaker we interviewed, 'When you hire people to pore over detail and make judgements, and then elevate them into management without training, it's inevitable that detail and judgement will become the default for their managing style.'[279] Good funder managers give their grantmakers space and encouragement, and won't micromanage their every move. You should ensure that you talk to the people who report to you about how they prioritise their time, asking them questions about how they do this rather than telling them exactly what to do.

- *Live up to the values*: Managers should clearly live by the values that a funding organisation claims are important. As one senior grantmaker told us:

'As a manager in grantmaking it's really important to remind your team of the values that underpin the organisation – you should also be the person that calls colleagues to account if those values aren't being met.'[280]

It's also important to have integrity and to be someone whom people want to follow. One grantmaker praised their manager for 'identifying with and expressing moral values without taking herself too seriously'.[281]

What are some good management no-brainers?

Good management no-brainer no. 1: Schedule regular team meetings and one-to-one catch-ups

One of the most basic steps you can take to be a good manager of grantmakers is to make sure that you have regular team meetings – with a clear set purpose – and individual catch-ups in your calendar. Scheduling these as recurring events and trying to avoid too many cancellations or postponements is one of the most basic building blocks to having a well-managed, happy and productive team.

It's very important that these regular meetings and catch-ups have a predictable structure and agenda that you use every time. This means that you won't forget to ask crucial quality-of-life questions (e.g. 'How do you feel about your job?') and it will help your colleagues to understand what the meetings are for and how they need to prepare for them. You can also use the meetings as a tool for making sure that a grantmaker is clearly aware of their own objectives, and that their work is aligned to them. One way of doing this is to encourage the use of a personal development plan (see Chapter 9 for more on these).

Good management no-brainer no. 2: Ask others regularly and openly for their input into your decisions

This is a simple one. One of the key tasks of being a manager is to make decisions. When you do this, you should always try to take soundings from others who may have useful contributions to make. Small steps like making two-way debriefs common practice after key meetings can help to normalise the sharing of ideas and the giving of feedback.

Some bad managers confuse the authority they have with the idea that they do not need to listen to others or to study the evidence. Don't be that person. Whenever you think someone else may have something valuable to add to a decision, involve them. You'll rarely regret it, and your colleagues will value your inclusiveness immensely.

Good management no-brainer no. 3: Give your team members incentives that align with impact

If you manage grantmakers within a mission-driven funding organisation, your deepest desire is probably for those team members to help your organisation to make grants that achieve that mission. Unfortunately, grantmaking is a strange business full of unintended consequences. This can lead to bad incentives in grantmaking that are actually opposed to the mission of your organisation, for example:

- If you tell grantmakers that they must disperse at least, say, $1 million within a tight time frame, their incentive will be to make a relatively small number of relatively big grants to the 'usual suspects', which won't require much background research.

- If you put in place lots of anti-fraud checks, you may incentivise grantmakers to pursue applications that favour incorporated organisations with constituted boards and offices – characteristics that some grantseekers simply don't have.

Good grantmaking managers need to be acutely aware that it is very easy to introduce perverse incentives like this. Here are some practical steps you can take to make sure that your grantmakers are nudged towards doing the right things, not the wrong things:

- Ensure that your team and everyone in it regularly and collectively reviews progress against team goals and how you are contributing to the overall mission, strategy and objectives of your organisation. This will keep people's eyes on the prize.

- Constantly survey your grantmakers' work environment for processes and technology that cause pain and irritation, like a slow and infuriating funding management system. Where such problems occur, team members will be motivated to choose and process grant applications that minimise their own personal pain rather than making the right choices. Don't make ticking the right box more tempting than making the right grant.

- Work consciously to create psychological safety within your team.[282] This means encouraging an environment in which people can openly share doubts and fears they have about decisions that are being made. *This includes you.* You need to show vulnerability sometimes if you expect others to do so.

A psychologically safe team is, in short, one in which people feel comfortable discussing issues and concerns. The concept was developed by Amy Edmondson, a professor at Harvard Business School, back in the 1990s. Psychological safety isn't about being 'nice', she says. It's about giving candid feedback, openly admitting mistakes and learning from each other.

Good management no-brainer no. 4: Be an inclusive leader of diverse teams

Grantmaking has a history of being dominated generally by privileged, highly educated, white people (see Chapter 3). As a grantmaking manager, you will have the ability to influence whether your organisation and team look and behave like the society it serves or more like a golf club from the 1950s.

It will be much easier for a funder to succeed if it is made up of diverse, confident staff who are more effective at talking to people from different communities, vetting and interpreting their bids, and giving them support when they need it. It will also be more effective as a funder, as your diverse workforce swaps skills and life lessons to make sure that everyone gets better at their job.

This means being guided by various values and activities, such as humility, awareness of your own biases, curiosity about others and a desire to make a visible commitment to diversity. Below we list specific steps you should consider taking with your current team, including some suggestions that Juliet Bourke and Andrea Titus shared in their article 'The Key to Inclusive Leadership',[283] published in the *Harvard Business Review* in March 2020:

- *Acknowledge and reward work to improve diversity, inclusion and equitable practices*: There's nothing more demotivating for a colleague than for them to make an attempt to improve the inclusiveness of a workplace and then be shot down by their senior colleagues. So encourage this kind of innovation while being prepared to create the space and psychological safety required to nurture this kind of activity.

- *Ensure that team events are inclusive*: Be sensitive to the fact that different people have different constraints on how and where they bond or socialise. Some people don't drink, while others have childcare obligations. Think carefully and ask before you schedule events that people are obliged to come to.

- *Work in the open*: Run daily, weekly or fortnightly 'stand-ups' where your team gets together to review individual and team progress against goals, and to discuss whether anything is stopping them from moving forwards. For more on how to run these types of sessions, we suggest checking out the UK government's 'Agile Tools and Techniques'.[284]

- *Value collaboration over hierarchy*: Coach the team and run meetings in ways that encourage collaboration and give space to all members rather than prioritising your own or more senior members' views.

If you're wondering if there are ways you can build your own skills in relation to these issues, please check out Chapter 9 where we describe some of the courses and training you might go on.

Good management no-brainer no. 5: Build effective feedback loops and peer reviews across the team

> It is a sector with no accountability model. There's absolutely no feedback loops.[285]
>
> — ANNA DE PULFORD, director of the Dulverton Trust

One of the reasons why funding organisations can seem slow or poor at improving working practices is that they are terrific places to hide or bury mistakes. Unlike a high-profile government agency where a bad mistake might be followed by an investigation or an inquiry, bad grants or bad handling of grantees can often be made to vanish quietly, with the help of the sheer power that comes with control over a lot of money.

As a manager, you will have to listen and build feedback loops if you want your team to get any feedback on its actions. What does this mean in practice? Well, here are some key steps you can take:

- *Organise team peer reviews with other teams*: If your organisation is large enough to have more than one team, you can arrange sessions in which your peers give you honest assessment and feedback on your impact and your ways of working.

- *Collect anonymous feedback*: Many people feel shy about giving bad feedback to or criticising others, and this is especially acute in professional grantmaking, given its wild power imbalances. So take steps to enable people both outside and inside your organisation to give you feedback about your decisions and ways of working. See Chapter 6 for more on how to do this effectively.

- *Work with researchers*: As we describe in detail in Chapter 7, good grantmakers should have a healthy relationship with research and researchers. As a team you should be regularly discussing research findings that relate to projects you have commissioned, especially with the people who did the research in the first place.

Good management no-brainer no. 6: Reflect on grantmaking decisions routinely

In other sectors such as social care it is expected that team members will review each case relating to an individual they are supporting with their line manager or a dedicated practice expert on a regular basis and receive feedback on their performance. These meetings also serve to show whether any changes should be made in the wider organisation, in light of new evidence raised.

Applying a broadly similar model, reviewing grant decisions will give grantmaking colleagues the space and time to share their knowledge and best practice. It will also make a space to discuss 'edge cases' or innovative grants that push your risk appetite or usual ways of working.

Can the five values behind Modern Grantmaking help me be a better manager?

In Chapter 1 we introduced five values that we think underpin the wider reform movement we see taking place across grantmaking. These are:

- humility
- equity
- evidence
- service
- diligence.

Consider these and then glance back at the advice in the previous section, and you'll see that they overlap closely. For example, encouraging awareness of the problem of power imbalance is clearly closely connected to humility. Living up to your organisation's purported values is about diligence. Encouraging learning is clearly about evidence.

So, if you are stuck with a particular management dilemma and you're wondering what to do, we suggest pulling up these five values and seeing if they help you to work out the right choice.

Is there any specific management advice for funder CEOs?

This book is not specifically for the CEOs or executive directors of grantmaking organisations, although we believe there's plenty here that will be useful to people doing these jobs.

One person who has looked directly at this most critical of roles is Fay Twersky, who was vice president of the William and Flora Hewlett Foundation. In 2016 she conducted research into 'what it takes to successfully lead a philanthropic organization', published free online as the report *Foundation Chief Executives as Artful Jugglers*.[286]

Her study was based on interviewing a sample of current and retired CEOs, and those who work with them, from a range of funders – mostly independent and family foundations – but also including CEOs from community and corporate foundations.

The lessons that emerged clustered around three essential elements of the foundation CEO's role:

- *Engaging the board*: This means a range of skills including being adept at discerning donor intent and values, facilitating alignment between boards and the work of the foundation, and fundamentally making sure that everyone gets on with everyone else.

- *Cultivating a healthy organisation:* As Twersky puts it:

    If you want to provide first-rate service to your customers, you have to treat your employees in a first-rate fashion. Successful CEOs recognize that foundation culture functions the same way. A foundation cannot have strong, trusting, productive grantee relationships without having strong, trusting, productive staff relationships.

- *Achieving impact*: This is where the rubber hits the road. Foundation CEOs are ultimately responsible for the impact that their organisations create. This means they're fundamentally responsible for the components of this impact: knowledge, strategy, responsiveness to change and ultimately leadership that models 'behaviours of compassion and generosity'.

Twersky's report is short, clear and full of interesting insights from current US foundation leaders. We strongly recommend taking a look at it especially if you're in the top job or thinking seriously about it.

What are the traits of a bad leader or manager of grantmakers?

> I came across one large US foundation that had various international branch offices. It turned out that a previous CEO of that funder had never visited them! That is really bad leadership.[287]
>
> — ANONYMOUS EXECUTIVE DIRECTOR of foundation

Sometimes there's only so much a person can learn about management and leadership by studying what good looks like. Sometimes the quickest and most useful way to learn it is to get down in the muck.

Let's start our journey into the depths with a game. We call this Bad Boss Bingo. All 11 characteristics in it are taken directly from the fun and bluntly named book *Why CEOs Fail: The 11 Behaviors that Can Derail Your Climb to the Top – and How to Manage Them* by David L. Dotlich and Peter C. Cairo.[288] All we have done here is put them into a grid (below) – we think this is a great set, albeit perhaps one that needs a trigger warning!

Arrogance	Melodrama	Volatility
You're right and everybody else is wrong	You always grab the center of attention	Your mood shifts are sudden and unpredictable
Excessive caution	**Habitual distrust**	**Aloofness**
The next decision may be your first	You focus on the negatives	You disengage and disconnect
Mischievousness	**Eccentricity**	**Passive resistance**
You know that rules are only suggestions	It's fun to be different just for the sake of it	Your silence is misinterpreted as agreement

Once you've considered all the squares, pause for a minute or two and consider how each one matches up against any of the less than *world-class* leaders you might have come across in your time in grantmaking. Note that this is a serious and scientific exercise – any cathartic enjoyment you derive from it is nothing to do with us.

How do I manage well both upwards and downwards?

If you are trying to be a good manager yourself, it is very important that you learn about common grantmaker management mistakes so that you can avoid them as much as possible. The next section deals with a few of the key ones.

Are there specific mistakes I should try to avoid as a manager of other grantmakers?

There are a lot of management mistakes that are not specific to grantmaking, such as being secretive and controlling, micromanaging and failing to give praise and recognition to people on a regular basis. Because this kind of advice is readily available, we're keeping our mistakes to ones that are specific to the business of being a Modern Grantmaker.[289]

Mistakes to avoid no. 1: Ignoring poor performance

Evaluating staff performance within funding organisations is much harder than in a regular business. This is because you can't easily ask whether they made enough widgets per hour or sold enough stuff. As one anonymous senior manager at a US foundation said to us, 'This makes for challenges in managing people who have performance issues, because you can't say something clear like "You didn't make your quota."'[290]

But bad performance by grantmakers is a real thing, and the harms that come from it can be immense. As a young nonprofit founder, one of your authors once lost 10 months of his life waiting for a grantmaker to transfer the money for a start-up grant that had been awarded and was then sloppily not executed. We wonder how many other nonprofits had their impact undermined by that one grantmaker and whether they were ever held to account.

The lack of hard numbers about performance, together with most people's aversion to having difficult conversations, means that funding organisations can – in the worst cases – become Petri dishes for breeding poor performance.

As a grantmaking manager you should be hyper-aware that a single underperforming or incompetent grantmaker can wreak havoc for hundreds or thousands of people you will never meet. So make sure that you have the tools for identifying and understanding poor performance and for resolving the problem. Grantees desperately need you to do this for them, even if it can be difficult at times.

Mistakes to avoid no. 2: Ignoring super-slow staff turnover

Grantmaking is a field where people often stay in the same jobs for an extremely long time. There are organisations in which twentieth and twenty-fifth anniversaries of employment are not that uncommon.

When we see these anniversaries we can comfort ourselves that this is because we are an organisation so uniquely blessed with talent that the best people want to stay with us for ever. But the truth is that grantmaking can be a comfortable life for people who aren't looking to challenge themselves. And even the very best people can go off the boil if they are not challenged and refreshed every now and then. Slow turnover and super-long tenure can therefore lead to a lack of engagement and a sense of 'phoning it in' or, worse, an intransigence and unwillingness to adapt to changes in the world and related new ways of working.

We like and admire the way in which the William and Flora Hewlett Foundation has put a cap of eight years on how long grantmakers can stay in the same role. It's smart and balances 'too long' against the danger of 'too short'. We would encourage every funder board in the world to discuss this HR policy idea at least once.

So, in short, be sure to talk regularly to your team about what they'll do next and how their careers will keep evolving beyond their current roles.

Mistakes to avoid no. 3: Not being authentic and open

New managers who lack self-confidence are in danger of thinking that any sign of weakness will undermine their authority.[291] This can manifest itself in behaviours that include micromanagement, secretiveness and a general denial of their own humanity. For example, one grantmaker we interviewed talked about how their CEO kicked their leg under the table when they tried to share an important mistake and lesson learned with their board.

A façade of invulnerability creates unnecessary distance and breeds resentment between colleagues. To avoid this mistake, take steps to build trust with your team. Show them that you understand that your role is to support them to do their job as well as they can, not to do it for them. For example, you should regularly ask your team members how you can help them do their jobs better – rather than always asking what they can do for you. You could also be honest about which of your skills or weaknesses you're working to improve, to show clearly that you don't think you've got all the answers.

Mistakes to avoid no. 4: Not giving recognition

Recognition and praise cost nothing, and yet are worth everything. There are various simple steps you can take to offer recognition, such as:

- When colleagues give you (as a manager) praise or credit for work done by your team members, correct them politely but clearly and tell them who did the actual work.

- Never have a team meeting or gathering of any kind in which you don't celebrate the work of at least a couple of your named colleagues.

- Raise others up when they do well and, no matter what, don't steal other people's glory.

Mistakes to avoid no. 5: Forgetting that you have to manage both downwards and upwards

Being a manager in a grantmaking organisation is often a busy life. It's easy to become fixated on just one problem – the problematic grant that haunts your dreams. If you can't balance your time between managing both downwards and upwards, people around you will soon become frustrated. Try to carve out and protect your time so that you don't end up facing just one way.

How do I manage upwards to a board or a founding donor?

Knowing how to manage your own bosses is part of any job. But it's unusually important in grantmaking organisations because the bosses are very often the board members who actually make the final grantmaking decisions. This makes the boards of funders much more like regular staff than the board members of an ordinary business, where the board will only very rarely make direct operational decisions, generally allowing the CEO and team to make most day-to-day decisions. In most funders the board is very active, not just in setting direction but in making the most critical decisions about who gets money and who doesn't.

Here are our top tips for managing upwards, garnered from interviewing a range of people who have been doing this for a long time:

- *Get to know board members well*: The single most frequently cited piece of advice we heard was the importance of simply getting to know your board members or your founding donor well enough. At a practical level this means making sure that you have allowed plenty of time to nurture the relationship. You should also spend time talking to them outside the formal constraints of a board meeting itself.

- *Use your strategy document as a lever*: In conversations with your board members, you should refer regularly and repeatedly to the strategy and mission to which you have all signed up. Reminding them of its existence and of the commitments it contains can be a way of avoiding conflict and resolving dilemmas without your ever having to say, 'I think you're wrong.' If your organisation doesn't have a good strategy that everyone is signed up to, go to Chapter 4 to find out how to develop one.

- *Consider a chair's fund*: Some grantmaking teams suffer because they want to have a clear strategy and to deliver on it, but their board members keep meeting new people and recommending brand new ideas. In an ideal world you'd explain why it's important to stick to a strategy, but this isn't always going to wash. So, as we suggested in

Chapter 4, consider advocating for a ring-fenced chair's fund which can be used to pay for unexpected initiatives. This shielding mechanism can help keep other, more strategic, priorities on track.

- *Keep the conversation two-way*: Try to relate to your board members as professional peers, constantly asking for feedback and giving feedback. If you resist being framed as a 'junior partner', you are more likely to be respected.

- *Watch like a hawk for divergent motivations*: It is extremely likely that at some point your board's wants and needs will be different from the wants and needs of the team of professional grantmakers within your funding organisation. Keep a constant eye out for this, and when you see it happening try to discuss ways of bringing the groups back together before any significant conflicts occur.

- *Remind boards regularly that site visits are not the whole truth*: One thing that funder board members most like to do is go on trips to see the projects, people and organisations that their money is supporting. As a responsible funder you should work to develop your board's evidence comprehension skills so that they can understand the difference between a heartfelt story and measured evidence of impact. You should also make sure that everyone is very clear about the concept of opportunity costs – the cost and impact of a project not done or not funded.

- *Set up a programme of skills development sessions for board members*: If a board or board member has a weakness in some critical skill or issue, it's not reasonable to expect that they'll just improve on their own – they won't. So consider suggesting to your board members that you co-design and then have professionally delivered a programme of ongoing skills development for the board itself, focusing on areas of mutual priority.

How do I go about hiring new grantmakers?

> Going from school to university into grantmaking – I don't know if that's the right way of doing it. I don't mean that as a criticism of anyone who's done it but I think there's something about working in a situation where you're trying to help folk going through difficult times or working in a community centre that just gives you something additional.[292]
>
> — ANONYMOUS GRANTMAKER

If you are a manager or a leader in a funding organisation, it is likely that at some point you will have the task of hiring grantmaking staff. There were certainly times in our grantmaking lives when scheduling, arranging and conducting employment interviews felt like the only thing we were doing!

For this book we spoke with managers and chief executives of various funding organisations who have hired many hundreds of grantmakers between them. We asked them for specific lessons they wanted to share, and in the list below you'll find their top tips. We have also included some suggestions made by Tessa Ann Taylor in her article 'Diversity, Inclusion and Culture: How to Build Great Teams', published in *The New York Times*.[293]

Hiring tip no. 1: Communicate your funder's mission and strategy clearly to applicants

Some funders tend to be a little secretive about what they're really trying to do and what their priorities really are. This is a big problem with recruiting because it means that people will approach your organisation with a potentially wrong or distorted view of what you're about. So make sure that your job ads and interviews are really clear about what you're about.

Hiring tip no. 2: Ensure that your recruitment approach and materials are accessible and inclusive

If your online job application form is so old and clunky that it doesn't work with screen readers and other accessibility software, you will rarely receive applications from people with visual impairments. If you use gendered wording in your job advert – e.g. 'dominant' this and 'superior' that – you'll probably get more applications from men than from women.[294] There's lots of practical advice online about how to be inclusive in recruiting. Use this advice when you are running recruitment exercises, and if you're still not sure what to do, hire a specialist consultant.

You may also want to work with community leaders or connectors to help spread the word about any job opportunities, in addition to advertising these through the trade press and recruitment websites.

Hiring tip no. 3: State the salary range clearly and unambiguously

There are a growing number of people who feel that it is not acceptable to post job adverts that do not clearly state the salary level of a role. You should always state the salary range for any job in a funder, especially since the problematic connection between power and money runs deep in grantmaking.

Hiring tip no. 4: Implement anti-bias measures at the sifting and interview stages

As with hiring for any job, you'll need to put measures in place to ensure that candidates who don't look and sound like the interviewers have a good shot at getting it. We recommend reading '7 Practical Ways to Reduce Bias in Your Hiring Process' by Rebecca Knight in the *Harvard Business Review* and *Diversity, Equity and Inclusion: The Pillars of Stronger Foundation Practice*, published by the Association of Charitable Foundations in the UK.[295]

Hiring tip no. 5: Don't ask for a university degree unless it's essential

Not everyone has the same chance to go to university or to make it through to graduation successfully. While you doubtless want smart people in your organisation, consider not using a degree as a minimum qualification because people with incredible experience and skills may not have a degree, and you don't want to miss out.

Hiring tip no. 6: Watch out for candidates who want to be famous

Funders make a mark on the universe primarily by backing people and organisations that do great work. But sometimes it's tempting to think

Modern Grantmaking

that we don't need our partners, that we can be the solution and the star in every scene. As one foundation CEO told us, 'We've had one or two situations where people have drunk their own Kool-Aid – then it became important for them that they were recognised on the conference circuit, or sitting on august commissions, which took them away from their day jobs.'[296] So make sure that your prospective recruits aren't obsessed with their own reputation.

Hiring tip no. 7: Look for people with experience of working in organisations that have been on the receiving end of grant funding

It doesn't matter if a candidate is extremely highly educated: if they have never worked for a nonprofit or other social impact organisation their ability to really empathise with and understand grantees will be reduced. Hiring people who have worked for recipients of grant monies also means that you will gain insights into grantees, which is always very helpful when you have to make tricky decisions. This doesn't mean that you should never hire people from academia or business but, if your grantmaking team doesn't have anyone who knows what it's like to be on the other side of the funding relationship, the chances are you're going to make some massive mistakes.

So those are our tips on recruitment. But once you've made a job offer your obligations are not over. There is more to do. You should ensure that you:

- try to help your new colleague integrate into the organisation by carrying out *structured pairing*, where you carefully partner them with an existing colleague who is particularly suited to making the new employee feel welcome, and who can help them learn how to navigate their way around the organisation;

- let a new recruit know about staff groups and forums that are available such as LGBTQIA+ networks;

- make sure that grantmakers are directly exposed to any user testing and user research that is being done by colleagues working on the experience of grantseekers and grantees – this is vital to ensure that new recruits start to develop an empathy straight away.

So that winds up our chapter on managing well, both upwards and downwards. But what about managing yourself – keeping your own self on track? That's what's coming up in Chapter 9.

Chapter 8 checklist

1. Do you know your own strengths and weaknesses as a manager? Has this been informed by anonymous feedback?

....

2. Are you clear about the values that underpin your own approach to management?

....

3. Do you understand common bear traps when it comes to management and have a plan for how to keep avoiding them?

....

4. If you work with a board, have you taken the time to build the respectful peer relationships that you will need to succeed?

....

5. Do you regularly check and act to make sure that the power imbalance between funders and grantees isn't undermining the work of any team members?

....

6. Have you asked your team in the last couple of months if you have micromanaged them?

....

7. Have you taken an active step to deliver on your organisation's equity, diversity and inclusion plan in the last seven days (i.e. one that wasn't forced on you because of a crisis as a result of institutional failures)?

....

8. Have you talked about mistakes you've made at work with your own team within the last three months?

....

9. If there is underperformance in your team, do you feel confident about taking action?

....

9

HOW DO I KEEP DEVELOPING MY SKILLS?

> We've all seen that senior management person who never asks what they can do better. Don't be that person.[297]
>
> — ANONYMOUS GRANTMAKER

In most professions there are strong incentives to keep learning and to continue training. Grantmaking differs from other occupations in that external incentives for self-improvement are largely absent. It is not at all like aviation or medicine where there are regular checks to ensure that you are doing your job to the required standards. By contrast, as a grantmaker, you cannot be struck off for not meeting standards because there are no standards, and you cannot lose your licence because there are no licences.

The usual disciplining effect of market forces doesn't apply either. There's virtually no chance that bad work within a funder will lead to that organisation going bankrupt, as it would in most businesses. If your department 'loses' money every year – well, that's your job!

It is also quite unlikely that your board will ever fire you because you haven't worked hard enough to improve your grantmaking skills. They may fire you because they think you don't share their vision, because they don't like your 'attitude' or just because (in the words of one of our interviewees) 'it's Wednesday'. But what they're very unlikely to do is make a cool, calm, data-driven evaluation of your performance and skills and dismiss you on that basis.

Furthermore, you will not experience much pressure from your 'clients' to continually improve. Grantseekers and grantees have a multitude of reasons to keep quiet even if they think you're absolutely terrible at your job. They may well criticise and denounce you in private, but you're very unlikely to hear about it.

Why is a lack of good incentives a problem for Modern Grantmakers?

The grantmaking life can be horribly busy, especially if there's an emergency such as a pandemic. This means that it's extremely tempting to kick self-improvement plans down the road into the distant future so you can just focus on getting the job done for now. This may be noble, but over time it leads to grantmakers working very hard but not necessarily as effectively as they could. We all need to take time out to learn and improve if we're going to be the partners that our grantees deserve.

The lack of the right incentives also contributes to one of the dark secrets of the grantmaking sector – that, despite the number of people working their socks off, grantmaking can also be an ideal career for people who just want a quiet life and a reliable salary. You may be shocked by this, and you may only know grantmakers who work too hard for their own good, but our research interviews revealed a consensus that there are people within the grantmaking universe who exploit a lack of pressure and of board scrutiny to take life easy.

We should say that, if you do encounter someone like this, you shouldn't be too hasty to judge them. Given plenty of job security and a lack of pressure at work, we are all likely to find that, bit by bit, our efforts decline over time. When we see this happening we should blame the system, not the person.

So the lack of pressure to improve is real and is a genuine problem for all of us. But what can you do about it?

How can I create my own incentives to keep improving?

We assume that anyone reading this page is probably already a driven and motivated grantmaker. But we're all human, which means that we often won't do things we know we should. For example, did you floss your teeth *twice* every single day this week?

It is very easy for grantmakers to go for long periods without taking any active steps to improve their skills and knowledge. Unless you have an exceptional boss, it's very unlikely that anyone will call you out for neglecting to improve yourself.

Before we get into the details of *how* you can get better, we want to emphasise the importance of you putting structures in place yourself that will *nudge* you to get better. This means setting up mechanisms that will encourage you to take time out to improve. Here are a few tricks you can try:

- If you have a manager you get on well with, ask them to tell you something that you could do better in your catch-up each week. To avoid dodging this question, bring a copy of the agenda with this item on it to each catch-up.

- Find an 'extremely critical friend' (in the words of one foundation CEO we spoke to) and schedule a regular meeting with them, at least a few times a year, in which they ask you difficult questions about what isn't going well with your work, and what you might do or change to improve it.

- Use a 360-degree review mechanism for your staff performance reviews, even if your organisation doesn't usually make use of this tool. This means that you will get feedback not just from your boss, but also from your colleagues, people you manage and (with some distortion) from grantees and stakeholders. Ideally, once the results are in, you should share these with the people who have contributed and let them know how you're going to act on their feedback.

- Run 'safe-space' meetings within your organisation or with other trusted funders, where the main purpose is explicitly to discuss mistakes you have made and how they could be avoided next time.

You could also run monthly or fortnightly retrospectives with your team, which are meetings that encourage people to learn from failure.[298] In these meetings everyone in the group shares what they think has gone well and what could have gone better since the last such meeting. Once these positives and negatives are clearly laid out, the team agrees what changes need to be made to improve.

What is the most valuable thing I can do to keep getting better as a grantmaker?

When you are thinking of developing your personal skills, it is easy to leap straight into the menu of activities you could engage in – courses, mentoring, seminars, retreats, books and so on. We think that the most valuable single step you can take is to write a short plan to help you choose between the myriad self-improvement options out there. These are normally called *personal development plans*.

Why should I bother with a personal development plan?

We get it – the world of HR contains a lot of tedious concepts, acronyms and jargon and a personal development plan doesn't sound massively exciting. But it is both useful and simple. Here's one we made earlier (opposite).

What's going on in this personal development plan?

The purpose of this one-page plan is to give a busy grantmaker a single, easy-to-digest page that helps remind them of the steps they need to take to improve their own skills.

Each row in the table represents a different area of focus. In this case there are rows that relate to living up to key Modern Grantmaking values and doing basic grantmaking well, as well as skills that aren't specific to grantmaking such as facilitation.

Within each row you can see that our fictional grantmaker has set out their goals – indicators that will determine whether or not these development goals are being met – and a quick summary of their progress.

You can put whatever you want in each row – your own personal history as a grantmaker may mean that you need to specialise in very different areas. But we think that the structure with the four columns is a good, simple mechanism to capture your plans for any conceivable skill area.

How do I keep developing my skills?

Area	Activity	Goal	Progress
Humility and equity Modern Grantmaking values (Chapter 1)	Participate in a programme for leaders who want to be more inclusive – to lead diverse teams, serve diverse customers and work with diverse stakeholders – by end of December	To improve cultural intelligence, apply this learning back in role and also extend professional network	Course booked
Evidence Modern Grantmaking values (Chapter 1)	Shadow head of customer insight for a day by end of March to learn more about how we gather, analyse and use customer feedback – by end of December	To better understand how to further develop our funding services based on customer feedback	Complete
Mutually beneficial conversations Grantmaking no-brainers (Chapter 2)	All grantholders in my portfolio to complete a quick questionnaire about my practice and behaviours – by end of February	To gather and analyse feedback with my line manager, leading to any practical changes to approach	Complete
Participatory grantmaking Big questions (Chapter 5)	Write and present a virtual workshop on findings from stage 1 of the participatory grantmaking project we ran with other funders – by end of April	To help other funders to learn from our experiences in participatory grantmaking	Complete
Facilitation skills Big questions (Chapter 5)	Attend Felicity Facilitate's Two-Day Practical Course – by end of May	To be better able to facilitate tricky meetings	Course booked

It can take time to build up a development plan, and it should be a two-way process in which you propose what you think you could benefit from doing, and other people tell you whether that seems like a good priority for you. While you could write this sort of plan on your own, we strongly suggest that you get input from others to make it better.

We hope that all funding organisations will have put in place clear career development pathways that encourage and support the use of personal development plans. However, we understand that this may not always happen.

If you work for a funder that is surprised by the concept of a personal development plan and considers it newfangled, don't fret. Simply propose that you create one for yourself, and then start using it in one-to-one meetings with whoever you report to. Explaining by doing will work much better than explaining using abstract language.

What activities will improve my skills as a grantmaker?

For a grantmaker, there are an enormous number of informal activities to take part in, formal courses to enrol on, books to read and how-to web pages to scan. Here we share some examples that we know others have found useful in their skills development.

Activity no. 1: Shadow someone who works for a nonprofit

The most common self-improvement activity mentioned by people we interviewed for this book was shadowing, or observing someone who works for a grantee. What this means is observing someone who works or volunteers at a nonprofit or other social impact organisation up close, learning about the sorts of jobs they do and how they spend their days.

Shadowing can be done as formally or informally as both parties would like, but it is important for a grantmaker to carefully consider the power imbalance before asking a grantee if they can follow them around. Many people may feel pressurised to say 'yes' to being shadowed when they really want to say 'no'. So you should work out a way of allowing people to decline without worrying about their future funding.

It is also important to separate your desire to learn about their work from your monitoring or evaluation of their work. You will need to make it *very* clear that your shadowing is not a site visit or an inspection. It may be a good idea to shadow someone who is doing work that is not funded by your organisation, so as to avoid the impression that you're an admiral turning up on a naval ship, wearing white gloves and looking for specks of dirt on any insufficiently scrubbed surface.

Shadowing can range from a one-off activity lasting a day to something more meaningful such as showing up one day a week for several weeks. Ultimately, it's up to you to decide with the prospective grantee what you should do. Whatever you discuss, be mindful that even the simple act of observing someone's normal working day is likely to require additional preparation and may well introduce stress into the life of someone who is already working under pressure.

Activity no. 2: Reverse mentoring

> Reverse mentoring between a grantmaker and a senior member of staff or board member can be really powerful when expectations, goals – for instance about supporting a purposeful power shift and boundaries – are clear at the outset and enough time and space is given for a relationship and trust to develop.[299]
>
> — SACHA ROSE-SMITH, director of programmes and learning at the School for Social Entrepreneurs

Reverse mentoring pairs less experienced employees with senior team members for an unconventional learning experience. What makes it different from the usual flow of knowledge is that the more junior employee then 'mentors' the more senior colleague, relating ideas and experiences that the more senior colleague may never have previously encountered.

In these schemes the more senior colleague usually shares their concerns about strategic issues, leadership questions and how they approach their work. The more junior colleague – acting as a mentor – then offers support, advice and insights from their different perspective. Being part of a reverse mentoring scheme – either as the mentor or as the mentee – can challenge and expand the thinking of people at both ends of the experience.

As Sacha Rose-Smith told us, these schemes tend to be most useful not as one-offs, but when they are established and seen as a normal part of working life. They also work best when the individuals taking part have been properly briefed on the scheme's purpose, their respective roles and expectations, and what to do if a match doesn't work out – which is especially important for the junior colleague in the exchange.

Activity no. 3: Service design training

In Chapter 6 we tackled the question 'How can I improve the experience of grantseekers and grantees?' In summary, our answer was: think of your funding as a high-quality professional service offered to grantseekers, and design it by deploying the right professional skills.

Chapter 6 offers specific steps to providing a better service, but that's not the same as directly acquiring professional training in *service design*. This is the name given to the discipline of designing services that are accessible, inclusive and highly usable.

There are a range of courses, both online and offline, that will teach you the various skills of a service designer. Taking one of these courses will give you some of the skills you need to improve your grantseeker and grantee experiences directly, and will make you better able to work with contractors if that is required.

Skills that you're likely to learn about during service design training include:

- user-centred design;
- user research;
- agile project management.

We think that learning about service design is really important to make sure that you're not inadvertently erecting barriers that make life difficult for grantseekers and grantees.

Activity no. 4: Undertake training in equity, diversity and inclusion, as well as in power and privilege

In Chapter 3, and indeed throughout this book, we've made the case that grantmakers who don't think hard about issues of power, privilege, discrimination, inclusion and diversity are much less likely to have a positive impact than those who are familiar with them.

A wide range of courses and training providers are now available that can help you to understand how to make your own behaviour (and that of your colleagues) more equitable, inclusive and non-discriminatory. This can be hugely valuable in making all members of your workplace feel safe and respected, and helping you be more empathetic in your relationships with grantseekers and grantees.

Discrimination is complex, multi-layered and often intersectional. We recommend that you consider training on different issues to build up your skills and reflect on your own attitudes over a period of time. We also strongly recommend paying experienced grantees or nonprofits with lived experience of the issues to run these sessions for you, and that you keep a dialogue open with them about changes that you yourself are committed to making as a result of the training.

Finally, be careful that you are not just signing up to courses that focus on keeping on the right side of discrimination laws. In the grantmaking game some of the worst failures involving bias, prejudice, and poor practice may well be legal, but that doesn't make them acceptable.

Activity no. 5: Improve your understanding of what it takes to make systems change

The term 'systems change' may make some of you groan. We accept that some of what's been written and said on the subject can be pretty impenetrable. However, the idea itself is sound and important.

The best way to confront and deal with complex social phenomena is by changing the systems that perpetuate them. The ways in which groups of people have successfully changed systems in the past bears little resemblance to traditional grantmaking norms: single grants made to single organisations with little coordination. A grantmaker who doesn't understand this – and who thinks that the world changes one discrete project at a time – isn't a brilliant ally to people who are devoting their lives to tackling some of the hardest and most entrenched problems in the world.

So what specifically can you work on to make sure that you understand systems change and that you can work empathetically with people who are serious about change? Here are some suggestions:

- *Gen up on the existing research available on funders and systems change.*[300] Many organisations have developed and shared systems change learning publicly. Social Innovation Exchange (SIX) has compiled some global multi-funder reflections on opportunities and challenges, while the Bridgespan Group recently published work on funding movements within the Black-led racial justice ecosystem. We also recommend taking a look at *Stanford Social Innovation Review*'s article 'Five Ways Funders Can Support Social Movements' (2018).

- *Study some of the biggest system changes in history.*[301] Systems change isn't new, even if the phrase itself is relatively recent. From the abolition of slavery to the enfranchisement of women to the banning of CFCs (chlorofluorocarbons), there are numerous stories about how large coalitions of people have worked to change systems that seemed fixed and immovable, including Adam Hochschild's *Bury the Chains: The British Struggle to Abolish Slavery* and Duncan Green's *How Change Happens.*

- *Consider specific learning opportunities.*[302] Organisations such as the School of System Change, an initiative by Forum for the Future, in the UK run learning programmes to which you can sign up.

Activity no. 6: Take a course in research methods or research ethics

In Chapter 7 we talked about how understanding research practices can help you become a better grantmaker. There are various free introductions to this huge but important area of knowledge, for example Coursera's course on 'Understanding Research Methods'.[303] University STEM (science, technology, engineering and mathematics) departments offer many more such courses for those who want to go a bit deeper. And, if you're really serious, research companies may be able to create a bespoke programme for your pre-existing skill level.

As we mentioned in Chapter 7, you can also take a course to understand research ethics. However, it is likely to make more sense if you have learned something about research methods first.

We strongly recommend doing some kind of research methods course as preparatory work for commissioning professional researchers. Being familiar with some of the basics of research will help you to ask the right questions when talking to specialists and may enable you to understand their language and working practices a bit better.

Activity no. 7: Join a fellowship programme

What exactly, you may ask, is a fellowship? Well, despite taking many shapes, fellowships generally invite people to become part of a multi-stage learning journey together with others, normally while continuing with their day jobs.

For example, Churchill Fellowships are offered each year to 150 'exceptional people' from across the UK and a wide variety of sectors.[304] Their goal is to 'learn from the world about the UK's crucial issues and bring those global insights home'. In practice, fellows are funded to spend four to eight weeks overseas researching a project of their own choosing, which they believe can make a major difference to their profession or community when they return. Their key duty on their return is to share what they have learned and to try to put it into practice.

There are also a few fellowships specifically for grantmakers. Grant Givers' Programme, run by Ten Years' Time, is an eight-session, UK-based course that 'explores the best ways in which philanthropy can be used to advance social change'.[305] It is aimed at people who work in grantmaking but who have less than five years' working experience. It is designed to 'enable people to take a step back from the everyday work of grant making, and to look at the sector more critically'. People we spoke to who went through it were extremely positive about it, and talked with gratitude about the value of being brought into a new community of other grantmakers.

We're big fans of this sort of grantmaker-specific fellowship which combine new skills with a sense of camaraderie and shared purpose. US equivalents include the Equity in Philanthropy Fellowship from the Rockwood Leadership Institute and the Momentum Fellowship from Philanthropy Northwest.[306] We urge you to strongly consider them.

Activity no. 8: Dive deep – do a master's degree in a specialist subject

At the most ambitious end of the scale, you can sign up to a full higher education degree in an area that relates directly to your grantmaking. For example, if you are working for a funder with a major interest in environmental grantmaking, you could consider a master's in sustainable development. Or, if you fund a lot of schooling projects, you might enrol on a master's course in education to learn all about the evidence base for schooling interventions.

For long-serving funder staff, a course like this could even be done as part of a sabbatical agreement, if your organisation is open to it. We suggest that, if you are interested in something like a master's degree, you should start a conversation with your manager about whether your organisation would be interested in financially supporting you to develop your skills as well as giving you the time and space to do so. We recognise that the cost implications of higher education can be an insurmountable barrier for many.

Activity no. 9: Learn more about digital technology and grantmaking

No matter what area a grantmaker works in, the world that funders now operate in is entirely pervaded by digital technologies. These technologies are powerful, but they also mean that the ways of delivering and measuring impact in a wide variety of areas have shifted rapidly. As a grantmaker, you may want to consider dedicated training on the impacts of digital technology on grantmaking and civil society at large to help you ensure that the funding decisions you make are right for the digital era.

A good brief introduction to this topic is Alix Dunn's *How to Fund Tech*. If you are based in the UK you can join the meet-ups arranged by 'Funders Who Tech', run by Tom Steinberg.[307]

What if I just want to read something helpful rather than signing up for a course?

Not everyone wants to learn things through a course or a mentoring programme. Sometimes we just want to read something well written on a topic of interest. So where should a grantmaker look for guides written specifically for them?

First, of course, there are books on grantmaking, most commonly on philanthropic grantmaking. We've talked about these throughout the chapters, dropping them in wherever they seemed helpful. But not everyone searching for some knowledge wants to pick up a whole tome on the subject. So we want to point you to two different organisations that offer rich online libraries that are particularly relevant to grantmakers: GrantCraft by Candid and the Association of Charitable Foundations.

Candid's GrantCraft

Candid is an organisation that resulted from the merger of two US nonprofit sector stalwarts, the Foundation Center (established in the

1950s) and GuideStar (founded in the 1990s).[308] This is what Candid does:

> Every year, millions of nonprofits spend trillions of dollars around the world. Candid finds out where that money comes from, where it goes, and why it matters. Through research, collaboration, and training, Candid connects people who want to change the world to the resources they need to do it.

Candid now offers an enormous array of information and services. The service that is most helpful for a grantmaker looking to improve their skills is GrantCraft.

Originally founded by the Ford Foundation as an independent project back in 2001, GrantCraft has since been absorbed by Candid and is run as one of its websites. In two decades it has become an enormous online resource filled with guides, case studies and much more – well over 1,000 documents in all, covering a huge range of different issues.

We've cited GrantCraft advice elsewhere in this book. If you have identified a specific part of grantmaking you want to be better at, we think it is highly likely that you will find something relevant on their site.

Association of Charitable Foundations

The ACF is the industry body for grantmaking organisations in the UK.[309] It runs conferences and networking events, and is well known to pretty much everyone who works within the UK grantmaking sector. Its web page on 'Practice Publications' has a number of guides and reports that are free to ACF members, such as guides on how to manage endowments, how to be more transparent and what it means to be good at impact and learning.

Can I just sign up to a grantmaking course that will teach me everything I need to know?

> Why is there no academy or good-quality accredited course co-sponsored by a network of funders each year to provide a more standard professional development pathway for grantmakers?
>
> There are so many people tasked with giving away literally billions of pounds, and we don't invest in them or their skills. That is a travesty. And the counter that each funder is unique, special, with different requirements simply isn't true. There are some basic requirements relevant to every funder. It's about ego.[310]
>
> — ANONYMOUS SENIOR GRANTMAKER

We've explained in the sections above how you can go about picking and choosing learning opportunities that suit you. However, not everyone will know or feel confident about what grantmaking skills they should be trying to acquire. Some people may well prefer the reassurance that comes with taking part in an education programme that offers a well-rounded mix of different skills, all chosen and packaged up by someone who really understands the business of grantmaking.

In another profession this would have been done for all of us before we even started our jobs. For instance, the General Medical Council in the UK accredits university courses that teach medicine. The lack of such institutions in grantmaking is one of the things that raises the question of whether grantmaking is a profession in any meaningful sense.

There are no such training gatekeepers in grantmaking, so someone who just wants to 'do the required course' to 'become a certified grantmaker' can't just pick an accredited programme from a list and sign up to it. You've got to do more homework about how to learn and take a bit more of a gamble on your choice.

In this section we look at what your options are like if you'd like to enrol on a grantmaking programme that contains a full menu of skills, not just a single dish.

What grantmaking courses and programmes do universities offer?

Unlike other professions, grantmaking skills are not taught at most universities, which makes the few that do teach it especially important. Even more confusingly, most university certificates and degree programmes that contain the word 'philanthropy' are actually *fundraising* degrees for people aiming at careers in nonprofit organisations. Take care that you don't sign up to one of these by accident!

There are a number of universities in the US and UK that offer extended grantmaker education:

- The Lilly Family School of Philanthropy, Indiana University (US);
- The Business School (formerly Cass), City University of London (UK);
- Loyola University Chicago (US);
- Centre for Philanthropy, University of Kent (UK);
- The Center for Social Sector Leadership, Haas School of Business, University of California, Berkeley (US);
- Centre for the Study of Philanthropy & Public Good, University of St Andrews (UK).[311]

Some of these organisations offer both master's programmes (MA and MSc) for grantmakers, as well as certificates and diplomas. The main differences between the full master's degrees and certificates is the intensity and duration of the study involved. Most universities look for students to study full time for a year or two before they consider them worthy of a master's, but just a few weeks or months (on a more part-time basis) for diplomas and certificates. Unsurprisingly, shorter courses are generally priced lower than longer ones.

What do you get from putting serious time and money into a university course like this? Well, they're all different, but here's a summary of one master's programme, the Grantmaking, Philanthropy and Social Investment MSc at the Business School (formerly Cass) in London. Its teaching covers:

- developing a clear understanding of the principles and practice of philanthropy and grantmaking, and of the importance of all aspects of risk assessment, probity of applications, ethical frameworks and relationships with external communities and agencies;

- examining grant-giving and other investment categories such as loans, endowments, contracts, social bonds and impact investing;

- providing a solid background in the history and theory of philanthropy and grantmaking (with examples both from the UK and abroad) as well as studying the application of social investment practice as a business process.[312]

One way of differentiating the university courses above is to examine related books and papers. Grantmaking and philanthropy courses are heavily shaped by their academic founders and leaders. This means that it is possible to learn something about the course by reading books by those individuals.

For example, Dr Peter Grant leads the Business School course described above, and has published *The Business of Giving: The Theory and Practice of Philanthropy, Grantmaking and Social Investment*.[313] The University of Kent team is led by Dr Beth Breeze, the co-author of *Richer Lives: Why Rich People Give*.[314] The founding dean of the Lilly Family school in Indiana is Gene Tempel who has published a large number of papers that you can find by searching for 'E. R. Tempel' in Google Scholar.

A little time spent looking at the publications and writings of these individuals will almost certainly give you a sense of where a professor or a whole programme is coming from.

What does PEAK Grantmaking offer in the way of grantmaker education?

Universities are not the only source of rounded programmes for grantmakers. One of our favourite non-university education providers is PEAK Grantmaking.[315] PEAK Grantmaking is a US-based nonprofit that describes itself as a 'member-led community of professionals who specialize in grants management for funding organisations'.

PEAK's mission is to 'advance grantmaking so grantmakers and grantseekers can best achieve their missions'. Its way of doing this is to 'connect members of the grantmaking profession, offer educational opportunities for grants management professionals at all levels, and guide grantmakers in strengthening practices'.

Its member-led community of grantmakers is '5,000 strong', and over 300 funders have organisational memberships. It is clearly a vibrant and growing community, according to its annual reports.

PEAK offers a huge array of events for members and resources for people to study in their own time. What makes it particularly notable from our perspective is that all this work is founded on a 'Grants Management Professional Competency Model' which gives shape and structure to the learning.

This model contains various 'cross-cutting competencies' that can help a grantmaker work out where to focus, including:

- *Communications*: listen to others and communicate effectively.

- *Diversity, equity and inclusion*: promote diversity, equity and inclusion in grantmaking practices.

- *Ethics, integrity and accountability*: act with integrity and accountability.

- *Financial management*: implement financial policies and controls to ensure effective and efficient deployment of financial resources for grantmaking.

- *Knowledge management*: capture and apply knowledge to promote learning and improvement.

- *Process and change management*: plan and monitor processes efficiently and effectively.

This model can then be deployed by learners to work out which resources to use, which events to attend and who to network with from among the many thousands of PEAK community members. It is, in some ways, the equivalent of a university syllabus.

PEAK's model is also useful because the competencies set out in it are also connected to different phases of the grantmaking journey, so if there is some part of the process that you feel you could do better, they can connect you directly to relevant support.

What does the effective altruism movement offer in the way of grantmaker education?

We have not dwelled much in this book on effective altruism, the philosophical and social movement that advocates using evidence and reasoning to determine the most effective ways to benefit others. Effective altruism is a kind of all-encompassing theory about how grantmaking should work, and one that has found favour especially among people with a more scientific mindset. It isn't without its critics, but that would take a whole other book to explore.

We will therefore just note that Peter Singer's Coursera course on 'Effective Altruism' is a free and relatively quick introduction to a somewhat radical approach to spending money on social impact.[316] You may well find it interesting and challenging, but you will also find that it doesn't really tackle the logistics and politics of working within an institutional funder. That's because it's focused mainly on the private giving decisions of individuals.

A final thought on skills development

Before we wrap up this chapter, we have one final plea. Whatever you decide to do in terms of your skill development, we ask you to remember one thing: that a huge part of your job is managing grants that have already been made.

The management of current grants is often treated as the less glamorous side of grantmaking – less 'surprising people with huge cheques' and more 'filing dull reports'. This in turn means that little attention is paid to doing it well, or to honing the skills to do it better. This is a temptation you should push back against because, if you get good at grant management, you can make a huge difference. So try to make sure that all your skills development work isn't just about choosing the next grantee.

One of the best ways of learning anything about grantmaking, of course, is from other grantmakers, especially those who work for other funding organisations. In the next and final chapter we'll talk about how you can do that.

Chapter 9 checklist

1. Do you have a current personal development plan?

....

2. Do you discuss this regularly with your manager?

....

3. Do you know the three next areas of skill that you wish to improve, and have you written them down?

....

4. In the last six months have you been on a skill development course, exercise or activity that you actively chose to participate in?

....

5. Is your organisation good at supporting colleagues with their skills development?

....

10
HOW DO I BECOME A GRANTMAKING REFORMER?

Modern Grantmaking is grantmaking that embodies the values of humility, equity, evidence, service and diligence.

— GEMMA AND TOM

So here we are at last in the concluding chapter to this book. Whether you stuck it out grimly from page 1 or skipped straight here to get The Answer – welcome!

This final chapter has been written to give you three things:

- a quick summary of the most important take-aways from this book;
- an encouragement to be bold and unabashed about your identity as a grantmaking reformer, with some advice on how to team up with other reforming grantmakers;
- guidance on how to take your next steps towards Modern Grantmaking, and how you can start to influence your own organisation at the same time.

With that all set out, let's get started.

What are the most important lessons in this book?

- Traditional grantmaking is flawed in a myriad of ways. In response to these problems, there is a growing community of professional grantmakers who think that better is not only possible but a moral imperative.

- The values that lie at the heart of this reform community are the foundations of what we call Modern Grantmaking. This is grantmaking that embodies the values of humility, equity, evidence, service and diligence.

- The first and pre-eminent of these Modern Grantmaking values is humility. A grantmaker who has real humility will be naturally drawn towards a lot of good grantmaking practices even without a guidebook or a mentor. A humble grantmaker will lean towards making unrestricted grants, and will listen carefully because they won't assume they know it all. (Chapter 1)

- All grantmakers should treat grantees as essential partners, not simply as recipients of money. This isn't just because it's morally right to treat people with dignity, but also because to treat them in any other way will undermine their work. (Chapter 2)

- Even if you are not one of the big cheeses in your funding organisation, you can still push your organisation towards being more diverse and inclusive in terms of the grants it makes, the people it employs and the culture it creates. (Chapter 3)

- All funders – including those that don't accept unsolicited applications – should work hard to ensure that their funding is as accessible as possible. The traditional grantmaking assumption that 'people who really want our money will work for it' is as empirically wrong as it is pointlessly macho. Improving access to your funding is a matter of justice, not of bureaucratic efficiency. (Chapter 6)

- Every time you develop a new programme of funding aimed at supporting a particular group of people, you absolutely have to involve them deeply in the design and delivery of the programme, otherwise it's both unfair and a perfect recipe for undermining your organisation's impact. (Chapters 3 and 6)

- In situations where making and understanding impact really matter, don't ask grantees to be responsible for conducting their own evaluations. Bring in independent research specialists with a strong ethical mindset to reduce the burden on grantees and to avoid the conflict of interest when grantees are asked to mark their own homework. (Chapter 7)

- All grantmakers need to resist the temptation to rest on their laurels and let their skills ossify. You have to fight for the time and resources to continue to develop your skills throughout your career.
(Chapter 9)

- Make sure that you haven't accidentally encouraged, nudged or strong-armed a nonprofit into doing something that they, deep down, don't believe is a good idea. So keep your random ideas to yourself and always default to less restricted funding over more. (Chapter 2)

- Grantmaking as a whole will change only if people like you join others in declaring publicly that grantmaking needs reform, and that you are part of that reform movement. To learn more about how to get involved, keep reading.

What does it mean to be a grantmaker who identifies as a reformer?

We believe that grantmaking will get better more quickly if individual grantmakers start identifying themselves clearly as members of grantmaking reform movements. But if this is to happen there must be clear movements to join and grantmakers who are willing to say 'That's me'.

This shouldn't be too much of a leap. It is already quite common for grantmakers to stand in public solidarity with causes that originate from outside grantmaking. Plenty of grantmakers identify, for example, as feminists or as social justice advocates. What is somewhat less common, however, is for grantmakers to publicly identify themselves as belonging to or supporting reform movements that exist *within* grantmaking.

We believe that significant changes to grantmaking norms and practices are much more likely to catch on if there are widely recognised reform movements within the sector that many people feel a part of. Such internal movements already exist in many other professions. For example, *open science* is a movement that has been challenging what counts as normal and acceptable practices within scientific professions. In business and some parts of government *agile* has taken on a similar role. In medical practice *evidence-based medicine* was similarly once an insurgent movement that has now totally changed that profession.

So we encourage you, as a grantmaker, to consider whether any of the nascent movements that exist within grantmaking are ones that you could feel comfortable allying yourself to, especially in public. If you conclude that you are comfortable with an affiliation, please don't be shy about it. Put it on your social media profiles, put it on your T-shirt, add it to your CV or résumé, talk about it when you start presentations and flag it up in reports you write. Be a reformist grantmaker and be proud of it.

Are there grantmaker reform movements I can join?

Yes, absolutely. Reform-minded groups in grantmaking are bubbling up all over the place – here are just a few to whet your appetite.

One US-based group that we think is very encouraging is the Trust-Based Philanthropy Project.[317] This movement, which describes itself as 'a five-year, peer-to-peer funder initiative to address the inherent power imbalances between foundations and nonprofits', is notable because its demands are clear and challenge the status quo.

Trust-Based Philanthropy stands out from the crowd because it takes clear positions on grantmaking practices (such as 'Give multi-year unrestricted funding'), some of which will make some funders uncomfortable. It also treats power imbalances as a serious problem. We think any movement that has a kind of chance of being successful is always going to make at least some people uncomfortable, so we give this collaboration a thumbs up for taking a clear stand on many issues.

We'd encourage all our readers to sign up to Trust-Based Philanthropy's newsletter or to follow them on Twitter. We give big kudos to the people at the Headwaters Foundation, the Robert Sterling Clark Foundation and the Whitman Institute, together with all the other funders that have backed it.

But Trust-Based Philanthropy doesn't have to be the only slogan on your baseball cap or coffee mug. There are others that are well worth considering too. Next up in awesome and memorable naming choices is the work of Jessamyn Shams-Lau, Jane Leu and Vu Le.[318] In their book *Unicorns Unite: How Nonprofits & Foundations Can Build EPIC Partnerships* they have done the world a service by wresting the term 'unicorns' back from Silicon Valley to do more useful work than celebrating tech billionaires, deploying it to celebrate funder–grantee partnerships that are serious about the business of slaying 'the dragons of injustice and inequity once and for all'.[319] If you've ever dreamed of being both a unicorn *and* a better grantmaker at the same time, this community will be perfect for you.

Here in the UK one of the most promising signs of a reforming grantmaker wave is the Grant Givers' Movement. 'A non-hierarchical gathering of those working in the grant-giving sector', it is a 'space for those who feel passionate about making positive change in and through philanthropy to do so with collective power behind them'.[320]

We absolutely love the reference to 'collective power' here. This is language that is very common among organisations backed by funders but relatively uncommon in being applied to funders themselves. We think the Grant Givers' Movement is a super-exciting, energetic network, and we hope that it builds international alliances too. So, wherever you are in the world, head over to **grantgiversmovement.org** and sign up.

Some reform movements are emerging from specific sub-sectors of the broader grantmaking universe. One of note here is #ShiftThePower, a hashtag movement that originated in the community philanthropy sector, which is predominantly located in developing countries.[321] Born at a single conference in Johannesburg in 2016, it has been sustained for over five years and is widely used to draw together people in both philanthropy and civil society who feel that grantmaking can and should be more participatory and inclusive. Moreover, the community brought together by this hashtag has come together in person at the pre-pandemic Pathways to Power Symposium in 2019, showing how the right brands and the right ideas can lead to real movements.[322]

Finally, an emerging force is Future Foundations in the UK, which describes itself as 'supporting minoritised racial groups working in the UK Trust and Foundation sector to connect, create and champion a vision of a just future'.[323] Its aim is to 'radically shift UK Philanthropy' so that 'communities of colour are appreciated for their abundance, and are no longer viewed through a deficit lens'.

Is Modern Grantmaking a movement I can join?

We don't know whether Modern Grantmaking is a name that anyone will want to be identified with, let alone one that will become the slogan or banner for a whole movement. But we chose the name partly so it can be used in talking about grantmaking or in descriptions of people without being too wordy or too pretentious. We want people to feel confident about saying, 'I'm part of the Modern Grantmaking community' or 'Is that really Modern Grantmaking?' or to simply use #ModernGrantmaking.

Modern Grantmaking also benefits from a clear definition of what it is – *grantmaking that embodies the values of humility, equity, evidence, service and diligence* – which we hope will mean that people can make a choice quickly about whether or not they'd like to be associated with it.

So, even with our typical British reticence, we'll say it clearly: we think Modern Grantmaking is a useful name when flying the flag of reform. If you want to use it, go ahead – we made it for everyone and it's not something we will seek to own or control.

If you'd like to be connected to other funders who are starting to get into Modern Grantmaking, we can help you. Just visit our website at **ModernGrantmaking.com** for a variety of ways to join in. We'll be running events, hosting guest writers, publishing posts and offering supporting materials that will help you to make use of this book. It's free to subscribe, so why not sign up?

How can I get started with Modern Grantmaking?

This book contains a lot of different ideas and things to try, and knowing what to do next can be a bit overwhelming. We get that.

To help you make sense of it all, this section of the book gives you some simple recommendations.

Over the next few pages we will guide you through a four part exercise to help you to identify some:

- decisions you can make that are entirely within your control
- changes you can make in collaboration with your colleagues
- reforms that can be made only if the board and top leadership agree
- changes that will make your organisation a better member of the community that it serves

So grab a pen or pencil, and let's go.

Step 1: Choose some decisions you can make that are entirely within your control

This book contains many choices that cannot be made by a single grantmaker working on their own. You can't generally decide a new strategy on your own or change your organisation's recruiting policies. But it also contains quite a few choices you can make that are entirely up to you. These changes include:

- how you talk to and listen to grantseekers and grantees;
- how you do background research on grants;
- what you choose to work on when it comes to your own skills development.

The chapters that contain the most stuff you can do alone are Chapters 1, 2, 3, 7, 9 and this one, 10. Why not check them out and then try filling in this simple table?

Priority	What is the decision or practice?	How do I get started?
1		
2		
3		

Step 2: Choose some changes you can make in collaboration with your colleagues

There are plenty of ideas in this book that can be acted on as long as you can persuade one or two other people to join you. These changes include:

- running team meetings differently;
- revising the way you use evaluation and research;
- changing the way your funder's application guidance or forms work.

The chapters that contain the most stuff you can do together with colleagues are Chapters 3, 4, 5, 6, 7, 8 and this one, 10.

Priority	What is the decision or practice?	How do I get started?
1		
2		
3		

Modern Grantmaking

Step 3: Choose some changes that can be made only if the board and top leadership agree

Here's where things get a bit more ambitious and a lot more political – and potentially difficult. These changes include:

- changing practices and policies to meaningfully promote diversity, inclusion and equity;

- moving towards unrestricted funding and away from project funding;

- changing positions on difficult issues like endowments.

These really gnarly issues are concentrated mostly in Chapters 3, 4 and 5.

Priority	What is the decision or practice?	How do I get started?
1		
2		
3		

Step 4: Choose some changes that will make your organisation a better member of the community it serves

Lastly, the highest and most difficult of tiers. This relates to the role that the organisation plays in the outside world and involves the toughest of choices. These changes include decisions such as:

- Who should have the power to decide where our money goes?
- How can we be more transparent?
- How can we collaborate so that our research is of use not just to us but to many other people?

Priority	What is the decision or practice?	How do I get started?
1		
2		
3		

Does this book ever end?

Thanks for asking!

Yes it does. It ends here.

Please don't be shy to contact us with your thoughts and questions, either online at **ModernGrantmaking.com**, via Twitter @GemmaCBull and @Steiny, or by email at **hello@ModernGrantmaking.com**.

Bye!

ACKNOWLEDGEMENTS

We would never even have thought of writing this book if we hadn't worked alongside so many inspiring people in nonprofits and in funding organisations.

Modern Grantmaking as a concept comes only partly from our own experiences: the vast majority of ideas and practices included in this book come from people who work as grantmakers and for nonprofits that are trying to make the world a more tolerant, more equal and more sustainable place.

Some of these kind people gave up lots of precious time to be interviewed by us and to answer our questions, including Ngozi Lyn Cole, Jake Hayman, Ben Harrison, Dan Paskins, Jen Bokoff, John Palfrey, Alexandra Garita, Anna de Pulford, Stephen King, Jo Wells, Dr Tiago Peixoto, Eric Sears, Helen Turvey, Sarah Drummond, Lilli Geissendorfer, John Rendel, Ciorsdan Brown, Will Somerville, Sacha Rose-Smith, Jenny Oppenheimer, Michael Feigelson, Alison Goldsworthy, Simon and Jane Berry, Stephen Bediako, Jayne Engle, Pia Infante, David Sasaki, Stephen Tall, Louisa Syrett, Johnny Chatterton, Geeta Gopalan, Maggie Jones, Chris White, Dr Jennifer Rubin, Katherine Sladden, Rebecca Eastmond, Lisa Weaks, Chris Stone, Sufina Ahmad, Paul Lenz, John Bracken, Stacy Donahue, Jo Andrews, Dan Sutch, Alice Kershaw, Diana Samarasan, Mary Ann Bates, Jon Cracknell, Wietse van der Werf, and Angela Murray. We also interviewed many people who asked to remain anonymous – you know who you are, and we hope you know how grateful we are.

Others volunteered to read draft chapters or even the full manuscript. These heroes, who never shied from the liberal application of the red pen, include Hannah Paterson, Morena Shepherd, Caroline Fiennes, Stuart Hobley, Dr Natalie Byrom, Ruth Levine, Rene Olivieri, Lynne Tinsley, Dr Genevieve Maitland Hudson, Paul Waters and Fran Perrin. Still others kindly offered incredibly helpful advice, such as Phil Buchanan, Tricia Levesque and Edgar Villanueva, Rhodri Davies, David Callaghan, Julie Broome, Meg Massey and Ben Wrobel.

The book would have remained a series of Google docs if it wasn't for the production prowess of Jacqueline Harvey who provided sterling copyediting support, Catherine Dunn who proofread the book, Andrew Chapman who typeset it, and Jamie Keenan who created the cover design.

Thanks also to Janet Haven, Ruth Ibegbuna, Swee Leng Harris, Forest Gregg, Rebecca Williams, Cassie Robinson, Tom Nealon and Tom Longley who simply gave us a lot of wisdom and moral support.

We'd also like to thank Omar the insatiable cat whose on-camera tail and unstoppable food-theft habit brought levity to many a long Zoom call.

Now the soppy bit: we are filled with love and gratitude for both of our families who probably never want to hear about grantmaking ever again but unfortunately will almost certainly have to. And to Anna Powell-Smith for everything, always.

We also want to acknowledge that this book is a two-author endeavour, and each of us absolutely couldn't have done it without the other person. One of the great miracles of the pandemic era is that we wrote this book without a single argument or creative flounce.

Lastly, we'd like to acknowledge the long-term impact of an unnamed grantmaker back in 2003. After they had passed on the good news of a grant award to Tom's nascent nonprofit, the money failed to appear for 10 dreary months of thumb-twiddling. This *may* have shaped his views on the profession of grantmaking and ultimately led him to mention to Gemma that someone really should write a book that helps grantmakers do better.

NOTES

Introduction

[1] **'I went looking ...'**: Authors' interview with Lisa Weaks, 15 September 2020.

[2] **while many funders have been innovating ...**: Naomi Orensten and Ellie Buteau, 'Foundations Respond to Crisis: A Moment of Transformation?', The Center for Effective Philanthropy, https://cep.org/portfolio/foundations-respond-to-crisis1.

[3] **'All I do is read ...'**: Authors' interview with anonymous grantmaker, 2020.

[4] **the Grant Givers' Movement**: https://www.grantgiversmovement.org.

[5] **#ShiftThePower**: https://globalfundcommunityfoundations.org/what-we-stand-for/shiftthepower.

[6] **Resourcing Racial Justice**: http://resourcingracialjustice.org.

[7] **20th-century environmentalists ... and 21st-century tech entrepreneurs ...**: Rachel Carson, *Silent Spring* (London: Penguin, 2000); Eric Ries, *The Lean Startup: How Constant Innovation Creates Radically Successful Businesses* (London: Portfolio Penguin, 2011).

[8] **There are over 10,000 ...**: Cathy Pharoah and Catherine Walker, 'Foundation Giving Trends 2019', Association of Charitable Foundations, https://www.acf.org.uk/policy-practice/research-publications/foundation-giving-trends-2019; 'Canadian Foundation Facts Webpage', Philanthropic Foundations Canada, https://pfc.ca/resources/canadian-foundation-facts; and 'Key Facts on U.S. Nonprofits and Foundations', candid, https://www.issuelab.org/resources/36381/36381.pdf.

[9] **a book to help you with your own giving**: Phil Buchanan, *Giving Done Right: Effective Philanthropy and Making Every Dollar Count* (New York: PublicAffairs, 2019); William MacAskill, *Doing Good Better: How Effective Altruism Can Help You Help Others, Do Work that Matters, and Make Smart Choices about Giving Back* (London: Guardian Faber, 2016); and Caroline Fiennes, *It Ain't What You Give, It's the Way that You Give It* (London: Giving Evidence, 2012).

[10] **we recommend the following reading ...**: Morgan Simon, *Real Impact: The New Economics of Social Change* (New York: Nation Books, 2017); *After the Gold Rush: The Report of the Alternative Commission on Social Investment*, March 2015, https://www.sibgroup.org.uk/sites/default/files/files/FBEFinalPowerPoint%20DCMS%20Data%20Pack%20Final%20v%2003-08-2020.pdf;

[11] **the most well known of these ...**: Rob Reich, *Just Giving: Why Philanthropy Is Failing Democracy and How It Can Do Better* (Princeton, NJ: Princeton University Press, 2018); and Anand Giridharadas, *Winners Take All: The Elite Charade of Changing the World* (London: Allen Lane, 2019).

[12] **the connection between major funders, people of colour and indigenous peoples ...**: Edgar Villanueva, *Decolonizing Wealth: Indigenous Wisdom to Heal Divides and Restore Balance* (San Francisco, CA: Berrett-Koehler, 2018).

[13] **high-profile journalists have also been flagging concerns**: Roxanne Roberts, 'Why Does Everybody Suddenly Hate Billionaires? Because They've Made It Easy', *Washington Post*, 13 March 2019, https://www.washingtonpost.com/lifestyle/style/why-does-everybody-suddenly-hate-billionaires-because-theyve-made-it-easy/2019/03/13/00e39056-3f6a-11e9-a0d3-1210e58a94cf_story.html; and Elizabeth Kolbert, 'Gospels of Giving for the New Gilded Age', *The New Yorker*, 20 August 2018, https://www.newyorker.com/magazine/2018/08/27/gospels-of-giving-for-the-new-gilded-age.

[14] **'As a grantmaker it's so tempting to coast ...'**: Authors' interview with Paul Lenz, 8 September 2020.

[15] **the best available data ...**: Carol Mack, 'Funding on a Finite Planet', speech given at the Association for Charitable Foundations Conference, 8 November 2019, https://www.acf.org.uk/news/funding-on-a-finite-planet-carol-macks-speech-at-acf-conference.

[16] **networks such as the Global Alliance for Green and Gender Action, or the Global Greengrants Fund**: Global Alliance for Green and Gender Action, https://gaggaalliance.org; and Global Greengrants, https://www.greengrants.org.

[17] **the UK's Equality Act 2010**: https://www.legislation.gov.uk/ukpga/2010/15/contents.

1. What is Modern Grantmaking?

[18] **'five-year, $1 billion investment ...'**: 'Building Institutions and Networks', Ford Foundation, https://www.fordfoundation.org/work/our-grants/building-institutions-and-networks.

[19] **'Philanthropy and grantmaking is coming to the end of another cycle ...'**: Authors' interview with Jayne Engle, 1 October 2020.

[20] **'There are now a number of new leaders ...'**: Authors' interview with anonymous foundation CEO, 2020.

[21] **'In the US democracy funding space ...'**: Authors' interview with anonymous grantmaker, 2020.

[22] **We enjoyed ...**: Paul Vallely, *Philanthropy: From Aristotle to Zuckerberg* (London: Bloomsbury Continuum, 2020).

[23] **'It is (we are) a period play ...'**: Villanueva, *Decolonizing Wealth*, p. 17.

[24] **at the time of writing ...**: Valentina Di Liscia, 'New Documents in Purdue Case May Pressure Institutions to Rename Sackler-Funded Spaces', Hyperallergic, 28 October 2020, https://hyperallergic.com/597819/new-documents-purdue-pharma-sackler.

[25] **'Even newer funders ...'**: Authors' interview with Sufina Ahmad, 26 August 2020.

[26] **'Humility is one of the key values for grantmaking ...'**: Authors' interview with anonymous grantmaker, 2020.

[27] **'Humility is characterized by ...'**: Darren Walker, 'Foreword', in Villanueva, *Decolonizing Wealth*, p. 13.

[28] **'They are in no way qualified ...'**: Authors' interview with anonymous grantmaker, 2020.

[29] **'If the primary virtue of grantmaking ...'**: Authors' interview with anonymous foundation CEO, 2020.

[30] **'Grantmaking is done well ...'**: Authors' interview with Stephen Bediako, 18 May 2020.

[31] **'We had this director of a foundation ...'**: Authors' interview with anonymous grantmaker, 2020.

[32] **'In an ideal world ...'**: Authors' interview with Maggie Jones, 27 May 2020.

[33] 'I think that the most important thing for anybody ...': Authors' interview with Ruth Levine, 30 March 2020.
[34] 'There's a lot of theatre ...': Authors' interview with anonymous grantmaker, 2020.
[35] 'Site visits tend to play into funders' sense of specialness ...': Authors' interview with Dr Genevieve Maitland Hudson, 19 October 2019.
[36] 'One day one of the veteran grantmaking directors ...': Authors' interview with anonymous former foundation CEO, October 2020.
[37] 'Hello grantees! My name is Catherine the Great ...': Authors' interview with anonymous grantmaker, 2020.
[38] 'Our survival doesn't depend ...': Authors' interview with anonymous grantmaker, 2020.
[39] 'Funders and nonprofits need to work collaboratively ...': Buchanan, *Giving Done Right*, p. 109.
[40] 'Grantmaking is easy ...': Authors' interview with anonymous foundation board member, 2020.
[41] 'You have a duty ...': Authors' interview with Anna de Pulford, 7 October 2020.
[42] 'Many people treat grantmaking ...': Authors' interview with anonymous grantmaker, 2020.
[43] 'A colleague of mine once joked ...': Authors' interview with anonymous grantmaker, 2020.
[44] 'The GPR provides an opportunity ...': 'Grantee and Applicant Reception Report Page', The Center for Effective Philanthropy, https://cep.org/assessments/grantee-perception-report.
[45] 'Modern grantmaking requires a transformation ...': Authors' interview with Sufina Ahmad, 26 August 2020.

2. What are the no-brainers of Modern Grantmaking?

[46] 'Try not to be an asshole': Authors' interview with anonymous grantmaker, 2020.
[47] 'Every time we've been able ...': Authors' interview with anonymous international development nonprofit founder, 2020.
[48] over 800 funding organisations ...: 'A Call to Action: Philanthropy's Commitment during COVID-19', Council on Foundations, https://www.cof.org/news/call-action-philanthropys-commitment-during-covid-19.
[49] 66% of funders who took part in a survey ...: Orensten and Buteau, 'Foundations Respond to Crisis: A Moment of Transformation?'.
[50] a spicy Twitter thread ...: John Rendel @john_rendel, 7.41 a.m., 1 March 2019, https://twitter.com/john_rendel/status/1101386953767952385.
[51] **Headwaters Foundation (Montana, US)**: 'High-Impact General Operating Grants for Our Most Rural Communities', Headwaters Foundation, https://www.headwatersmt.org/funding/go-grants.
[52] **Blagrave Trust (UK)**: https://www.blagravetrust.org.
[53] **Luminate (US and multi-country)**: 'Our Commitment to Unrestricted Funding', Luminate, https://luminategroup.com/posts/news/our-commitment-to-unrestricted-funding.
[54] **The Peter Cundill Foundation (Canada, Bermuda, UK)**: The Peter Cundill Foundation: https://www.thepetercundillfoundation.com.
[55] **Pears Foundation (UK)**: https://pearsfoundation.org.uk.

[56] **The Trans Justice Project (US and Puerto Rico):** Trans Justice Funding Project, https://www.transjusticefundingproject.org.

[57] **It has also very helpfully published analysis…:** 'Insights on Core Funding', Esmée Fairbairn Foundation, https://esmeefairbairn.org.uk/latest-news/esmee-insights-on-core-funding/.

[58] **'No one can really achieve change …':** Authors' interview with Dan Paskins, 9 July 2020.

[59] **'should give multi-year grants …':** Authors' interview with Ruth Levine, 30 March 2020.

[60] **90% of attempts to change systems take 20 years:** Susan Taylor Batten, Edward M. Jones, Leslie MacKrell and Jerry Petit-Frere, 'Guiding a Giving Response to Anti-Black Injustice', The Bridgespan Group, 25 August 2020, https://www.bridgespan.org/insights/library/philanthropy/guiding-a-giving-response-to-anti-black-injustice.

[61] **a programme called Sustaining Grants:** 'Major Grant Recipients', Cummings Foundation, https://www.cummingsfoundation.org/grants/grant_recipients.htm#sus-grant.

[62] **'Long-term financial support is rare for nonprofits …':** Cummings Properties blog, https://blog.cummings.com/?p=2666.

[63] **'a lot of talk …':** Authors' interview with anonymous grantmaker, 2020.

[64] **GrantCraft … have helpfully created three broad categories:** 'Types of Funder Collaboratives', GrantCraft, https://grantcraft.org/content/takeaways/types-of-funder-collaboratives.

[65] **One recent example of a pooled fund …:** 'CLF Expands Support for COVID-19 Global Response', Clara Lionel Foundation, 13 April 2020, https://claralionelfoundation.org/news/clf-expands-support-for-covid-19-global-response/.

[66] **'Too often funders behave …':** Authors' interview with anonymous grantmaker, 2020.

[67] **an essential piece of reading is Bridgespan's report …:** Alison Powell, Susan Wolf Ditkoff and Kate Hassey, *Value of Collaboration Research Study: Literature Review on Funder Collaboration* (Boston: The Bridgespan Group), https://cdn.givingcompass.org/wp-content/uploads/2019/07/09170013/bridgespan-2019-value-of-philanthropic-collaboration-study-literature-review.pdf.

[68] **Case study of a good funder collaboration:** Authors' interview with Jo Andrews, 21 August 2020.

[69] **'When our organisation was small and new …':** Authors' interview with anonymous activism nonprofit founder, 2020.

[70] **A study of grant application forms by the University of Bath:** Marcelle Speller, Philip Hodgson, Alistair Brandon-Jones, Dimo Dimov and Julian Padget, 'UK Third Sector Grant Making: A Summary of Research 2019', The University of Bath, https://researchportal.bath.ac.uk/en/publications/uk-third-sector-grant-making-a-summary-of-research-by-the-univers.

[71] **'Another study claimed …':** Tom Neill, 46% of Grants Cost More than They're Worth, Time to Spare blog, https://blog.timetospare.com/grants-cost-more-than-they-are-worth.

[72] **'It isn't fair for a funder …':** Authors' interview with Wietse van der Werf, 29 May 2020.

[73] **'It's really important to have the courage …':** Authors' interview with Stephen King, 15 September 2020.

[74] **here are some suggestions from our interviewees …:** Authors' interviews with anonymous grantmakers, 2020.

[75] 'We first approached a really big beast funder...': Authors' interview with anonymous nonprofit CEO, 2020.

[76] 'Nonprofit leaders are like Ginger Rogers ...': Buchanan, *Giving Done Right*, p. 13.

[77] 'The No. 1 thing that nonprofits have said to me ...': Edgar Villanueva, interviewed by David Bornstein, 'A Call to Modernize American Philanthropy', *New York Times*, 27 November 2018, https://www.nytimes.com/2018/11/27/opinion/philanthropy-minorities-charities.html.

[78] 'Listen more than you talk ...': Lindsay Austin Louie and Fay Twersky, 'Seven Habits of Excellent Work with Grantees: Practical Tips for Program Staff', The William and Flora Hewlett Foundation, https://hewlett.org/seven-habits-of-excellent-work-with-grantees-practical-tips-for-program-staff.

[79] 'We're really just beginning to learn ...': Naomi Orensten and Ellie Buteau, 'Foundations Respond to Crisis: A Moment of Transformation?', The Center for Effective Philanthropy, https://cep.org/portfolio/foundations-respond-to-crisis1.

[80] listening to and learning from ...: Buchanan, *Giving Done Right*, p. 53.

[81] 'I was talking to someone who runs a foundation ...': Authors' interview with anonymous foundation CEO, 2020.

[82] 'It's very easy for a funder to make a minor request ...': Authors' interview with Helen Turvey, 28 September 2020.

[83] 'Pre-COVID, our nonprofit ran several face-to-face training sessions ...': Authors' interview with anonymous nonprofit founder, 2020.

[84] 'One time, a funder looked at my salary as the executive director ...': Authors' interview with Esra'a Al Shafei, 16 September 2020.

[85] also means not investing in upcoming and current leaders ...: Manmeet Mehta, Michael Zakaras and Nathaniel Heller, 'How We Shift the Status Quo in Philanthropy', Ashoka, November 2020, https://medium.com/change-maker/how-we-shift-the-status-quo-in-philanthropy-7820d5a97dcd.

[86] a number of US-based funders have agreed to support a 'pay-what-it-takes' approach ... : Jeri Eckhart-Queenan, Michael Etzel and Sridhar Prasad, 'Pay-What-It-Takes Philanthropy', *Stanford Social Innovation Review*, Summer 2016, https://ssir.org/up_for_debate/article/pay_what_it_takes_philanthropy.

[87] 'Multi-year general operating support is working ...': Authors' interview with Jen Bokoff, 16 September 2020.

[88] 'Working with the Center for Effective Philanthropy ...': Authors' interview with Stephen King, 15 September 2020.

[89] 'Maybe it doesn't have to take ...': Authors' interview with anonymous grantmaker, 2020.

[90] The Association of Charitable Foundations ... has developed a helpful safeguarding framework specifically for funders: *Safeguarding for Foundations: Thinking Through Your Approach* (London: Association of Charitable Foundations, 2018), https://www.acf.org.uk/downloads/member-briefings/ACF_Safeguarding_June_2018_FINALv2.pdf.

[91] International Child Safeguarding Standards: *The International Safeguarding Standards ... and How to Implement Them* (London: Keeping Children Safe, first launched 2002), https://www.keepingchildrensafe.global/wp-content/uploads/2019/12/KCS-CS-Standards-191213.pdf.

[92] 'You don't go into grantmaking thinking you're going to manage safeguarding ...': Authors' interview with anonymous grantmaker, 2020.

[93] Only one in 100 funders ... share information on past grants, and only 10% ... have a website: 'The Foundation Transparency Challenge', GlassPockets by Candid, http://glasspockets.org/transparency-challenge.

[94] 360Giving, which runs the excellent GrantNav website: https://grantnav.threesixtygiving.org.

[95] GlassPockets: https://glasspockets.org.

3. What should I do about privilege?

[96] 'The sheer power of grantmaking! ...': Authors' interview with Ngozi Lyn Cole, 3 July 2020.

[97] 'If you're a funder who brings in Black and brown expertise ...': Ruth Ibegbuna @MsIbegbuna, Twitter, 20 August 2019, 9.11 a.m., https://twitter.com/msibegbuna/status/1163725172152635392.

[98] 'In ten years working for disability charities ...': Authors' interview with anonymous senior executive of a UK disability nonprofit, December 2019.

[99] 'A set of unearned benefits ...': Sian Ferguson, 'Privilege 101: A Quick and Dirty Guide', Everyday Feminism, https://everydayfeminism.com/2014/09/what-is-privilege.

[100] 'There is only one complete unblushing male ...': Erving Goffman, *Stigma: Notes on the Management of a Spoiled Identity* (first published 1963; New York: Simon & Schuster, 1986), p. 128.

[101] 'Privilege is a hard concept for people to understand ...': John Amaechi, 'What Is White Privilege?', BBC Bitesize, 7 August 2020, https://www.bbc.co.uk/bitesize/articles/zrvkbqt.

[102] The US sociologist and historian ...: W. E. B. Du Bois, *The Souls of Black Folk* (Seattle, WA: CreateSpace Independent Publishing Platform, 4 Feb 2018). William Edward Burghardt Du Bois was an American sociologist, historian, civil rights activist, Pan-Africanist, author, writer and editor, and the first African American to receive a doctorate from Harvard University.

[103] In her much cited 1988 article ...: Peggy McIntosh, 'White Privilege and Male Privilege: A Personal Account of Coming to See Correspondences through Work in Women's Studies', https://www.collegeart.org/pdf/diversity/white-privilege-and-male-privilege.pdf.

[104] 'Power is not intrinsically bad ...': Katie Boswell, Fatima Asif, Oli Kelly-Dean and Angela Kail, 'A Rebalancing Act: How Funders Can Address Power Dynamics', New Philanthropy Capital, 17 March 2020, https://www.thinknpc.org/resource-hub/power-dynamics.

[105] 'I once talked to a very wealthy board member ...': Authors' interview with anonymous senior grantmaker, 2020.

[106] In a recent survey ...: 'Discrimination, Prejudice & Isomorphism: A Short Report', Grant Givers' Movement, December 2018, https://www.grantgiversmovement.org/discrimination-prejudice.

[107] 'There is a massive power and privilege imbalance ...': Authors' interview with Sufina Ahmad, 26 August 2020.

[108] 'A group that has privilege and power is criticized ...': Vu Le, 'How Funder Fragility Is Similar to White Fragility and What Funders Can Do about It', Nonprofit AF, https://nonprofitaf.com/2019/01/how-funder-fragility-is-similar-to-white-fragility-and-what-to-do-about-it.

[109] 'Inherent structures within grantmaking elevate a particular experience ...': Authors' interview with Jenny Oppenheimer, 26 August 2020.

Notes

[110] **In the UK, foundation boards are 99% white:** Keiran Goddard, 'Foundation Trustee Boards: The Good, the Bad and the Data', Association of Charitable Foundations, https://www.acf.org.uk/news/foundation-trustee-boards-the-good-the-bad-and-the-data.

[111] **In the US nearly 90% of foundation executives are white, and 40% of American foundations have boards that are entirely white:** 'The State of Change: An Analysis of Women and People of Color in the Philanthropic Sector', Council on Foundations, https://www.cof.org/sites/default/files/documents/files/2017-Gender-Diversity-Report.pdf; Drew Lindsay, 'Foundations Show Little Interest in Making their Boards More Diverse, Report Says', *The Chronicle of Philanthropy*, 28 February 2018, https://www.philanthropy.com/article/foundations-show-little-interest-in-making-their-boards-more-diverse-report-says.

[112] **Male board members in the UK ...:** Goddard, 'Foundation Trustee Boards'.

[113] **the CEOs of the top 20 funders in the UK ...:** Desk research based on grantmaking data included in Cathy Pharoah and Catherine Walker, 'Foundation Giving Trends 2019', Association of Charitable Foundations, https://www.acf.org.uk/policy-practice/research-publications/foundation-giving-trends-2019.

[114] **'it [is] abundantly clear that foundations are not sufficiently diverse ...':** 'Diversity, Equity and Inclusion: The Pillars of Stronger Foundation Practice', Association of Charitable Foundations, https://www.acf.org.uk/policy-practice/stronger-foundations/dei-working-group.

[115] **'My boss allows me to be bullied ...':** Authors' interview with anonymous grantmaker, 2020.

[116] **The Grant Givers' Movement:** https://www.grantgiversmovement.org.

[117] **More than 95 instances of prejudice or discrimination ... discrimination in the sector:** 'Discrimination, Prejudice & Isomorphism: A Short Report', Grant Givers' Movement, https://www.grantgiversmovement.org/discrimination-prejudice.

[118] **'The question for Black and indigenous grantmakers ...':** Authors' interview with Paul Waters, 23 October 2020.

[119] **The Story of the Disability Rights Fund:** Outline kindly provided by Diana Samarasan, founding executive director of the Disability Rights Fund and the Disability Rights Advocacy Fund.

[120] **'In Peru, we've funded groups of people ...':** Diana Samarasan, interviewed by Beverly Bell, 'The Global Disability Rights Movement: Winning Power, Participation, and Access', *HuffPost*, 5 October 2014, https://www.huffpost.com/entry/the-global-disability-rig_b_5651235.

[121] **The Trust-Based Philanthropy Project is ...:** https://trustbasedphilanthropy.org/.

[122] **Trust-Based Philanthropy Self-Reflection Tool:** Trust-Based Philanthropy Project, https://trustbasedphilanthropy.org/resources-articles/self-reflection.

[123] **Workplace Equality Index:** 'UK Workplace Equality Index', Stonewall, https://www.stonewall.org.uk/creating-inclusive-workplaces/workplace-equality-indices/uk-workplace-equality-index; version for multinational organisations, https://www.stonewall.org.uk/global-workplace-equality-index.

[124] **'three-quarters of [US] foundations have no written policy on board diversity':** Gara Lamarche, 'Democracy and the Donor Class', *Democracy: A Journal of Ideas*, Fall 2014, https://democracyjournal.org/magazine/34/democracy-and-the-donor-class.

[125] **any training where senior leaders ...:** Villanueva, *Decolonizing Wealth*, p. 63.

[126] **A shout-out here ...:** 'Where our Money Comes From', Lankelly Chase Foundation, https://lankellychase.org.uk/about-us/ourinvestmentstrategy.

[127] **It spent over $460 million ...**: '2019 Audited Financial Statements and Footnotes', Ford Foundation, https://www.fordfoundation.org/about/library/financial-statements/2019-audited-financial-statements-and-footnotes.

[128] **starting a programme called BUILD ...**: 'Reflections on the First Year of BUILD', Ford Foundation, https://www.fordfoundation.org/work/learning/learning-reflections/reflections-on-the-first-year-of-build.

[129] **'Almost certainly, providing deeper, more intensive support ...'**: Darren Walker, 'What's Next for the Ford Foundation?', Ford Foundation, 11 June 2015, https://www.fordfoundation.org/ideas/equals-change-blog/posts/whats-next-for-the-ford-foundation.

[130] **'Turning the oil tanker at Ford ...'**: Authors' interview with anonymous grantmaker, 2020.

[131] **the Rooney Rule ...**: David Roth, chief of IT, quoted in Chantal Forster and Satonya Fair, 'As Foundations Reimagine Themselves, They Should Give Attention to DEI in Operations', Inside Philanthropy, https://www.insidephilanthropy.com/home/2019/8/26/as-foundations-reimagine- themselves-they-should-give-attention-to-dei-in-operations.

[132] **'Back in 2016 Walker found himself criticised' ...**: Darren Walker, 'Ignorance Is the Enemy Within: On the Power of our Privilege, and the Privilege of our Power', Ford Foundation, 12 September 2016, https://www.fordfoundation.org/ideas/equals-change-blog/posts/ignorance-is-the-enemy-within-on-the-power-of-our-privilege-and-the-privilege-of-our-power. Subsequent quotations are from this source.

[133] **The Ford Foundation website now has a page on diversity, equity and inclusion**: 'Diversity, Equity and Inclusion', Ford Foundation, https://www.fordfoundation.org/about/people/diversity-equity-and-inclusion.

[134] **The foundation also has a separate policy on disability inclusion**: Noorain Khan and Catherine Townsend, 'Turning the Tide, Together: Disability Inclusion at Ford', Ford Foundation, 17 April 2019, https://www.fordfoundation.org/ideas/equals-change-blog/posts/turning-the-tide-together-disability-inclusion-at-ford.

[135] **'Ford's orientation, being a social justice funder and tackling inequality ...'**: Authors' interview with anonymous grantmaker, 2020.

[136] **Comic Relief has been criticised for perpetuating the 'white saviour' archetype**: Rob Preston, 'Comic Relief Caught Up in Another "White Saviour" Controversy', *Civil Society*, 1 March 2019, https://www.civilsociety.co.uk/news/comic-relief-defends-itself-over-latest-white-saviour-controversy.html.

[137] **Comic Relief decided to take steps to address this**: 'A Big Step in the Right Direction: Comic Relief Funding for BAME-Led Organisations', Charity So White, https://charitysowhite.org/blog/a-big-step-in-the-right-direction-comic-relief-funding-for-bame-led-organisations.

[138] **Democracy Frontlines Fund (US)**: https://www.democracyfrontlinesfund.org.

[139] **'movement-funding mainstay'**: Philip Rojc, 'Newcomers to Movement Funding Join a Collaborative Effort to Support Black-Led Groups', Inside Philanthropy, 18 September 2020, https://www.insidephilanthropy.com/home/2020/9/18/newcomers-to-movement-funding-join-a-collaborative-effort-to-support-black-led-groups.

[140] **Resourcing Racial Justice (UK)**: http://resourcingracialjustice.org.

[141] **'with funders who simply wanted to outsource their work on racial justice' ... 'It's a great example ...'**: Authors' interview with anonymous grantmaker, 2020.

[142] **Diversity, Equity and Inclusion coalition (UK)**: Harriet Whitehead, 'Charitable Foundations Form Thirteen-Strong Coalition to Tackle Sector's Inclusion Issues', Civil Society, 14 October 2019, https://www.civilsociety.co.uk/news/foundations-form-thirteen-strong-coalition-to-tackle-sectors-inclusion-issues.html.

[143] 'We went out to diversify our workforce ...': Authors' interview with anonymous grantmaker, 2020.

[144] 'Think of the buzzword phrase ...': Authors' interview with anonymous nonprofit leader, 2020.

[145] 'My proposal for investment ...': Authors' interview with anonymous grantmaker, 2020.

[146] One or two training sessions ...: Edward H. Chang et al., 'Does Diversity Training Work the Way It's Supposed To?', *Harvard Business Review*, 9 July 2019, https://hbr.org/2019/07/does-diversity-training-work-the-way-its-supposed-to.

[147] 'Thinking about inequality demands ...': Joy Warmington, 'Stronger Foundations Blog – Don't Rest on Your Foundations', Association of Charitable Foundations, 3 October 2019, https://www.acf.org.uk/news/stronger-foundations-blog-dont-rest-on-your-foundations.

[148] 'any authentic process ...': Gita Gulati-Partee and Maggie Potapchuk, 'Paying Attention to White Culture and Privilege: A Missing Link to Advancing Racial Equity', *The Foundation Review*, 6(1), 2014, https://www.racialequitytools.org/resourcefiles/2_Gulati_AB3.pdf.

[149] 'Organizational designers now recommend ...': Villanueva, *Decolonizing Wealth*, p. 108.

4. How do I help my funder develop a good strategy?

[150] 'I want my organisation to have a purpose ...': Authors' interview with anonymous foundation CEO, 2020.

[151] 'A strategy is a framework ...': Ann Latham, 'What the Heck Is a Strategy Anyway?', Forbes, 29 October 2017, https://www.forbes.com/sites/annlatham/2017/10/29/what-the-heck-is-a-strategy-anyway/?sh=28d92d827ed8.

[152] I always used to joke ...': Authors' interview with Ruth Levine, 30 March 2020.

[153] There is plenty of grant-making still happening ...': Authors' interview with Jo Andrews, 21 August 2020.

[154] Organisations without good, clear strategies ...: Barbara Kibbe, 'Five Things Strategy Isn't', *Stanford Social Innovation Review*, 14 March 2014, https://ssir.org/articles/entry/five_things_strategy_isnt.

[155] 'Funding big projects ...': Conor O'Clery, *The Billionaire Who Wasn't: How Chuck Feeney Secretly Made and Gave Away a Fortune* (New York: PublicAffairs, 2013), p. 335.

[156] 'Things *will* go wrong ...': Authors' interview with Ben Harrison, 14 April 2020.

[157] 'One bad thing that you see ...': Authors' interview with anonymous foundation CEO, 2020.

[158] The William and Flora Hewlett Foundation: Aimée Bruederle, 'Tying Grant Practices to our Foundation's Values', The William and Flora Hewlett Foundation, https://hewlett.org/tying-grant-practices-to-our-foundations-values.

[159] Disability Rights Fund: About page, https://disabilityrightsfund.org/about.

[160] The Joseph Rowntree Foundation: About page, https://www.jrf.org.uk/about-us.

[161] Malala Fund: About page, https://www.malala.org/about.

[162] If you want to boost your own skills ...: Kris Putnam-Walkerly, *Delusional Altruism: Why Philanthropists Fail to Achieve Change and What They Can Do to Transform Giving* (Hoboken, NJ: Wiley, 2020); Buchanan, *Giving Done Right*; Caroline Fiennes, *It Ain't What You Give*; and Paul Brest and Hal Harvey, *Money Well Spent: A Strategic Plan for Smart Philanthropy*, 2nd edn (New York: Bloomberg Press, 2018).

Modern Grantmaking

[163] **'One division which happens too much ...'**: Authors' interview with Dan Paskins, 9 July 2020.

[164] **AI transcription tools**: For more information see Jonas P. DeMuro and Brian Turner, 'Best Transcription Services in 2021', TechRadar, https://www.techradar.com/uk/best/best-transcription-services.

[165] **'The more things you do ...'**: Brest and Harvey, *Money Well Spent*, p. 272.

[166] **Use 'red teaming' exercises ...**: Ivy Wigmore, 'Red Teaming?', WhatIs.com, https://whatis.techtarget.com/definition/red-teaming; and Bryce G Hoffman, *Red Teaming: How Your Business Can Conquer the Competition by Challenging Everything* (New York: Crown Business, 2017).

[167] **Support and enable a chosen community ...**: Case study, including quotations, kindly provided by Alexandra Garita, executive director of Prospera – International Network of Women's Funds, September and December 2020.

[168] **A recent article ...**: Mengyao Liu et al., 'The Acceptability of Using a Lottery to Allocate Research Funding: A Survey of Applicants', *Research Integrity and Peer Review*, 5, art. 3 (2020), https://researchintegrityjournal.biomedcentral.com/articles/10.1186/s41073-019-0089-z.

[169] **'Lots of funders in the UK have links to colonialism ...'**: Authors' interview with Jenny Oppenheimer, 26 August 2020.

[170] **If you discover that your organisation's money ...**: Julia Travers, 'Making Amends: How Funders Can Address Slavery's Legacy', Inside Philanthropy, https://www.insidephilanthropy.com/home/2019/9/19/making-amends-how-funders-can-address-slaverys-legacy.

[171] **'various asset-building projects ...'**: Villanueva, *Decolonizing Wealth*, p. 41.

[172] **Make sure that you review your strategy ...**: Dana O'Donovan, Gabriel Kasper and Nicole L. Dubbs, 'How Adaptive Strategy Is Adapting', *Stanford Social Innovation Review*, 24 May 2018, https://ssir.org/articles/entry/how_adaptive_strategy_is_adapting.

5. What big questions should all funders debate from time to time?

[173] **'There are these two young fish swimming along ...'**: David Foster Wallace, 'This Is Water', Kenyon commencement speech, 2005, http://bulletin-archive.kenyon.edu/x4280.html.

[174] **Website excerpt ...**: The National Lottery Community Fund, https://www.tnlcommunityfund.org.uk.

[175] **'In the last financial year ...'**: Matthew O'Reilly, 'Why We Are Suspending Unsolicited Applications', The Indigo Trust, https://indigotrust.org.uk/2018/04/09/why-we-are-suspending-unsolicited-applications. For more on US grant writing costs and benefits, see Ted von Hippel and Courtney von Hippel, 'To Apply or Not to Apply: A Survey Analysis of Grant Writing Costs and Benefits', *PloS One 10*(3): e0118494, 4 March 2015, https://www.ncbi.nlm.nih.gov/pmc/articles/PMC4349454.

[176] **'We worked very openly for some time ...'**: Authors' interview with anonymous former foundation CEO, 2020.

[177] **'We're a funder with a single, clear social change goal ...'**: Authors' interview with anonymous foundation director, 2020.

[178] **Case study: When risk management becomes discrimination**: Authors' interview with anonymous grantmaker, 2020.

[179] **people working together as a group may become more risk averse:** Marielle Brunette, Laure Cabantous and Stéphane Couture, 'Are Individuals More Risk and Ambiguity Averse in a Group Environment or Alone? Results from an Experimental Study', *Theory and Decision*, 78(3), March 2015, pp. 357–76, https://www.researchgate.net/publication/268803206_Are_individuals_more_risk_and_ambiguity_ave rse_in_a_group_environment_or_alone_Results_from_an_experimental_study.

[180] **But there is one risk-related argument ...:** Lateefah Simon, 'If Philanthropy Won't Take Risks, Who Will?', PND by Candid, 9 March 2016, https://philanthropynewsdigest.org/commentary-and-opinion/if-philanthropy-won-t-take-risks-who-will. For a view that challenges the notion of applying the concept of risk to funders, see Nathan Washatka, 'Philanthropy and Risk Taking', *Philanthropy Daily*, 25 April 2019, https://www.philanthropydaily.com/philanthropy-and-risk-taking.

[181] **a systematic review ... :** 'Every £1 Spent on Public Health in UK Saves Average of £14', *BMJ*, https://beta-www.bmj.com/company/newsroom/every-1-spent-on-public-health-in-uk-saves-average-of-14.

[182] **'A focus on root causes isn't somehow superior ...':** Buchanan, *Giving Done Right*, p. 69.

[183] **Prevention-based grantmaking often focuses ...:** 'Joint Action for a Healthier, Fairer Future', UK Prevention Research Partnership, https://ukprp.org/what-we-fund/actearly; 'Early Action Funders Alliance: Challenging Funders to Act Earlier', Global Dialogue, https://global-dialogue.org/programmes/early-action-funders-alliance.

[184] **'giving grants and support to organisations working in Islington ...':** 'Strategy', Cripplegate Foundation, https://www.cripplegate.org/about-us/strategy.

[185] **Clear themes and a lack of geographical specificity ...:** Screen capture from the Stanton Foundation's home page, https://thestantonfoundation.org.

[186] **the wide range of issues supported by Cripplegate Foundation:** 'Organisations We Support', Cripplegate Foundation, https://www.cripplegate.org/support-funding/organisations-we-support.

[187] **place-based funding rose in popularity:** 'Place-Based Funding', Institute for Voluntary Action Research, https://www.ivar.org.uk/our-research/place-based-funding.

[188] **'We made a change to push our responsibility ...':** Authors' interview with anonymous senior foundation executive, 2020.

[189] **Here are some suggestions:** Ben Wrobel and Meg Massey, *Letting Go: How Philanthropists and Impact Investors Can Do More Good by Giving Up Control* (Potomac, MD: New Degree Press, 2021); Cynthia Gibson, *Participatory Grantmaking: Has Its Time Come?*, Ford Foundation, 2017, https://www.fordfound.org/media/3598/has-the-time-come-for-participatory-grant-making.pdf; Cynthia Gibson and Jen Bokoff, *Deciding Together: Shifting Power and Resources through Participatory Grantmaking*, GrantCraft, 2018, https://grantcraft.org/wp- content/uploads/sites/2/2018/12/DecidingTogether_Final_20181002.pdf; and Sam Kaner et al., *Facilitator's Guide to Participatory Decision-Making*, 3rd edn (San Francisco, CA: Jossey-Bass, 2014).

[190] **Understanding the blockers ...:** Paraphrased from Hannah Paterson, 'Grassroots Grantmaking: Embedding Participatory Approaches in Funding', Winston Churchill Memorial Trust, https://www.wcmt.org.uk/sites/default/files/report-documents/Paterson%20H%202019%20FINAL.pdf; and 'Participatory Grantmaking', 2020, https://hannahpaterson.com.

[191] **'Funders can be too simplistic ...':** Authors' interview with Louisa Syrett, 6 December 2019.

Modern Grantmaking

[192] 'What's the alternative to a mix of philanthropic and government support ...?': Buchanan, *Giving Done Right*, p. 21.

[193] 'Endowments, philanthropic and other, are of deep concern ...': Authors' interview with Jo Andrews, 24 July 2020.

[194] **One person who should know ...**: Seb Ellsworth, 'All Foundations Can Do More to Align Their Investments with Their Mission', *Third Sector*, https://www.thirdsector.co.uk/seb-elsworth-foundations-align-investments-mission/finance/article/1699779.

[195] 'disinvest every penny of philanthropic capital ...': Authors' interview with Jake Hayman, 24 March 2020.

[196] **The Association of Charitable Foundation's guide on investments**: *Investment: The Pillars of Stronger Foundation Practice*, Association of Charitable Foundations, https://www.acf.org.uk/policy-practice/practice-publications/investment-the-pillars-ofstronger-foundation-practice.

[197] **Lankelly Chase's investment strategy**: 'Where Our Money Comes From', Lankelly Chase, https://lankellychase.org.uk/about-us/ourinvestmentstrategy.

[198] **The Forum for Sustainable and Responsible Investment**: https://www.ussif.org.

[199] 'It's quite hard to judge grantmaking ...': Authors' interview with Dan Paskins, 9 July 2020.

[200] 'Who are you being transparent for and why? ...': 'Transparency and Engagement', Association of Charitable Foundations, https://www.acf.org.uk/policy-practice/stronger-foundations/transparency- and-engagement.

[201] **GrantAdvisor UK**: https://grantadvisor.org.

[202] 'Grantmakers should set ourselves to a much higher standard ...': Authors' interview with Jayne Engle, 1 October 2020.

[203] '2020 has given us a global pandemic ...': Authors' interview with Pia Infante, 7 October 2020.

[204] **publicly available reports and articles on GrantCraft**: https://grantcraft.org/gcsearch/?fwp_search=spend+down.

[205] **Case study** provided by Pia Infante and Rachel Dearborn from the Whitman Institute, February 2020.

6. How can I improve the experience of grantseekers and grantees?

[206] 'As a funder you have a very interesting power dynamic ...': Authors' interview with Angela Murray, 22 June 2020.

[207] **Here are a few anonymous quotes from grantseekers ...**: Authors' interviews with anonymous grantseekers, 2020.

[208] 'The challenge in foundations ...': Authors' interview with Dan Sutch, 7 April 2020.

[209] 'In the funders I've worked for previously ...': Authors' interview with Sufina Ahmad, 26 August 2020.

[210] 'When it comes to being a nonprofit ...': Authors' interview with Helen Turvey, 28 September 2020.

[211] 'Modern grantmakers design funding services ...': Authors' interview with Ngozi Lyn Cole, 3 July 2020.

[212] 'A good user experience in grantmaking ...': Authors' interview with Angela Murray, 22 June 2020.

[213] **'We always tried to treat applicants with respect ...':** Anonymous vice president quoted in William Ryan, 'A Customer Service Approach to Decision Giving Fostering a Culture of Respect', GrantCraft, https://grantcraft.org/content/case-studies/a-customer-service-approach-to-decision-giving.

[214] **'Not having any concept of human-centred design ...':** Authors' interview with anonymous foundation CEO, 2020.

[215] *The Field Guide to Human-Centered Design*: https://www.designkit.org//resources/1.

[216] **'Modern grantmaking respects ...':** Authors' interview with Sarah Drummond, 23 June 2020.

[217] **An example of design iteration in a large funder:** Case study kindly provided by anonymous grantmaker, 2020.

[218] **'Size doesn't cut it for funders ...':** Authors' interview with anonymous grantmaker, 2020.

[219] **HotJar:** https://www.hotjar.com.

[220] **anonymous feedback survey:** 'Dulverton Trust Anonymous Feedback Survey', The Dulverton Trust, https://www.dulverton.org/feedback-form.

[221] **How a smaller funder rebuilt its grantmaking model around listening:** Authors' interview with Jo Wells, 5 October 2020.

[222] **Example questions used by the Center for Effective Philanthropy's Grantee Perception Reports:** 'Grantee and Applicant Perception Report', The Center for Effective Philanthropy, https://cep.org/assessments/grantee-perception-report/.

[223] **We recommend checking out ...:** 'Governance Principles for Agile Service Delivery', https://www.gov.uk/service-manual/agile-delivery/governance-principles-for-agile-service-delivery.

[224] **books on service design:** Lou Downe, *Good Services: How to Design Services that Work* (Amsterdam: BIS, 2020), https://good.services; Tim Brown, *Change by Design: How Design Thinking Transforms Organizations and Inspires Innovation*, rev. and updated edn (New York: HarperCollins, 2019).

[225] **Case study of design infrastructure for grantees: The Mental Health Pattern Library:** Case study kindly provided by Sarah Drummond, CEO of Snook. For more information see 'Mental Health Pattern Library: Connecting the Dots of Mental Health Learnings and Research', Snook, https://wearesnook.com/work/mental-health-pattern-library.

[226] **'You should share as much information as possible ...':** Authors' interview with Ruth Levine, 30 March 2020.

[227] **'I think a lot of funders ask questions ...':** Authors' interview with anonymous grantmaker, 2020.

[228] **'Some funders don't always get back ...':** Authors' interview with anonymous grantmaker, 2020.

7. How should I make use of research?

[229] 'For funders, using research means ...': Authors' interview with Dr Tiago Peixoto, 24 September 2019.

[230] *research*: studious inquiry or examination ...': https://www.merriam-webster.com/dictionary/research.

[231] we recommend reading ...: Buchanan, *Giving Done Right*, p. 135.

[232] Centers for Disease Control and Prevention's cornucopia of resources: 'CDC Evaluation Resources', Centers for Disease Control and Prevention, https://www.cdc.gov/eval/resources/index.htm.

[233] 'You can't just rely on your judgement ...': Authors' interview with Caroline Fiennes, 16 March 2020.

[234] *cognitive biases*: For more on cognitive bias, see Dan Ariely, *Predictably Irrational: The Hidden Forces that Shape our Decisions* (New York: Harper, 2009) and *The Honest Truth about Dishonesty: How We Lie to Everyone – Especially Ourselves* (New York: Harper, 2013); and Richard H. Thaler and Cass R. Sunstein, *Nudge: Improving Decisions about Health, Wealth and Happiness* (New York: Penguin Books, 2009).

[235] consider the phenomenon known as *confirmation bias*: Max Rollwage et al., 'Confidence Drives a Neural Confirmation Bias', *Nature Communications*, 26 May 2020, https://www.nature.com/articles/s41467-020-16278-6.

[236] 'Modern Grantmaking is about understanding what is working ...': Authors' interview with Geeta Gopalan, 2 July 2020.

[237] 'It's all too complicated ...': Authors' interview with anonymous grantmaker, 2019.

[238] 'Too many funders get their own grantees ...': Authors' interview with Stephen Hall, 10 September 2020.

[239] 'When I first started in this role ...': Authors' interview with anonymous grantmaker, 2020.

[240] 'although we're seeing some green shoots of change': Authors' interview with Ngozi Lyn Cole, 3 July 2020.

[241] the Hewlett Foundation's bracingly honest report *Hard Lessons* ...: Prudence Brown and Leila Fiester, 'Hard Lessons about Philanthropy & Community Change from the Neighborhood Improvement Initiative', March 2007, The William and Flora Hewlett Foundation, http://www.hewlett.org/wp-content/uploads/2016/08/HewlettNIIReport.pdf.

[242] an evaluation of a large education initiative ...: Valerie Strauss, 'Bill Gates Spent Hundreds of Millions of Dollars to Improve Teaching. New Report Says It Was a Bust', *The Washington Post*, 29 June 2018, https://www.washingtonpost.com/news/answer-sheet/wp/2018/06/29/bill-gates-spent-hundreds-of-millions-of-dollars-to-improve-teaching-new-report-says-it-was-a-bust.

[243] 'Meta-analyses of seven studies show ...': Anthony Petrosino, Carolyn Turpin-Petrosino, Meghan E. Hollis-Peel and Julia G. Lavenberg, '"Scared Straight" and Other Juvenile Awareness Programs for Preventing Juvenile Delinquency', *Cochrane Database of Systematic Reviews*, 4, 2013, https://www.cochranelibrary.com/cdsr/doi/10.1002/14651858.CD002796.pub2/full.

[244] 'Often you have to retrofit the way you do evaluation ...': Authors' interview with Jen Bokoff, 16 September 2020.

[245] 'One problem that grantmakers ...': Authors' interview with anonymous grantmaker, 2020.

Notes

[246] **We find that charities spend 15.8m hours every single year:** Will Thompson, 'Charities Spend 15.8 Million Hours Reporting to Funders – That's Too Much', Time to Spare, https://blog.timetospare.com/charities-spend-15-8-million-hours-reporting-to-funders-thats-too-much.

[247] **a RAND report ...:** Sandraluz Lara-Cinisomo and Paul Steinberg, 'Meeting Funder Compliance: A Case Study of Challenges, Time Spent, and Dollars Invested', RAND, 2006, https://www.rand.org/content/dam/rand/pubs/monographs/2006/RAND_MG505.pdf.

[248] **'when one Bridgespan client added up the hours ...':** Ann Goggins Gregory and Don Howard, 'The Nonprofit Starvation Cycle', *Stanford Social Innovation Review*, Fall 2009, https://ssir.org/articles/entry/the_nonprofit_starvation_cycle.

[249] **'If you're a funder that wants to follow your heart ...':** Authors' interview with Stephen Tall, 10 September 2020.

[250] **'Not all research is born equal ...':** Authors' interview with Ruth Levine, 30 March 2020.

[251] **'you either need to hire someone ...':** Authors' interview with anonymous grantmaker, 2020.

[252] **a whole (if politically slanted) book on this ...:** Martin Morse Wooster, *Great Philanthropic Mistakes* (Washington, DC: Hudson Institute, 2010).

[253] **the work on poverty ...:** Andreas Adriano, 'Poverty Fighters', International Monetary Fund, June 2020, https://www.imf.org/external/pubs/ft/fandd/2020/06/MIT-poverty-fighters-abhijit-banerjee-and-esther-duflo.htm.

[254] **private funder communities for sharing questions ...:** Ariadne, https://www.ariadne-network.eu; The Funders Network, https://www.fundersnetwork.org; Environmental Funders Network, https://www.greenfunders.org.

[255] **Candid's database of over 16 million US grants:** 'Foundation Directory Online' (some elements are subscription based), Candid, https://fconline.foundationcenter.org/.

[256] **GrantNav's website ...:** https://grantnav.threesixtygiving.org.

[257] **Google Scholar:** https://scholar.google.com.

[258] **'You should do a rigorous causal impact evaluation ...':** Authors' interview with Mary Ann Bates, 17 September 2020.

[259] **'Introduction to Research Ethics: Working with People':** https://www.futurelearn.com/courses/research-ethics-an-introduction.

[260] **'We had to hire a consulting firm ...':** Villanueva, *Decolonizing Wealth*, p. 58.

[261] **The Equitable Evaluation Initiative:** For further information see https://www.equitableeval.org/ee-framework.

[262] **'Where there are important gaps ...':** Authors' interview with Caroline Fiennes, 16 March 2020.

[263] **Magic Breakfast:** 'Magic Breakfast', Education Endowment Foundation, https://educationendowmentfoundation.org.uk/projects-and-evaluation/projects/magic-breakfast.

[264] **Not Too Late:** Authors' interview with Mary Ann Bates, 17 September 2020.

[265] **Further reading:** Mary Kay Gugerty and Dean Karlan, *The Goldilocks Challenge: Right-Fit Evidence for the Social Sector* (New York: Oxford University Press, 2018); Helen Kara, *Research Ethics in the Real World: Euro-Western and Indigenous Perspectives* (Bristol: Policy Press, 2018); and Fiennes, *It Ain't What You Give, It's the Way that You Give It*.

8. How do I manage well both upwards and downwards?

[266] 'So much of what we call management ...': Peter F. Drucker, *The Practice of Management* (New York: Harper Business, 2006)

[267] recorded more than 95 instances of prejudice or discrimination: 'Discrimination, Prejudice & Isomorphism: A Short Report'.

[268] 'I am far from alone ...': Villanueva, *Decolonizing Wealth*, p. 90.

[269] 'Out of the crooked timber of humanity ...': Immanuel Kant, *Idea for a Universal History with a Cosmopolitan Purpose*, quoted by Isaiah Berlin in *The Crooked Timber of Humanity: Chapters in the History of Ideas*, 2nd edn (Princeton, NJ: Princeton University Press, 2013).

[270] Classic macho, alpha 'leading from the front' ...: For more on different perspectives on leadership, we recommend Tomas Chamorro-Premuzic and Michael Sanger, 'What Leadership Looks Like in Different Cultures', *Harvard Business Review*, 6 May 2016, https://hbr.org/2016/05/what-leadership-looks-like-in-different-cultures; Robert K. Greenleaf, *Servant Leadership: A Journey into the Nature of Legitimate Power and Greatness* (New York: Paulist Press, 1977); and Susan Cain, *Quiet: The Power of Introverts in a World that Can't Stop Talking* (London: Penguin Books, 2013).

[271] 'It is super important to approach the work ...': Authors' interview with John Palfrey, 20 October 2020.

[272] 'As a manager you have a responsibility ...': Authors' interview with anonymous grantmaker, 2020.

[273] A good grantmaking manager compensates for this by showing real trust: Stav Ziv, '10 Traits of a Great Manager, according to Google's Internal Research', The Muse, https://www.themuse.com/advice/10-behaviors-make-great-google-manager.

[274] 'A good manager shows an active interest ...': Authors' interview with anonymous grantmaker, 2020.

[275] an active commitment to equity, diversity and inclusion: Vivian Hunt, Dennis Layton and Sara Prince, *Diversity Matters*, McKinsey & Co., 2015, https://www.mckinsey.com/business- functions/organization/our-insights/~/media/2497d4ae4b534ee89d929cc6e3aea485.ashx; and Vijay Eswaran, 'The Business Case for Diversity in the Workplace Is Now Overwhelming', World Economic Forum, 29 April 2019, https://www.weforum.org/agenda/2019/04/business-case-for-diversity-in-the-workplace.

[276] 'What is it to be a good leader in grantmaking ...': Authors' interview with anonymous grantmaker, 2020.

[277] For a useful perspective on equity and funding organisations ...: Kris Putnam-Walkerly and Elizabeth Russell, 'What the Heck Does "Equity" Mean?', *Stanford Social Innovation Review*, 15 September 2016, https://ssir.org/articles/entry/what_the_heck_does_equity_mean#.

[278] 'balances being really supportive and enthusiastic ...': Authors' interview with anonymous grantmaker, 2020.

[279] 'When you hire people to pore over detail ...': Authors' interview with anonymous grantmaker, 2020.

[280] 'As a manager in grantmaking ...': Authors' interview with anonymous grantmaker, 2020.

[281] 'identifying with and expressing moral values ...': Email from anonymous grantmaker, 2020.

Notes

[282] **Work consciously to create psychological safety ...**: Amy Edmondson, 'Psychological Safety and Learning Behavior in Work Teams', *Administrative Science Quarterly*, 44(2), June 1999, pp. 350–383, https://journals.sagepub.com/doi/abs/10.2307/2666999.

[283] **some suggestions that Juliet Bourke and Andrea Titus shared ...**: Juliet Bourke and Andrea Titus, 'The Key to Inclusive Leadership', *Harvard Business Review*, 6 March 2020, https://hbr.org/2020/03/the-key-to-inclusive-leadership.

[284] **the UK government's 'Agile Tools and Techniques'**: https://www.gov.uk/service-manual/agile-delivery/agile-tools-techniques#daily-standup.

[285] **'It is a sector with no accountability model ...'**: Authors' interview with Anna de Pulford, 7 October 2020.

[286] **Fay Twersky's work on top leadership in foundations**: Fay Twersky, *Foundation Chief Executives as Artful Jugglers*, The Center for Effective Philanthropy, 2014, http://arizonagrantmakersforum.org/wp-content/uploads/2014/11/Artful-Jugglers.pdf.

[287] **'I came across one large US foundation ...'**: Authors' interview with anonymous foundation executive director, 2020.

[288] **All 11 characteristics in it are taken...**: David L. Dotlich and Peter C. Cairo, *Why CEOs Fail: The 11 Behaviors that Can Derail Your Climb to the Top – and How to Manage Them* (San Francisco, CA: Jossey-Bass, 2003).

[289] **Because this kind of advice is ...**: See for example, 'The 10 Mistakes of a New Manager', RealityHR, https://www.realityhr.co.uk/10-mistakes-new-manager.

[290] **'This makes for challenges in managing people ...'**: Authors' interview with anonymous grantmaker, 2020.

[291] **Not being authentic and open**: Bill George, *Authentic Leadership: Rediscovering the Secrets to Creating Lasting Value* (San Francisco, CA: Jossey-Bass, 2004).

[292] **'Going from school to university into grantmaking ...'**: Authors' interview with anonymous grantmaker, 2020.

[293] **some suggestions made by Tessa Ann Taylor ...**: Tessa Ann Taylor, 'Diversity, Inclusion and Culture: How to Build Great Teams', *New York Times*, 19 April 2018, https://open.nytimes.com/diversity-inclusion-and-culture-steps-for-building-great-teams-ca157bd98c07.

[294] **e.g. 'dominant' this and 'superior' ...**: D Gaucher, J Friesen and A. C. Kay, 'Evidence That Gendered Wording in Job Advertisements Exists and Sustains Gender Inequality', *Journal of Personality and Social Psychology*, 101(1), 109–128, 2011. https://doi.org/10.1037/a0022530

[295] **We recommend reading ...**: Rebecca Knight, '7 Practical Ways to Reduce Bias in Your Hiring Process', *Harvard Business Review*, 12 June 2017, https://hbr.org/2017/06/7-practical-ways-to-reduce-bias-in-your-hiring-process; *Diversity, Equity and Inclusion: The Pillars of Stronger Foundation Practice*, Association of Charitable Foundations, https://www.acf.org.uk/downloads/ACF_DEI_Thepillarsofstrongerfoundationpractice_final.pdf.

[296] **'We've had one or two situations ...'**: Authors' interview with anonymous grantmaker, 2020.

9. How do I keep developing my skills?

[297] **'We've all seen that senior management person ...'**: Authors' interview with anonymous grantmaker, 2020.

[298] **monthly or fortnightly 'retrospectives' with your team**: 'Agile Tools and Techniques', https://www.gov.uk/service-manual/agile-delivery/agile-tools-techniques#retrospective-meetings.

[299] **'Reverse mentoring between a grantmaker ...'**: Authors' interview with Sacha Rose-Smith, 15 July 2020.

[300] **Gen up on the existing research available on funders and systems change**: Social Innovation Exchange (SIX), https://socialinnovationexchange.org/insights/themes/system-change; Batten et al., 'Guiding a Giving Response to Anti-Black Injustice'; Carlos Saavedra, 'Five Ways Funders Can Support Social Movements', *Stanford Social Innovation Review*, 9 July 2019, https://ssir.org/articles/entry/five_ways_funders_can_support_social_movements.

[301] **Study some of the biggest system changes in history**: Adam Hochschild, *Bury the Chains: The British Struggle to Abolish Slavery* (London: Picador, 2012); and Duncan Green, *How Change Happens* (Oxford: Oxford University Press, 2018).

[302] **Consider specific learning opportunities**: the School of System Change, https://www.forumforthefuture.org/school-of-system-change.

[303] **Coursera's course on 'Understanding Research Methods'**: Dr J. Simon Rofe, 'Understanding Research Methods', Coursera, https://www.coursera.org/learn/research-methods#instructors.

[304] **Churchill Fellowships**: 'Churchill Fellowships', Winston Churchill Memorial Trust, https://www.wcmt.org.uk/what-we-do/churchill-fellowships.

[305] **Grant Givers' Programme, run by Ten Years' Time ...**: https://tenyearstime.com/grant-givers-programme/.

[306] **US equivalents include ...**: 'Momentum Fellowship', Philanthropy Northwest, https://philanthropynw.org/momentum-fellowship-0; and Jeremiah E. Headen, 'The Inaugural Equity in Philanthropy Fellowship Announced!', Rockwood Leadership Institute, https://rockwoodleadership.org/announcing-the-2020-equity-in-philanthropy-fellows.

[307] **A good, brief introduction ...**: Alix Dunn, 'How to Fund Tech', https://www.howtofund.tech/buy-the-guide.

[308] **Candid's GrantCraft**: https://grantcraft.org.

[309] **Association of Charitable Foundations**: https://www.acf.org.uk.

[310] **'Why is there no academy ...'**: Authors' interview with anonymous senior grantmaker, 2020.

[311] **a number of universities in the US and UK**: Lilly Family School of Philanthropy, Indiana University (US), https://philanthropy.iupui.edu/; the Business School (formerly Cass), City University of London (UK), https://www.cass.city.ac.uk/study/masters/courses/grantmaking-philanthropy-and-social-investment; Loyola University Chicago (US), https://www.luc.edu/philanthropy/about_nmps.shtml; Centre for Philanthropy, University of Kent (UK), https://research.kent.ac.uk/philanthropy; Center for Social Sector Leadership, Haas School of Business, University of California, Berkeley (US), https://haas.berkeley.edu/cssl/about-us; Centre for the Study of Philanthropy & Public Good, The University of St Andrews (UK): https://www.philanthropy.scot/.

[312] **developing a clear understanding ...**: MSc/Postgraduate Diploma: Grantmaking,

Philanthropy and Social Investment, October 2021, https://www.cass.city.ac.uk/_data/assets/pdf_file/0016/571111/2021-22-MSc-Grantmaking_Philanthropy_and_Social_Investment_Overview.pdf.

[313] **Dr Peter Grant leads the Business School course ...**: Peter Grant, *The Business of Giving: The Theory and Practice of Philanthropy, Grantmaking and Social Investment* (London: Palgrave Macmillan, 2011).

[314] **The University of Kent team is led by Dr Beth Breeze ...**: Beth Breeze and Theresa Lloyd, *Richer Lives: Why Rich People Give* (London: Directory of Social Change, 2013).

[315] **PEAK Grantmaking**: 'Grants Management Professional Competency Model', PEAK Grantmaking, https://www.peakgrantmaking.org/resource/grants-management-professional-competency-model.

[316] **Peter Singer's Coursera course on 'Effective Altruism'**: https://www.coursera.org/learn/altruism.

10. How do I become a grantmaking reformer?

[317] **Trust-Based Philanthropy Project**: https://trustbasedphilanthropy.org.

[318] **awesome and memorable naming choices ...**: Jessamyn Shams-Lau, Jane Leu and Vu Le, *Unicorns Unite: How Nonprofits & Foundations Can Build EPIC Partnerships* (Wareham: Red Press, 2018).

[319] **'the dragons of injustice and inequity ...'**: Unicorns Unite, https://www.epicpartnerships.org.

[320] **'A non-hierarchical gathering ...'**: 'Championing Diversity in the Grant-Giving Sector', ACEVO, 11 October 2021, https://www.acevo.org.uk/2019/10/championing-diversity-in-the-grant-giving-sector.

[321] **#ShiftThePower**: https://globalfundcommunityfoundations.org/what-we-stand-for/shiftthepower.

[322] **Pathways to Power Symposium**: 'Pathways to Power: New Ways of Deciding and Doing', 18–19 November 2019, Global Fund for Community Foundations, https://globalfundcommunityfoundations.org/what-we-stand-for/shiftthepower/a-symposium-on-people-led-development-pathways-to-power-new-ways-of-deciding-and-doing.

[323] **Future Foundations in the UK**: https://www.future-foundations.co.uk; quotation from Twitter profile @FutureFoundsUK.

INDEX

Locators in **bold** refer to tables and those in *italics* to figures.

2027 initiative 97
360-degree reviews 269
360Giving 71, 167

academic research *see* research
Access to Justice Lab 224
accountability
 classic funder dilemmas 165–168
 private foundations 16–18
 risk appetite 145
 types of organisations *14*, 14
accreditation 280–283
 see also graduate qualifications; skills
African Americans 82–83
Ahmad, Sufina 30, 43, 87, 135–136
Amaechi, John 81
Andrews, Jo 112
anonymity of contributions to this book 22–23
anonymous feedback 253
application process
 ease and accessibility 56–57, 288
 good communication 59–60
 rejecting proposals 57–58
 time cost of applying for grants 56–57, 141–142
Arts and Health Repository 224
Association of Charitable Foundations (ACF) 69, 279
authenticity 258

Barp, Meghan 42
Bates, Mary Ann 228
Bediako, Stephen 34
beliefs about grantmaking 247
 see also values

bias
 cognitive bias 211
 confirmation bias 211–212
 and evidence 36–37, 212
 recruitment 263
 research methods 230
 research quality 235, 236
 strategy development 113
Big Philanthropy 16–18
Bill and Melinda Gates Foundation 216
The Blagrave Trust 48, 194–195
Blueprints for Healthy Youth Development 225
board members
 diversity 75–78, 87
 as final decision makers 156, 158
 gender 89
 Modern Grantmaking 296
 participatory grantmaking 160
 privilege 27, 103–104
 skills development 40
 strategy development 120
 traditional grantmaking 27–28, 40
 upwards management 260–261
 who is this book not for? 15
Bokoff, Jen 66, 217
Boswell, Kate 84
Bridgespan Group 51, 275
Buchanan, Phil 39, 59, 151, 162–163
budgets 213–214

Cairo, Peter C. 256
Campbell Collaboration 225
Candid 240, 278–279
careers
 grantmaker job roles 27–28
 management 245–248

Index

salary 65, 263
staff turnover 258, 268
who is this book for? 12–13
see also recruitment
causes for grants
  climate change 20–21
  negative consequences 17–18
  strategic priorities 19
  see also mission; social impacts
Center for Effective Philanthropy (CEP) 42
CEOs of funding organisations 12, 255
chair's funds 114
charitable donations 15
charitable organisations *see* nonprofits
Charity So White 100
chief executives of funding organisations 12
Churchill Fellowships 277
Clara Lionel Foundation (CLF) 53
classic funder dilemmas 139–140
  checklist 172
  final decision makers 156–161
  financial sustainability of grantees 162–163
  foundation investments 163–165
  perpetual vs. spending down funders 169–171
  prevention vs. cure 151–152
  risky projects 144–150
  thematic vs. place-based funders 153–155
  transparency and accountability 165–168
  unsolicited proposals 140–144
climate change 20–21
cognitive bias 211
Cole, Ngozi Lyn 75, 216
collaboration with other funders 52–55
  addressing privilege 96, 101–102
  strategy development 113–114
College of Policing 225
Comic Relief 100
communication with grantees
  good communication 59–60
  mutually beneficial conversations 60–61, 271
  rejecting proposals 57–58
  strategy development 112, 123–124, 126

community approach
  Modern Grantmaking 297
  participatory grantmaking 158, 159–161
  programme design 289
  strategy development 132–134
community research 231
confirmation bias 211–212
Convention on the Rights of Persons with Disabilities (CRPD) 92–93
core grants *see* unrestricted grants
corporate culture
  faking it 102–104
  inclusion 95, 288
  listening to grantees 61
  privilege 85–87, 85–89, 94–96
  and strategy 111
COVID-19 pandemic
  good communication 61
  pooled funds example 53
  restricted grants 46, 47
Cripplegate Foundation 153, *154*
crowdfunding 143–144
cultural context 232, 246
  see also corporate culture
Cummings Foundation 51
cure vs. prevention focus 151–152

de Pulford, Anna 40, 252
decision-making
  collaboration with other funders 53
  diligence 40–41
  ease and accessibility of application process 56–57, 288
  equity 34–35
  evidence basis 29, 36–37
  humility 33
  management no-brainers 249, 253
  Modern Grantmaking 294–295
  pace of grantmaking 67–68
  privilege 85–87
  rejecting proposals 57–58
  research 207–208
  strategy development 113
  traditional grantmaking 27–28
  types of organisations *14*, 16–17
  who makes the final decision? 156–161
  see also classic funder dilemmas
Democracy Frontlines Fund (US) 101

Modern Grantmaking

digital technology, impacts on grantmaking 278
diligence
   management 254
   as Modern Grantmaking value 31, 40–41
disabilities
   addressing privilege 75–76, 92–93
   Ford Foundation case study 98–99
   representing funding organisations 77–78
Disability Rights Advocacy Fund (DRAF) 92–93
Disability Rights Fund (DRF) 92–93, 116
discrimination
   addressing privilege 94–96
   awareness training 75–77, 274–275
   ease and accessibility of application process 56
   invite-only applications 62
   language use 24
   and management practices 244
   risk management 148
   in the workplace 90
   see also privilege
Ditkoff, Susan Wolf 54
diversity
   awareness training 75–77, 95–96, 274–275
   Ford Foundation case study 98–99
   gender 89
   in grantmaking organisations 87, 89
   management 247, 251–252
   and privilege 78–79, 95
   recruitment practices 95, 97, 98
   representing funding organisations 77–78
   strategy development 131
   workplace discrimination 90
Diversity, Equity and Inclusion (DEI) coalition 102
donors 15
Dotlich, David L. 256
Du Bois, W. E. B. 82–83, 84

Early Action Funders Alliance 152
Early Intervention Foundation 224
easy wins *see* no-brainers
Edmondson, Amy 251

Education Endowment Foundation (EEF) 238–239
effective altruism movement 284
Ellsworth, Seb 164
emergency grants 53, 114
endowments
   addressing privilege 96
   approaching your foundation investment 163–165
Engle, Jayne 26, 167–168
the environment, and climate change 20–21
Equitable Evaluation Framework 232
equity
   addressing privilege 95, 96
   management 247, 251, 254
   as Modern Grantmaking value 31, 34–35
   participatory grantmaking 159
   personal development plans 271
   strategy development 113
Esmée Fairbairn Foundation 49
ethics
   avoid short-changing grantees 65–67
   backing grantseekers' priorities 63–65
   paying up front 65
   rejecting proposals 57–58
   research 229–231, 276
   treating grantees well 60–61, 288
   see also values
evaluation of project success
   burdensome reporting 217–219
   failures 216–217
   grantee reports 211, 213–214, 218–219, 236
   how to find useful research 223–224
   independent research 225–227, 289
   influencing government spending 238–239
   outputs and outcomes 214–215
   and research 209, 210
   research quality 233–237
   site visits 261
   skills to manage 284
evidence
   management 249, 254
   as Modern Grantmaking value 31, 36–37

Index

personal development plans **271**
seeking research 219–220
evidence-based medicine 290
executive directors of funding organisations 12, 255
extractive research 230–231

facilitation skills **271**
failure, acknowledgement of 216–217
feedback
   backing grantseekers' priorities 64
   listening to grantees 61
   management no-brainers 252–253
   from managers 247
   participatory grantmaking 160–161
   performance reviews 257
   praise and recognition 259
   psychologically safe teams 251
   rejecting proposals 57–58
   strategy development 121, 123, 128–129
   transparency and accountability 166–168
   values surveys 42
Feeney, Chuck 114
fellowship programmes 277
feminist funding principles 133–134
Fiennes, Caroline 211
financial sustainability
   of grantees 162–163
   perpetual vs. spending down funders 169–171
Floyd, George, death of 101
Ford Foundation
   addressing privilege 98–99
   BUILD programme 26
   GrantCraft 279
foundation investments
   addressing privilege 96
   classic funder dilemmas 163–165
   upwards management 260–261
funder fragility 88–89, 90
funders, terminology 23
   see also funding organisations
funding criteria 70–72
funding organisations
   job roles 12
   mission clarity 49–50
   recruitment 95, 97
   strategic priorities 19
   types of organisations 13–15, *14*

   websites 62–63, 70–71
fundraising degrees 281–282
Future Foundations 292

Garita, Alexandra 133
gender diversity 89
general support grants *see* unrestricted grants
GlassPockets 71, 72, 167
goals *see* objectives
Goffman, Erving 80
Google Scholar 223
Gopalan, Geeta 212
governance
   opportunity funds 114
   people with disabilities 93
   Women's Funds Collaborative 133–134
Governance and Social Development Resource Centre (GSDRC) 225
government-funded organisations
   control of 16
   influencing government spending 238–239
   types of organisations 13–15, *14*
graduate qualifications 263, 277–278
   see also master's degrees
grant causes *see* causes for grants
Grant Givers' Movement 11, 90, 244, 291–292
Grant Givers' Programme 277
Grant, Peter 282
GrantAdvisor 167
GrantCraft 52, 170, 240, 278–279
Grantee Perception Reports (GPRs) 42
grantee reports 211, 213–214, 218–219, 236
grantee surveys 42
grantmaking
   challenges involved 9
   as profession 9–10
   as role 27–28
   traditional practices 11, 27–28
   who is this book for? 12–13
   see also Modern Grantmaking; reform in grantmaking
grantmaking accreditation 280–283
grantmaking organisations *see* funding organisations
grantmaking reform *see* reform in grantmaking

Modern Grantmaking

GrantNav 71
grantseeker experiences
  barriers to great experiences 198–199, 202–203
  checklist 204
  design infrastructure 200–202
  frustrations 18, 175–176, 179–180
  good service 38
  human-centred design 183–186
  improving the experience 173–174, 182
  investing in improvements 174
  invite-only applications 181
  iteration 184–186
  large funders 196–197
  listening to grantees 60–61
  Modern Grantmaking 180–181
  scale 188–189
  service quality and discrimination 176–178
  small funders 189–195
  training and upskilling 199–200
  user experience research 187–188
Great Recession (late 2007 to mid-2009) 155
Gregory, Ann Goggins 218
Gulati-Partee, Gita 104

Harrison, Ben 115
Hassey, Kate 54
Hayman, Jake 165
Headwaters Foundation 48
Hewlett Foundation 216, 220
hiring *see* recruitment
Howard, Don 218
hubris 33
Hudson, Genevieve Maitland 36–37
human resources (HR) *see* careers; management; recruitment; skills
humility
  management 246, 254
  as Modern Grantmaking value 31, 32–34, 288
  personal development plans **271**
  strategy development 119
  unsolicited proposals 143

Ibegbuna, Ruth 77
impact evaluation 228
  see also evaluation of project success

inclusion
  faking it 102–104
  recruitment 95, 97, 98, 262–263
  representing funding organisations 77–78
  strategy development 131
  workplace discrimination 90
  see also diversity
Indigo Trust 141–142
inequalities
  restricted grants 46
  unsolicited proposals 142, 143
  see also equity
Infante, Pia 169, 171
international grantmakers' reform community 12
International Initiative for Impact Evaluation 225
investments
  approaching your foundation investment 163–165
  perpetual vs. spending down funders 169–171
invite-only applications
  classic funder dilemmas 140–144
  grantseeker experiences 181
  no-brainers 62
  pros and cons **141**
Irfan, Fozia 102

Jameel Poverty Action Lab (J-PAL) 224, 239
job roles
  grantmakers 27–28
  management 245–248
  who is this book for? 12–13
  see also recruitment
job security 258, 267, 268
John Ellerman Foundation 135–136
Jones, Maggie 34
Joseph Rowntree Foundation 116

Kahneman, Daniel 211
King, Stephen 57
knowledge *see* resources for grantmakers; skills
Kolbert, Elizabeth 17

language use
  diversity and inclusion 103–104
  terminology 23–24
Le, Vu 88

Index

leadership
  addressing privilege 102–103
  bad traits 256–257
  funder fragility 88–89
  Modern Grantmaking 296
  professional researchers 220–222
  strategy development 118–121
  strategy use 111
  terminology 245
  see also management
Learning Network 52
learning to be a good grantmaker 247, 267
  see also skills
Lenz, Paul 18
Levine, Ruth 36, 51, 108, 220
listening to grantees 60–61
long-term grants
  as no-brainer 50–51
  perpetual vs. spending down funders 171
  unrestricted grants 47
lotteries, use in grantee selection 134–135
Luminate 48

Magic Breakfast project 238–239
'Magna Carta excuse' 50
Malala Fund 116
management
  bad managers 255–256
  checklist 265
  in funding organisations 243–244
  good managers 246–248
  job roles 245–248
  mistakes 257–259
  Modern Grantmaking 296
  no-brainers 249–253
  recruitment 262–264
  terminology 245
  upwards management 246, 259, 260–261
  values 248, 254–255
  see also leadership
master's degrees 277–278, 281–282
matched funding 157
McIntosh, Peggy 83–84
meetings, management no-brainers 249
mentoring 273
micromanagement 248

mission
  clarity of 49–50
  management no-brainers 250
  perpetual vs. spending down funders 170
  recruitment 262
  strategic priorities 19
  strategy development 108, 109, 126–127
  see also strategy; values
mission statements 49–50, 108, 126
mitigation vs. prevention 151–152
Modern Grantmaking
  contact details 298
  definition 31, 287, 292
  practices 30–31
  as reform 11, 25–27, 292–297
  values 31–32, 43
  see also reform in grantmaking
#ModernGrantmaking 292–293
monitoring and evaluation (M&E) 209–210
  see also research
multi-year grants *see* long-term grants
Murray, Angela 173

National Emergencies Trust (NET) 100
National Lottery Community Fund 18
National Science Foundation (US) 220
negative consequences 17–18
  see also opportunity costs
no-brainers 45
  avoid short-changing grantees 65–67
  backing grantseeker priorities 63–65
  collaboration with other funders 52–55
  ease and accessibility 56–57
  good communication 59–60
  long-term grants 50–51
  management 249–253
  mission clarity 49–50
  mutually beneficial conversations 60–61
  pace of grantmaking 67–68
  paying up front 65
  putting into practice 72–73
  rejecting proposals 57–58

Modern Grantmaking

safeguarding 68–70
transparency 70–72
unrestricted grants 46–49
unsolicited proposals 62–63
nonprofits
  current challenges 10
  experience of working for 264
  shadowing work 272–273
  terminology 23
  time cost of applying for grants 56–57, 141–142, 218
Not Too Late project 239

objectives
  achieving the mission 127
  divergent motivations 261
  mission clarity 49–50
  strategy development 109, 110, 114–115
O'Clery, Conor 114
open organisations *see* unsolicited proposals
open science 290
Open Society Foundations 157
openness *see* transparency
Oppenheimer, Jenny 89, 135
opportunity costs 18, 261
opportunity funds 114
opportunity statements 126
outcomes, vs. outputs 214–215

pace of grantmaking 67–68, 158
Palfrey, John 246
participatory grantmaking
  Disability Rights Fund 93
  meaning of 157, 159
  personal development plans **271**
  planning a scheme 160–161
  power dynamics 158
  #ShiftThePower 292
participatory research 231
partnerships *see* collaboration with other funders
Paskins, Dan 50, 120, 165
Paterson, Hannah 161
payment schedules 65
payments
  avoiding short-changing grantees 65–67
  making payment up-front 65
  pace of grantmaking 67–68
PEAK Grantmaking 282–283

Pears Foundation 49
peer review 134, 135, 237, 253
Peixoto, Tiago 205–206
people management *see* management
people-of-colour-led organisations 100
  see also race
people with disabilities *see* disabilities
performance reviews 257
personal development plans 270–272, **271**
skills development 268, 269
  see also skills
perpetual funders 169–171
personal development plans 270–272, **271**
  see also skills
Peter Cundill Foundation 49
philanthropy
  charitable donations 15
  distinction from grantmaking 16, 28
  slavery association 30
philanthropy courses 281–282
place-based funders 153–155
pooled funds 52–53
Potapchuk, Maggie 104
Powell, Alison 54
power dynamics
  addressing privilege 98–100
  anonymity 22–23
  backing grantseekers' priorities 63–65
  equity 35
  grantseekers 38
  management 246
  participatory grantmaking 158, 159
  privilege 78–79, 84, 87–89
  reform movements 291
  #ShiftThePower 11, 292
  Trust-Based Philanthropy Project 94
prevention vs. cure focus 151–152
private foundations
  legal obligations 16
  slavery associations 30
  types of organisations 13–15, *14*
  unaccountable status 16–18
privilege
  addressing privilege 21, 94–102
  awareness about 80–81

326

Index

board members 27
checking your privilege 78, 91–93
checklist 105
decision-making 85–87
definition 79
diversity awareness training 75–77
equity 34, 35
funder fragility 88–89
in grantmaking 84, 85–87, 89
historical context 82–84
power dynamics 78–79, 84, 87–89
social groups 79–80
unchecked privilege 78, 81–82, 87–88, 90
unearned benefits 80
professional development
  activities to improve skills 272–278
  board members 261
  checklist 285
  courses 280–283
  effective altruism movement 284
  importance of 18, 267–268
  incentives for improving 268–269
  lack of attention given to 267–268
  lack of training 9–10
  management of current grants 284
  personal development plans 270–272, **271**
  resources and books 278–279
professional researchers 206, 220–222, 225–227
  see also research
project success *see* evaluation of project success
Prospera – International Network of Women's Funds 132–134
Prudence Foundation 145
psychologically safe teams 251
public grant databases 223

qualifications *see* graduate qualifications; skills
qualitative impact evaluations 235
quantitative impact evaluations 235

race
  addressing privilege 101–104
  people-of-colour-led organisations 100
  and privilege 79, 82–84
Resourcing Racial Justice 11, 101–102
risk management and discrimination 148
slavery-philanthropy association 30, 135–136
workplace discrimination 90
RAND report 218
random selection of grantees 134–135
Rank, Rachel 167
recruitment
  2027 initiative 97
  addressing privilege 95, 97
  managing the process 262–264
  Rooney Rule 98–99
reform in grantmaking 287
  contact details 298
  endowments 164–165
  identifying as a reformer 290
  important lessons from this book 288–289
  international grantmakers' reform community 12
  Modern Grantmaking 11, 25–27, 292–297
  purpose of this book 11–12
reform movements
  examples of 291–292
  Modern Grantmaking 11, 27, 292–293
  Trust-Based Philanthropy 94, 291
rejecting proposals 57–58
Rendel, John 47
reporting 213–215
  see also evaluation of project success; research
research
  checklist 240
  common problems 213–219
  ethics 229–231, 276
  finding useful research 223–224
  further reading 239
  how to make use of 205–206, 219–239
  meaning of 206–207
  monitoring and evaluation (M&E) 209–210
  repositories 223, 224–225
  strategy development 112, 207, 238
  when to consider the role of 207–208, 210–212

327

research methods 206–207, 229–231, 276
research quality evaluation 233–237
resources for grantmakers
 collaboration with other funders 52
 skills development 278–279
Resourcing Racial Justice (UK) 11, 101–102
restricted grants
 avoiding short-changing grantees 65–66
 as common practice 47
 criticism of 46–47
 definition 46
 reasons for 48
reverse mentoring 273
risk
 attitudes to 144–150
 and discrimination 148
 session to clarify appetite for 147–149
Roberts, Roxanne 17
Rooney Rule 98–99
Rose-Smith, Sacha 273

safeguarding 68–70
salary
 funders vs. grantees 65
 recruitment 263
Samasaran, Diana 92
scale, funding organisations 142–143
Scared Straight 216–217
self-improvement *see* skills
service
 management 254
 as Modern Grantmaking value 31, 38–39
 skills development 274
service design training 274
service quality *see* grantseeker experiences
shadowing (skills development) 272–273
Shafei, Esta'a Al 65
Shawn Carter Foundation 53
#ShiftThePower 11, 292
short-term grants 50–51
Singer, Peter 284
site visits, grantee projects 261

skills
 activities to improve skills 272–278
 board members 261
 checklist 285
 courses 280–283
 effective altruism movement 284
 importance of development 18, 267–268
 incentives for improving 268–269
 lack of attention given to 267–268
 lack of training 9–10
 management of current grants 284
 personal development plans 270–272, **271**
 resources and books 278–279
slavery-philanthropy association 30, 135–136
social entrepreneurialism 162
social impacts
 foundation investments 164
 and management practices 244, 255
 new ideas about grantmaking 25–26
 private foundations 17–18
 systems change 275–276
 those in need 29
 see also evaluation of project success
Social Innovation Exchange (SIX) 275
social investment 15–16
spending down funders 169–171
staff *see* job roles; management; recruitment
staff incentives 250, 267–268
staff turnover 258, 268
Stanton Foundation 153
Strategic Alignment Network 52
strategic questions *see* classic funder dilemmas
strategy
 checklist 137
 communication 125
 community approach 132–134
 developing a good strategy 116–118
 development process 120–121, 131–132, 136
 drafting and revision 128–129
 examples 109–110, 116
 feedback and research 123–125

goals and priorities 114–115
how to use 111–112, 130–131
issues to be addressed 122
leadership 118–120
lottery use 134–135
meaning of 107, 108–109
planning day 126–127
recruitment 262
and research 112, 207, 238
righting wrongs 135–136
time required 115
written documents 110, 111–114
studious inquiry 206
success *see* evaluation of project success
sustainability *see* climate change; financial sustainability
Syrett, Louisa 162
systems change 275–276

Tall, Stephen 213–214, 219
tax status, private foundations 17
Taylor, Tessa Ann 262
team meetings 249, 252, 269
technology, impacts on grantmaking 278
terminology, language use 23–24
thematic funders 153–155
Thomas Paine Initiative 55
time resources
　cost of applying for grants 56–57, 141–142, 218
　strategy development 115, 118–120, 131
Time to Spare 218
traditional grantmaking
　addressing privilege 94–95
　criticism of 11, 288
　meaning of 27–28
　weaknesses 28–29
training
　courses 280–283
　diversity awareness 75–77, 95–96, 274–275
　fellowship programmes 277
　lack of 9–10
　master's degrees 277–278
　research methods 276
　service design training 274
　shadowing work 272–273
　university courses 280, 281–282
　see also skills

Trans Justice Funding Project 49
transparency
　classic funder dilemmas 165–168
　ease and accessibility of application process 56–57
　funding criteria 70–72
　invite-only applications 62
　management 258
　rejecting proposals 57–58
　Trust-Based Philanthropy Project 94
trust
　addressing privilege 94
　management 247
　reform movements 291
　unrestricted grants 47–48
Trust-Based Philanthropy 94, 291
Turvey, Helen 63
Tversky, Amos 211
Twersky, Fay 255

UK Prevention Research Partnership 152
unanticipated events budget 114
unchecked privilege 78, 81–82, 87–88, 90
'unicorns' 291
university courses 277–278, 280, 281–282
unrestricted grants
　addressing privilege 94
　definition 46
　examples 48–49
　as no-brainer 46–48, 289
　reasons to restrict 48
unsolicited proposals
　classic funder dilemmas 140–144
　no-brainers 62–63
　pros and cons **141**
up-front payments 65
upwards management 246, 259, 260–261

Vallely, Paul 28
values
　backing grantseekers' priorities 63–65
　diligence 40–41
　diversity 95
　equity 34–35
　evidence 36–37
　group exercise idea 44

329

humility 32–34
living up to 41–42, 248
management in accordance with 248, 254–255
mission clarity 49–50
for Modern Grantmaking 31–34, 43, 288
personal development plans **271**
service 38–39
strategy development 114–115, 135–136
Villanueva, Edgar 28, 60, 104, 135–136, 230, 244
vision statements 126
vulnerable people, safeguarding 68–70
see also disabilities
Vyriotes, Joyce 51

Walker, Darren 32, 98–99
Wallace, David Foster 139
Warmington, Joy 104

Waters, Paul 90
Weaks, Lisa 9
websites
crowdfunding 143–144
moderngrantmaking.com 292–293
need for a funding organisation website 62–63, 70–71
research methods 240
Wellcome Trust (UK) 220
What Works Centres 225
whistleblowing 17–18
whiteness 79, 82–84
see also privilege
the Whitman Institute (TWI) 171
William and Flora Hewlett Foundation 61, 116, 258
Women's Funds Collaborative (WFC) 133–134
Workplace Equality Index 95

XTreme Foundation 145

Made in the USA
Las Vegas, NV
21 December 2023